T0314303

DATAPUBLICS

The Construction of Publics in
Datafied Democracies

Edited by
Jannie Møller Hartley, Jannick Kirk Sørensen
and David Mathieu

BRISTOL
UNIVERSITY
PRESS

First published in Great Britain in 2023 by

Bristol University Press
University of Bristol
1–9 Old Park Hill
Bristol
BS2 8BB
UK
t: +44 (0)117 374 6645
e: bup-info@bristol.ac.uk

Details of international sales and distribution partners are available at bristoluniversitypress.co.uk

British Library Cataloguing in Publication Data
A catalogue record for this book is available from the British Library

ISBN 978-1-5292-2862-5 hardcover
ISBN 978-1-5292-2863-2 ePub
ISBN 978-1-5292-2864-9 OA Pdf

FSC
www.fsc.org
MIX
Paper | Supporting
responsible forestry
FSC® C013604

Contents

List of Figures, Tables and Boxes iv
Notes on Contributors v
Acknowledgements vii

1   Introduction: Datapublics Beyond the Rise and Fall Narrative 1
     Jannie Møller Hartley, David Mathieu and Jannick Kirk Sørensen

PART I   Agentic Publics
2   Deconstructing the Notion of Algorithmic Control over 27
     Datapublics
     David Mathieu
3   Counterpublicness and Hybrid Tactics across Physical and 49
     Mediated Spaces
     Mette Bengtsson and Anna Schjøtt
4   Stratified Public Formation in Mundane Settings 72
     Morten Fischer Sivertsen and Mikkeline Sofie Skjerning Thomsen

PART II   Cultivated Publics
5   Imagining Publics through Emerging Technologies 99
     Jannie Møller Hartley and Anna Schjøtt
6   Personalization Logics and Publics by Design 121
     Jannie Møller Hartley, Anna Schjøtt and Jannick Kirk Sørensen

PART III   Infrastructured Publics
7   Classifying the News: Metadata as Structures of Visibility 145
     and Compliance with Tech Standards
     Lisa Merete Kristensen and Jannick Kirk Sørensen
8   Infrastructuring Publics: Datafied Infrastructures of the 165
     News Media
     Lisa Merete Kristensen and Jannick Kirk Sørensen

9   Conclusion: Datapublics as a Site of Struggles 189
     David Mathieu and Jannie Møller Hartley

Index 201

List of Figures, Tables and Boxes

Figures

4.1	Four different types of publics	80
4.2	Space of public connections and lifestyles	81
4.3	The main topics of Danish Facebook groups	85
4.4	Space of Facebook groups and civic engagement	86
8.1	Prevalence of companies in the 'underwood' of third-party URLs	175
8.2	The long-tail of third-party presence at 361 news sites	177
8.3	The total number of third-party appearances at the media sites arranged by category	178
9.1	The (social) construction of datapublics	197

Tables

3.1	Public formation tactics	59
5.1	Three phases of the press	113
7.1	Characteristics and prevalence of metadata tags	156
8.1	Technologies sustaining journalistic news media	172
8.2	Number of URLs and prevalence of third-party URLs	176

Box

8.1	Other top ten third-party companies	176

Notes on Contributors

Mette Bengtsson is Associate Professor at the Department of Communication, University of Copenhagen. She researches political debate in a mediated, datafied world and is the principal investigator of the Carlsberg-funded project 'Tell Me the Truth: Fact-Checkers in an Age of Epistemic Instability'.

Morten Fischer Sivertsen is a sociologist and PhD student at Roskilde University, Department of Communication & Arts. His research interests include democracy, citizenship, media and audience studies and social inequality, which he analyses through primarily quantitative methods on survey data and digital data.

Jannick Kirk Sørensen is Associate Professor in digital media at Department of Electronic Systems at Aalborg University, Denmark. He researches media personalization in the intersection between computer engineering, user agency and media politics. With this point of departure, he focuses his research at the emerging paradoxes in current claims for algorithmic fairness and transparency. He is principal investigator of the Horizon Europe project 'Fair MusE' 2023–2026.

David Mathieu is Associate Professor at the Department of Communication and Arts at Roskilde University, Denmark. His current work focuses on audience and reception research, social media and research methodologies, with an emphasis on the changing nature of audience practices in the age of social media, digitalization of communication and datafication of society.

Lisa Merete Kristensen is Assistant Professor at the Department of Communication and Arts at Roskilde University. Her work is centred around metrics, tech stacks and technical infrastructures in journalism and the impact of these for media organizations and journalism. She is specialized in theories around the journalistic profession and is working with both digital methods and more qualitative research methodologies.

Jannie Møller Hartley is Associate Professor at the Department of Communication and Arts at Roskilde University. She is currently co-leading the Centre for Big Data at Roskilde University and the principal investigator of the Velux Funded research project DataPublics (2020–2023). Her research is situated in between the fields of journalism research, audience studies and data science, and ranges across subjects such as media ethics, #metoo and artificial intelligence in media.

Anna Schjøtt is a technological anthropologist and PhD candidate at the Media Studies Department at the University of Amsterdam. Her PhD research consists of multiple cases studies where she ethnographically explores how responsible artificial intelligence is conceptualized and pursued in practice in the media sector – predominately in Europe – with the aim to critically examine the politics of artificial intelligence design processes and their implications.

Mikkeline Sofie Skjerning Thomsen holds an MA in Rhetoric and is a partner in the sociological consulting company Analyse & Tal FMBA. Mikkeline and her team specialize in counting what is difficult to count. Through quantitative and qualitative analysis of large-scale data from social media platforms, Mikkeline explores citizenship, democracy, volunteering and hate speech within digital communities.

Acknowledgements

This volume comes out of the research project DataPublics at Roskilde University, Denmark. The project brought together different people, from different disciplines, with the overall aim to investigate the transformations of journalism and audiences in datafied societies.

The book has been born in difficult circumstances, which have impacted both the empirical field-sites and our analytical approaches. We were in the midst of a pandemic as the first thoughts on the book materialized. Around the same time US experienced the biggest crisis of its democracy with the storming of Capitol Hill. Later, as we were finishing up, a war in Europe loomed. The EU launched an AI-act, Elon Musk bought Twitter and OpenAI launched ChatGPT, all significant events when analysing media, publics and civic practices.

As significant these events were, they also forced us to re-evaluate and revisit some of our basic assumptions about publics, the role of the media and tech platforms, and the events naturally made the empirical reality more messy. Thus the empirical realities constantly entered our ongoing discussions on how we could capture and understand both processes of datafication and datafication of public formation.

While each of the chapters are the authors' own, the book is also co-authored. We have been deeply involved in each other's chapters, constantly forcing each other to re-evaluate how the empirical analysis or conceptual development in one chapter would contradict or support the conclusions in other chapters. Many of these overall discussions have been enriched by the multiple disciplines involved in the group, ranging from rhetoric, techno-anthropology, sociology, media and communication, journalism and data science.

Without the participation and willingness of citizens and media professionals to be interviewed and be part of our fieldwork, our analytical endeavours would have been a lot less thick and less grounded in empirical realities. Therefore, the biggest thank to all of you for letting us into your organizations and into your thoughts and struggles.

We would also like to thank the research groups 'Audiences and Mediated Lives' and 'Journalism and Democracy' at Roskilde University for invaluable feedback on earlier drafts of chapters. Also, thanks to our advisory board and great colleagues that have challenged us along the way, discussed our analytical points with us and provided valuable suggestions and constructive feedback. A special thanks to: Göran Bolin, Södertörn University, Tina Askanius, Malmø University, Lina Dencik, Cardiff University, Helle Sjøvaag, Stavanger University, Ike Picone, Vrije University Brussels, Hallvard Moe, Bergen University, Irene Costera-Meijer, Vrije University Amsterdam, Jan Fredrik Hovden, Bergen University, and Kim Schrøder, Anton Grau Larsen, Elisabetta Pettruci and Aske Kammer, all from Roskilde University. The crew at the AI-Lab at the University of Amsterdam and others from the university, in particular Thomas Poell and David Nieburg asked the hard, but necessary questions at the very end of the book writing process. We are thankful for the anonymous reviewers, who were both encouraging and assured coherence in the book as a whole as only an outside reader could provide.

Last, but not least, we are grateful for support from the Velux Foundation funding the research project DataPublics over these last three years, enabling the many seminars we have had discussing the book at locations such as Hornbæk beach, the Swedish woods, the Meat Packing District of Copenhagen, and various locations around Amsterdam.

Introduction: Datapublics Beyond the Rise and Fall Narrative

Jannie Møller Hartley, David Mathieu and Jannick Kirk Sørensen

Introducing datapublics

As we walked past the Parliament Christiansborg in central Copenhagen one dusky night in October 2020, scattered groups had gathered holding handwritten signs like 'my body, my choice' and were clapping instrumentally to the banging of pots and pans. The signs and banners they held protested COVID-19 policies; however, they also revealed the many issues and stakes among the protestors. Some felt forced to vaccinate, some were angry at the government's handling of the crisis, and others had shown up because they felt a loss of control over their lives. There were even some who did not believe the pandemic even existed. There was little sign of any journalists covering the events. Nonetheless, as the pandemic continued and the movement gathered in strength, with a small fringe resorting to more violent demonstrations, the media started taking an interest. They covered demonstrations and did portraits of conspiracy theorists or anti-vaxxers. On Twitter, people gathered in so-called 'hashtag publics' (Bruns and Burgess, 2015) to criticize or praise a programme produced on conspiracies and the people who believe them. Meanwhile, fact-checking initiatives rivalled to verify the statements on both sides of the divide with the help of flagging from Meta's content moderation algorithm used on Facebook. COVID-19 sceptics found each other in ever-larger numbers, but increasingly gathered in closed groups and subgroups on Facebook and other social media platforms. They slowly developed their own secret language, which constantly evolved to avoid being caught by an algorithm that scanned millions of text bites every minute across the global network to automatically recognize and red-flag words like 'covid' or 'vaccine'.

Just some months before this happened, something seemingly unrelated to the spread of the deadly pandemic happened. This event also raised a few eyebrows across the planet, primarily among data scientists and tech innovators. The San Francisco-based artificial intelligence (AI) research laboratory OpenAI created the third generation of an algorithm based on an autoregressive language model that uses deep learning to produce human-like text. The quality generated by GPT-3 was so advanced that it was difficult to distinguish it from a text written by a human. Because of its possibly dangerous effects, Microsoft announced on 22 September 2020 that it had licensed the 'exclusive' use of GPT-3. Others could still use the public Application Programming Interface to receive output, but only Microsoft has control of the source code. The company was worried about what the algorithm could be used for – and whether it had created a Frankenstein of Silicon Valley that could turn evil, corrupting and disrupting democracies with unstoppable consequences. The next generation of the GPT-3 – the ChatGPT launched in 2022 – gained much more attention for its ability to create human-like songs, texts and assignments, and it is feared how it will impact huge domains such as the music industry, media and education.

Many such AI models developed by OpenAI, Meta, Google and other similar providers of so-called large language models are not only being used in the battle against COVID-19 misinformation, flagging content produced by anti-lockdown protesters and others, but increasingly also implemented by news organizations. By using AI, news organizations hope to better distribute their content to users and reach new audiences by linking large amounts of data content with large amounts of audience data. In doing so, the traditional media also enter into a race with Big Tech companies to define the 'public' and cultivate publics through increasing amounts of data on these audiences.

What we can observe in these tales of turmoil in modern democracies and the race to the datafied forefront are the manifold civic practices acting and re-acting as publics in both mediated and non-mediated modalities and the massive media infrastructure supporting these practices and flows of data. The tales also highlight how democracy is fragile and susceptible to transformation, which, depending on the view and the political position of the interpreter, can be seen as either damaging, a crisis or a global moment of reckoning.

Whatever the normative position, these events are signs of publics in transformation and beg the question of how datafication processes play a role in those transformations happening in and out of data flows. From data in the form of public statistics on vaccinations, MeToo hashtags and comments to the metadata inherent in pictures of the 'Make America Great Again' movement's storming of Capitol Hill, everything is used to train large language models to develop AI products and services. Subsequently that data is fed back to citizens as representations and mirroring of themselves via metrics, such as likes, clicks and shares. In turn, users respond to this mirroring as they navigate the vast woodlands of data and form in publics around various clusters of datapoints, via hashtags or debates on social media. The examples also serve to testify to the importance of researching how datafication transforms both citizens' ability to form publics, the foundations for civic engagement practices, and the role of the media and technology in those processes in all modalities across the hybrid media system.

This book investigates datapublics by asking how the formation of publics is challenged, formed, cultivated and transformed in datafied democracies. In this context, datapublics should not be understood as yet another public concept – this time with 'data' added – but as a lens through which we can examine datafication processes and how certain publics are constructed in and out of data flows.

We argue however, that publics are also constructed through the agency and civic practices of users and citizens as they navigate the hybrid media environment (Chadwick, 2011). As we trace how logics of datafication are transforming practices of media and journalism, while also profoundly affecting the many ways in which citizens engage in datafied democracies, this book bridges the gulf between audience studies and media production studies.

The book also considers the dynamic interactions between different aspects of data and how they intersect at disparate junctures with the public. Importantly, we bring nuances to discussions of datafication and its impact on modern democracies by not taking publics or datafication for granted but examining them through historical, cultural and sociological, and techno-materialist approaches. In doing so, we also reveal some of the discourses and normative assumptions regarding what publics are, highlighting the discursive dimension of public formation and the role of technologies in the shaping of those discourses. For example, we show how technologies and publics are imagined and implicitly seen as inherently linked to discussions of specific ideals of democracy.

As a highly digitalized society characterized by high internet penetration and a traditionally strong media system, Denmark represents an exemplary case for many of the explorations in this book. While the Nordic region is our point of departure, we do venture on journeys taking us afar to other media systems, inquiring for example into global infrastructures of data, albeit from a Nordic media perspective. The purpose here is not to present empirical data from Denmark as a singular case, although the book does provide a unique contribution on this ground, but to study the many junctions between data and publics from a variety of perspectives that speak to each other and shed light on a complex, yet interrelated, set of phenomena.

Datapublics beyond the rise and fall narrative

The coming of new technologies and their role in shaping publics has been met with both hopes and concerns, both by the media and in public discourse, for example praising the discursive and mobilizing effects of hashtags for both democratizing processes in the revolutions in Iran and Egypt to campaigns like #blacklivesmatter or #metoo. But warnings have also been raised in connection with spreading of disinformation, the storming of Capitol Hill and a rise in alternative, populist news media. This ambivalent relationship between public formation and technology is nothing new. Ever since the dawn of media research, scholars have been drawn to explore the immense possibilities of new technologies or, conversely, to critically examine the potentially harmful effects of the same technologies. In these tales of technologies, there is a constant balancing of utopian and dystopian visions – or in Anderson's words, a 'rise or fall' narrative (2013, p 1007) – of how such technologies are essentially reconfiguring the relationship between human and machine.

The dialectics between dystopian and utopian tales of man versus machine can be found dating back to the invention of the printing press in the 15th century, which on one hand was perceived as a promise to revolutionize access to written texts, while scribes and the Church, on the other hand, feared its impact on their livelihood and culture (Chadwick, 2013, p 28). Equally, the introduction of the World Wide Web and the way it revolutionized news through the transition to online news has been met with high hopes for increased access to information, the possibility of interaction through hyperlinks and improved engagement with news by its audiences. A decade later, online news was considered superficial, clickbait and the monster that would drive readers into the hands of social media for good. Suddenly, the internet was also to blame for the economic problems of legacy media and for falling subscription rates for print media (Domingo, 2005; Møller Hartley, 2011). In current public debates, the word 'internet' seems to be used interchangeably with the terms 'AI' or 'algorithms'. However, the tale remains the same. It is a tale that touches upon the ancient conflict of man's ambitions 'to achieve mastery over nature' (Ingold, 2000, p 312) through the use of technology, but simultaneously a tale of how the corruptive powers of the same technology might destroy the very foundation of humans and nature. The corruptive powers, we argue, are currently in much public debate and academic literature linked to the processes of datafication.

Inspired in part by Ziewitz's notion of 'the algorithmic drama' (2016), we have identified a rise and fall narrative regarding the impact of datafication on the formation of publics, a drama comprised around the central narrative that public formation is in crisis, largely due to forces of datafication. The villain, Big Tech (with datafication as its corrupting power), is taking advantage of a passive and defenceless victim, the public. The hero of this compelling drama is of course journalistic media, who battles the villain, protecting the kingdom of democracy. While there is always a grain of truth in all dramas, the narrative is of course too simplistic and obviously misrepresents actual states of affairs. However, good stories have a tendency to be told and retold, attracting attention to the tellers, enchanting those ready to listen. As arguments get told over and over again, they become stable and at times doxic.

The concept of doxa can be helpful to understand the technological drama and the discursive effects it produces. Aristotle usefully distinguished episteme from doxa and endoxa (Aristotle, 1996). The term *doxa* refers to the domain of opinion, belief or probable knowledge – in contrast to *episteme*, the domain of certainty or true knowledge. In the tradition of rhetoric, doxa is constructed through argumentation, and can be used in argumentation, and as such also paves the way for certain solutions to the problem defined. When doxa has become more stable we can talk of *endoxa*, claims that were previously debated but that have now become common sense. The drama surrounding public formation in datafied democracies run the risk of becoming common sense, without solid backing in evidence, and thus this book also aims to influence and inform this debate with nuanced detailed empirical and conceptual analyses. We believe the story is currently being retold in many different versions, yet always involving our three protagonists. We see the story shaping many conversations about the place and role of technology in our societies.

This drama and its characters are strongly represented in public discourse, shaping, for example, policy making and politics, which naturally respond to the narrative of a democracy and public formation in crisis. The story can be heard in the words of EU Commissioner for Competition, Margrethe Vestager (2020), when she says: 'We have to take our democracy back. We cannot leave it to Facebook or Snapchat or anyone else.' The drama is also infused by some academic literature that have proved influential for public discourse, for example, the work of Shoshana Zuboff (2019) or the notion of filter bubbles (Pariser, 2011). The drama is often implicitly present in much academic work, or at least not explicitly challenged and hence passively endorsed and reproduced.

All dramas invoke a fight between good and evil and affirm the relevance of morality. But this should not come at the price of oversimplification, ignorance and Manicheism. The drama of public formation, in all its simplicity, presents significant blind spots and further lack crucial connections to wider historical developments on datafication and public formation. This is problematic, because certain solutions are often prescribed as a medicine to safeguard democracy against the problems identified discursively (but not supported empirically) in the public debate concerning technology, Big

Tech and datafication. By prescribing inadequate solutions, we might even make things worse, for example by reinforcing old media structures and not recognizing the hybrid nature of today's media landscape. Responding to this development, we believe that what we need now, perhaps more than ever, is not more technology-blaming for the failures of public formation. Instead, we see a need for empirically supporting our understanding of public formation as it takes place nowadays with the help of media, technology, data and beyond. In the following we expands on the different parts of this drama. We begin with the victims, the passive publics.

Publics: the passive victims of datafication

Challenged by disinformation, the commodification of audiences and the datafication of media use, among others, the public sphere is, according to many commentators, in terrible shape. In *Weapons of Math Destruction*, mathematician and writer Cathy O'Neil (2016) warns against the world of Big Data and its insidious, fast-growing control over almost every aspect of modern life. In the book *People vs. Tech* Jamie Bartlett argues that platforms such as social media 'ultimately hinder citizens from developing and evaluating their own controversial thoughts (for fear of permanent negative public appraisal), leading to the development of a "moral singularity" whereby no individual really has their own views, with moral and political reasoning delegated to machines' (2018, p 38). Such fears are also to some extent present in the academic literature, where datafication is largely seen as a top-down process, both ideological (Van Dijck, 2014) and material (Couldry and Mejias, 2019), against which media users seem to be defenceless.

In the surveillance capitalist system, citizens are losing their agency and autonomy because of a newly created market for algorithmic predictions sustained by Facebook, Google and other data-driven platforms (Pariser, 2011; Gillespie, 2014; Diakopoulos and Koliska, 2017; Zuboff, 2019). It is argued that public debate is dumbed down on social media, where trolling and hate are symptomatic of emotional users lacking the proper resources to participate in public debate, contributing to polarization, extremism, conspiracy or 'dark participation' (Quandt, 2018). In media, algorithms are said to form the new power dynamics of production and distribution (O'Neil, 2016; Beer, 2017; Noble, 2018), against which audiences have little control.

These are but a few examples of concerns that are part of a larger narrative that historically sees audiences as gullible, vulnerable, passive or otherwise problematic (Butsch, 2008; Livingstone, 2019). Each time a new medium has been introduced – from comics to cinema, television, video games, the internet and now social media – there have been concerns, even moral panic, over the implications of this medium for society. It is no surprise that the same concerns reappear in times of rapid transformation in the media-technology sector.

These claims largely pertain to how audiences have been and continue to be imagined by practitioners and commentators. These imagined audiences (at times imagined as publics) are often inserted within the view of communication as an instrument of power and control. However, the assumptions that actual audiences follow from imagined audiences or that attempts at control result in success have been historically challenged (Hall, 1980; Livingstone, 2007). Simultaneously, current transformations in the media landscape, often discussed regarding a material turn in media and communication in which infrastructures, data and algorithms play a prominent role, require a better understanding, not just in terms of how this materiality affects the political economy of media, but also cultural practices (Lievrouw, 2009).

Newer studies are pointing to algorithmic resistance (see, for example, Treré, 2018; Velkova and Kaun, 2019), for instance highlighting audiences' agency in the form of coping tactics in datafied daily lives (Møller Hartley and Schwartz, 2020). As pointed out by Kennedy et al (2015), questions about agency have been overshadowed by a focus on oppressive techno-commercial strategies such as data mining. Like Nick Couldry and Allison Powell (2014), we call for more attention to discussions of agency than theories of algorithmic power, or data power, have thus far made possible.

Journalism: the heroic cultivator of publics

The second main character in this unfolding technological drama that we want to draw attention to is journalistic media. If the problem is Big Tech, the solution is often journalism. Traditionally and normatively journalism has been perceived (and with good reason) as a public good, as a provider of trustworthy information to publics. As Unesco writes in its report on world press freedom: 'Like other public goods, journalism plays a critical role in promoting a healthy civic space. It provides citizens with trusted and fact-based information while at the same time acting as an independent watchdog and agenda-setter' (Unesco, 2022). Media scholar Jesper Strömbäck (2005) has shown how journalism is closely linked to normative ideals of democracy, securing access to information, deliberation and a watchdog function. Journalism is also the hero, because it is seen as addressing publics as citizens in opposition to other actors who promote commercial content, without concern for the democratically informed citizen. In the Public Service Media Manifesto launched by a collective of communication scholars and practitioners in 2021 it is stated that: 'Public Service Media content is distinctive from commercial media and data companies. It addresses citizens, not consumers' (Public Service Media Manifesto, 2021).

This act in the drama of public formation in the age of datafication is also the story of a hero in decline and in crisis. The risk for journalism is that Big Tech and emerging datafied technologies take over, taking the lead role as the villain, and drawing the passive citizens towards more entertaining content. And, in turn, preventing publicist media (that is, privately owned but with a public service mission), from helping citizens in their agentic practices to form publics. We have observed that more and better journalism is perceived in public discourse as the solution when it comes to discussions on fake news, misinformation and dark participation, which Big Tech is not controlling sufficiently, leaving the public sphere in a terrible state. The academic literature point to a platformatization of news (Van Dijck et al, 2018), the power of platforms over news (Nielsen and Ganter, 2022) and generally provide a gloomy picture of journalism's role as cultivators of publics in the platformatized and datafied age. It is as if journalism, too, is a defenceless victim of datafication and of the technologies developed by tech providers outside journalism.

The idealization of journalism as it once was (and its readers), as a professional ideology (Deuze and Witschge, 2018), which can be observed in public discourse, creates an almost textbook 'technophobic' (Dinello, 2005) response to the idea of new technologies entering the newsroom. However, the rapid development of technology and the greater access to datafication have also led news organizations to increasingly take on the role of 'technologists' (Dinello, 2005), preaching how technologies are also the answer to the current problems of news organizations – including ensuring both economic survival and a continued democratic role in society. To paint a picture of journalism as 'pure', as non-technological and non-commercial cultivators of democratic publics, is, we argue, as with many stories, too good to be true. Journalism research has highlighted the diverse normative roles of journalism (Strömbäck, 2005), the dual construction of audiences within journalism as *both* market and as citizens (Ang, 2002) and more recent research has highlighted that the tech versus media relationship is more muddled than initially assumed.

Studies have shown how platforms both support and shape practices and sensemaking in news organizations (Anderson, 2011; Tandoc, 2014). On social media platforms, for example, algorithms not only generate news feeds based on signals from networks and the preferences of advertisers, but also assume agency by presenting 'algorithmic publics' to actors in the newsrooms (Christin, 2020). Arguably, as they increasingly ground their decision-making practices on the algorithmic processing of audience and user data (Vu, 2014; Christin, 2020) and implement personalization algorithms (Schjøtt Hansen and Hartley, 2021), news media adapt to and negotiate these logics of datafication. When investigating public formation, we argue that it is necessary to better define the evolving role of journalism as cultivator of publics as it develops in tandem with emerging technologies. Thus, we also set out on a research agenda, where we wish to pay attention to the strong discourses (for example, of journalism as a watchdog) surrounding the role of journalism as cultivators of publics. And it means that we analyse its practices and values as both diverse, at times contradicting and not always and far from always constructing publics as citizens.

Big Tech: the infrastructural villain

The criticism surrounding the role and influence of Big Tech in public formation prevails in the popular, political and academic realms. Big Tech is often understood as what van Dijck et al (2018), among others, term 'The Big Five' or 'GAFAM', namely Google (Alphabet Inc.), Apple Inc., Facebook Inc. (Meta Platforms), Amazon.com Inc. and Microsoft Corp. In particular Google and Meta have become increasingly important constituents of contemporary societies, providing a variety of services and products needed for the production, distribution and circulation of journalistic content, and more broadly information, while reshaping tech businesses into platform economies. The role as villain in the drama we have at hand is often narrated by the helper, the journalistic media, as for example summarized in the introduction to a report by the Federation of Danish Media (Danske Medier) published as a reply to the ongoing negotiations of media support in Denmark:

> International tech giants largely control the flow of information in our society, and they have a decisive influence on the digital media industry in relation to the prioritization and dissemination of content, traffic generation and the purchase and sale of advertising space. The platforms of the tech giants must therefore be considered a central part of our infrastructure, but they are nevertheless in many respects still free of responsibility and at the same time pose a potential fundamental threat to the publicist media. (Danske Medier, 2021, p 4, our translation)

Big Tech is seen as creating a monopoly in public opinion, developing a new infrastructure of surveillance. It lacks transparency and accountability but introduces important biases in the algorithmic management of public debates (Introna and Nissenbaum, 2000; Helberger, 2019; Zuboff, 2019). The imposition of new technologies in the media sector, such as personalization algorithms, have instilled fears of echo chambers and filter bubbles (Sunstein, 2001; Pariser, 2011). While these discourses of filter bubbles and echo chambers are empirically unproven, they nonetheless guide many of these personalization initiatives and studies into the infrastructural relationship between publics and platforms (Zuiderveen Borgesius et al, 2016). Big Tech is seen as controlling how publics are shaped, by controlling the infrastructural flows of information, the data and the algorithms. They are sampling people in certain (unhealthy interest-based) groups, and at the same time criticized for preventing publics from forming, by shutting down and closing profiles, accounts or groups, or not showing certain results in searches. While we recognize the contribution from the vast and comprehensive literature on platformatization in media and communication research, we see a need for more empirical research into how platforms and technical infrastructures play a more complex and integrated role for public formation. In this book we emphasize and investigate both their infrastructural role and their public formation capacities. However, we also want to add nuance to the drama, by introducing other characters, namely by also looking at an underwood of small tech.

Going beyond the rise and fall narrative, we thus align ourselves with research highlighting the social construction of algorithms and their imaginaries (Bucher, 2018; Korn et al, 2019). We investigate how tech infrastructures are built into news distribution systems, but focus on how news organizations also accommodate, adapt, resist and even to some extent platformatize themselves, that is, they become and act like platforms. Thus, our endeavour leads us to reveal a much more complex picture of the infrastructures supporting public formation in the datafied era than the drama portrayed here.

Defining datapublics

How we perceive the extent of a crisis of public formation for democracy depends on how we define publics and their importance for democratic processes. Historically, classic theoretical developments concerning the concept of publics emerged in the Lippmann–Dewey debate, centred on Walter Lippmann's provocateur's view of the public as an impossibility, or in his own (1993 [1925]) words, 'a phantom'. Dewey (2012 [1927]) responded with a more positive view of the public as real and as a necessity for well-functioning societies and democracies. Dewey argued that publics were essential to decision-making processes; he went as far as to argue that state action results from the process of organizing publics and, thus, does not oppose publics since they appear when issues are deemed unmanageable by existing institutions (Dewey, 2012 [1927]). Dewey, therefore, had a processual view of publics and saw them as emergent and multiple phenomena formed as part of an entanglement with issues. He argued that the 'lasting, extensive and serious consequences of associated activity bring into existence a public' (Dewey, 2012 [1927], p 35). Thus, the public was formed by all those affected by indirect consequences: individuals who became subjectively effective once organized and self-aware and were helped along by modern communicative technology. While we stand with Dewey in recognizing the importance of issues as a shaping factor and publics as processual and multiple, we want to emphasize the role of the media. Further, we argue that publics are not only emerging in the void of state action, but often in tandem with state legitimization of issues and politics in general.

Some 35 years later, Habermas proposed the notion of the 'public sphere', which he defined as 'a realm of our social life in which something approaching public opinion can be formed. Access is guaranteed to all citizens' (Habermas, 2006 [1989], p 73). Habermas perceived the public sphere as a more stable zone of publicness 'located between the civil society and the state, grounded in the former addressing the latter' (Calhoun, 2017, p 24). This sphere, he argued, was made possible by new patterns of social organization that could sustain such a zone of publicness: newspapers, coffeehouses and the state being increasingly more attentive to public opinion, creating the infrastructures of publicness (Habermas, 2006 [1989]; Calhoun, 2017). The public was theorized as a mode of connection rather than as a process and body of people forming around an issue. This mode was characterized by rational debate and the 'mutual willingness to accept the given roles and suspend their reality' (Habermas, 1989 [1962], p 131), emphasizing how private interests (including those of the market) were suspended in search of the public good. Habermas' concept of the public sphere has been critiqued and further developed, including by Habermas (1988) himself, who argued for pluralism and for multiple publics that could advance democracies as long as they would engage in a rational search for truth.

Thus it is now widely acknowledged that there is not one public sphere, but rather multiple publics that are loosely connected and carry the potential to influence each other (Chadwick, 2011), as stressed here in the latest definition provided by Habermas. Furthermore, online spaces such as social media platforms afford high-speed communication and multimodality and are generally structured around weak ties, which enable the transition of communication to higher levels at a more rapid pace than in traditional offline public spheres (Kaiser and Rauchfleisch, 2019, p 242). Nancy Fraser's (1990) seminal work on counterpublics is an important addition to the analytical approach we take in this book, in that it allows a conceptualization of publics as hegemonic and part of and at times in opposition to wider publics. She argues that counterpublics 'function as spaces of withdrawal and regroupment [and] as bases and training grounds for agitational activities directed toward wider publics' (Fraser, 1990, p 68). With the emergence of social media, it is now possible for people to express themselves in public using a range of modalities (written word, spoken word, body language, pictures, video, sound, graphics, memes, and so on) in an ongoing, real-time process. In this process, fragments of communication can be taken up and circulated by others (liked, shared, commented, and so on) and gain a collective force, power and weight by the 'quantification of displayed adherence' (Fraser, 1990, p 68). Hence, social media is potentially a space where the public can form without traditional gatekeeping from journalistic mass media (information sharing, identity building, debating, and so on).

To capture some of these digital transformations to public formation, but focusing more on everyday connective action, the concept of 'networked publics' was developed (boyd, 2008, 2010; Ito, 2008). boyd argues that networked technologies restructure the public through distinct affordances that shape which forms of participation arise and how participation unfolds (boyd, 2010, p 39). Further networked publics are a form of mediated public, which both share characteristics with non-mediated and other mediated publics (boyd, 2008, 2010). However, they are also unique due to the structural affordances of the networked technologies – persistence, searchability, replicability and scalability – which are not typically present in face-to-face public life or become amplified in comparison to past media technologies. Following the popularity of Twitter as a platform and the increasing use of hashtags, Bruns and Burgess have suggested 'ad-hoc issue publics' or 'hashtag publics' (Bruns and Burgess, 2015). Highlighting the affective side and discursive elements of social movements forming on social media, Papacharissi (2015), suggests the notion of 'affective publics', grounded in empirical analysis of the Arab Spring and the Occupy movement.

The problem with these concepts, as noted by Møller Hartley et al (2021), is that they are to some degree platform-centric, without really defining publics. They add a digital or platform modality, claiming that digital public formations differ radically from offline spaces or to some degree are separate from offline spheres. In this book, we would like to emphasize the links between these spheres, and not focus alone on the digital, just because we are dealing with datafication and publics.

In some of these works, we have noticed that the concept of publics is used instead of related, perhaps more accurate, concepts such as, for example, audiences, segments or communities, without offering reflections or arguments for choosing to do so. For example, we might ask if Tarleton Gillespie's (2014) concept of the 'calculated public' qualifies as a public. With concrete examples, such as 'customers like you' and 'friends, and friends of friends', Gillespie's understanding of publics is primarily a commercial and not a political or democratic construct, not even in the broadest sense, although it might become so later or overlap with publics that have similar intentions and gather around a common issue. The same can be said of Christin's (2020) 'algorithmic public', which refers to the work of metrics inside newsrooms that might be powerful in guiding, constraining and controlling journalists at work but that does not refer to an intentional, collective entity. What we find useful in Christin's work is that she highlights the discursive role of data in the construction of 'a public' inside the newsrooms.

What unites these approaches is that, by adding 'public', they highlight how the commercial and datafied profiling of audiences is in opposition to, and at odds with, the normative understandings of publics as collectives, gathered around the deliberation of a certain issue. Applying the notion of the public to all sorts of contexts in which technology is said to be doing something to these publics might only feed into this vague impression that democracy is in disarray and that technology is responsible for it. The notion of the public should not be used to raise the stakes for criticism addressed to technology. Rather, a central question in this book is how citizens, audiences or communities are formed into publics and how these public formations are diversely intertwined with the technologies of data and the media (Møller Hartley et al, 2021).

Situating datafication in relation to public formation

In this book, we use the concept of publics to explore the modalities associated with their formation and to investigate their multiple intersections with data. Hence, instead of suggesting the notion of datafied publics – implying that data does something to publics – we suggest the concept of *datapublics* to explore the reciprocal influences that one may have on the other without presuming hierarchy or directionality. At the same time, we consider the notion of datapublics to provide analytical entry points for empirical investigations. This allows for careful empirical illustrations of how publics are constructed (differently) by multiple actors and practices in relation to data. The drama, if still a drama, is an interactive one, with several possible endings.

In our approach audiences and users of media or citizens are not publics per se and should not be conceptualized as such. However, they are all part of distinct but overlapping constructions of publics, defined by their position in the space of symbolic struggles for legitimization and visibility. We understand publics as characterized by the overlap between, on the one hand, the constructions of publics by the media often in the shape of audience imaginaries and as an abstract 'othering' and, on the other hand, citizens' civic engagement and agency struggling to legitimize certain publics.

This leads us to the other part of our concept, namely data. We suggest investigating data not only as a technological process – the dominant position in the literature, often labelled 'datafication' – but also as a discourse and a value system articulated through technology and various actors, including the public itself. The concept of datafication was initially used by Kenneth Cukier and Viktor Mayer-Schönberger (2014) to describe how data have become a resource that could be harvested through digital technologies, implying a highly commercial logic, as these data have become a newfound economic resource. In continuation, Helen

Kennedy, Thomas Poell and José van Dijck emphasized the processual nature of datafication by defining it as the 'process of rendering into data aspects of the world not previously quantified' (Kennedy et al, 2015, p 1). Datafication has also been approached as a colonization of our lifeworld (Mejias and Couldry, 2019) to emphasize how datafication moves beyond simple practices of producing data. Rather, it changes multiple aspects of everyday life. In this book, we lean on these previous definitions in understanding datafication as processes of quantification enabled through digitalization, where aspects of human interaction are counted and made accessible as a new source of information that is both valuable in itself and fundamentally transformative to how publics can form, take shape, be cultivated and legitimized.

However, we are also inspired by other understandings of datafication. In describing the current datafication of today's society, José van Dijck (2014) referred to 'datafication' as a discourse, or what she calls the 'ideology of dataism', which describes a 'widespread belief in the objective quantification and potential tracking of all kinds of human behaviour and sociality through online media technologies' (p 198).

Particularly useful for our work has been the conceptualization by Göran Bolin (2022) of data as value and processes of valorization from a Deweyan perspective. In this, he notes the marked distinction between when we 'through valuation, assign value to objects around us. [W]e do this in the form of either nominal values (good/bad, ugly/beautiful) or ordinal values (1, 2, 3 etc.)' (Bolin, 2022, p 171). Accordingly, Bolin argues that datafication is also the process of transforming quality into quantity, or, if exemplified with the distinction between private and public value, transforming 'soft' value forms such as equality and knowledge into numeric form (for example, equal numbers or grades [Bolin, 2022]).

This means that we pay attention to how such valorizations are being normalized, how such processes of valorization are contested and to what extent and how they are made possible by the data infrastructures. We are interested in the objective, symbolic forms that such valorizations take and the autonomy or loss of such results, for example, how some forms of civic engagement are valued more and for different reasons, or how systems of valorization technologies are imagined or resisted. It also means asking how the affordances of digital platforms allow for specific valorization and for publics to form in certain ways. Most importantly, we need to question how we, as researchers, have distinct and normative ideals of how a democracy should work (that is, what a 'good' public looks like and the role of the media in that process). The risk is that we overlook certain modalities of public formation or promote elite forms of participation, while marginalizing those in opposition to the elite. We need to step *outside* the technological drama so to speak.

These concepts point to the difficulty of distinguishing datafication from other related concepts such as digitalization, deep mediatization, metrification, platformatization, and so on. Notably, while digitalization enables datafication, the latter has a longer history, not least in the Western world. Data collection by the media is also nothing new; the media has collected demographic data on their audience, and later psychographics, without giving rise to major concerns. In the book *Beyond Measure*, Vincent (2022) brilliantly shows how metrics and standardizations have been around for centuries, which has historically produced and organized societies, as well as made it easier to trade across borders and keep track of citizens. In that perspective data becomes an organizing principle in societal processes with great importance for public formation.

Therefore, we emphasize historical approaches and avoid assuming that emerging technologies are dramatically new or have a dramatic impact just because they are introduced or their use is generalized. Instead, we should pay attention to how these technologies produce changes in means of power, in our capacity to imagine certain audiences as publics or in imagining certain effects of technology. Rather than taking datafication for granted, we focus on how processes of datafication are implemented, represented and valued and what effects these phenomena are producing in contexts in which publics are constructed and cultivated.

Another challenge concerns the role of the media as a prerequisite for political acts and orientations, as scholars argue that the digital is blurring the boundaries between the private and public domains (Marwick and boyd, 2014). The blurring is foremost a consequence of digital platforms increasingly becoming ingrained into our daily lives, serving no longer merely to link audiences to information platforms, but acting as personal communication platforms, debate forums for user-generated content and billions of 'small acts of engagement' (Picone et al, 2019) every second across the globe. Thus, digital traces in the form of data on civic and mediated practices is an increasing and continual presence across the sites, activities and relationships of everyday life, also creating a feedback loop (Mathieu and Pruulmann Vengerfeldt, 2020) to those same practices. As Dourish and Bell (2013) have pointed out, technology is not simple, but involves the 'mess' of its constituent or related parts, as well as those of the institutions, power relations that govern its use and the conflicting discourses that define it.

Not only should we consider the dialectics between data and publics, but we also encourage examining those in a variety of contexts, settings and situations that can be understood as hybrid (Chadwick, 2011), crossing over legacy and new media, offline and online contexts, and private and public forms of engagement. Such a dialectic is a rearticulation of the classical dichotomy structure versus agency, which in media studies often translates into a dichotomy between media and technology versus the audience. It is important to open up for the possibility that actors, including the public and journalists, can align with these structures or oppose them, evade them or change them to win the struggle over who has a right to be a public and how.

Outline of the book

In a hermeneutic fashion, this work has been assembled as a puzzle. Each individual study has been used to inform the whole picture that the book provides on public formation in datafied democracies, while providing distinct pieces of the puzzle from a unique empirical or conceptual angle. We articulate different methods aimed at unpacking the complex processes of public formation in the hybrid media system. We do not solely rely on qualitative investigations but use quantitative survey data, interviews, participant observations, protocol readings, walkthroughs, focus groups and document analysis. We situate our analyses and conclusions in newly gathered empirical data; however, we also draw on previous studies we have conducted individually and collectively.

The book is divided into three parts, each addressing different parts of the drama we have identified. Hence, the first part of the book is concerned with the role of publics, whom we perceive as agentic. We turn to audience research to explore the formation of publics from a sociocultural perspective, the mundane lives of citizens, the resources they engage and their concrete experiences with datafied media.

Chapter 2 develops an argument against the soft determinism implied in the way publics are said to be affected by data and algorithmic control. It introduces a sociocultural approach, focusing on media consumption as a distinct moment from media production, the actual locus of algorithmic control. A distinction is made between our 'uses of media' – what is essentially captured as data and turned into (limited) knowledge – and our sociocultural practices – which remain to date largely invisible and incomprehensible to the data episteme. The gap between uses and practices provides a reflexive space of agency for users to escape algorithmic control, inserting a narrative of hope after a decade of research that has traced a rather dark picture of the datafied society and its consequences for democracy.

Chapter 3 explores how the dynamics of datafication intervene and influence the public formation processes and presents a typology of public formation tactics. Using COVID-19 sceptic groups as a paradigmatic case study, it analyses how these marginalized and often ridiculed groups assert themselves in today's datafied, hybrid media system through going from an inward to an outward focus framed as mobilization tactics, counter-tactics and publicity tactics. The chapter discusses how quantification logics permeate the processes of publicness, how the collective is not necessarily connected through an issue but a common struggle for legitimacy as anti-mainstreamers, and how traditional mass media still plays a central role in recognizing the counterpublic as such.

Chapter 4 uses a mixed-method approach, drawing on the Multiple Correspondence Analysis of large-scale survey data and netnographic mapping of Facebook groups. It argues that the activities in these groups, which tend to attract the seemingly apolitical and publicly disconnected, on a broad scale maintain the simmering potential of the publicness of civil society. Challenging the classic notion of the private/public distinction, the chapter presents empirical evidence suggesting, first, that public formation occurs in seemingly 'private', mundane and non-political spaces, and, second, that it does so while linked to processes of social stratification, the resources of those citizens who engage and their habitual preferences (or civic 'lifestyles'), which does not enjoy equal social recognition.

The second section of the book investigates the imaginaries and values as a vital part of understanding what is at stake when new technologies enter the hybrid media landscape. Chapter 5 illustrates through a case study of the *New York Times* how data logics and imaginaries of digital technologies often construct conflicting and opposing narratives of 'the news users as publics' and the role of journalistic media as cultivators of such imagined publics. Further, by linking this case study to a historization of the increasingly datafied distribution and audience measurement technologies, the chapter explores how audiences and thus publics are constructed differently as new measurement technologies emerge, from democratic collectives to segmented consumers, and finally, with the introduction of personalized recommendations as aggregated datapoints. Thus, the chapter shows how such opposing narratives have always been present, but different weights have been given to user constructions at different times.

In Chapter 6, we enter news organizations to investigate the introduction of personalized content distribution as a next step in a greater datafied evolution. With rich empirical examples from ethnographic fieldwork and qualitative interviews, we show how publics are cultivated through what we label 'personalization logics': individualism; dataism; and binarity and pre-determinedness. These 'personalization logics', we argue, become drivers for how media organization (re)construct their audiences, namely as aggregated, predictable and controllable datapoints. Thus, this reconstruction of the audience allows the media organizations to engage in new form of publics cultivation – publics by design – as they now materially begin to shape and design the publics they wish to cultivate into these systems. Finally, we discuss the broader implications of these processes and the cultivation of publics as personalized aggregated 'dividuals' by news media (Deleuze, 1992).

The third section of the book investigates the role of large-scale providers of technological infrastructure in shaping, validating and creating publics. It does this through the lens of what could be termed the 'old' or 'traditional' leading characters in this endeavour: the institutions of journalism and media.

Chapter 7 zooms in on metadata as an infrastructure in the news distribution ecology linking news media to the demands of intermediaries, by examining the metatags of 260 European news websites and determining the extent to which they apply metatags that allow webpages to be featured in Google search results. Furthermore, the chapter examines how media organizations are compliant with the metadata library of Schema.org, which is organized by, among others, Yandex, Google and the World Wide Web Consortium. While a majority of media are compliant with Google and Schema.org libraries, only a few large organizations utilize these to the full extent. Finally, the chapter discusses the impact on publics in the context of access to information via the news delivered through search engines.

Chapter 8 examines the digital infrastructure connected to media website architecture and discusses effects of such infrastructures on journalistic ideals of providing the information needed to enable a democratic public (see Strömbäck, 2005; Fenton, 2010). By using the media tech stacks as our point of departure, the chapter presents a mapping and categorizing of the systems sustaining journalism in the efforts of cultivating publics.

Next, by mapping third-party web services found on 361 European media websites, we uncover that the media in general rely heavily on Big Tech-provided systems for the production and distribution of journalistic content. In addition, we observe a large quantity of 'small tech' which tend to be overlooked in narratives around the dominance of Big Tech.

Chapter 9 concludes the book by discussing how datafication processes are transforming how the public takes shape, as well as the journalistic values and the dilemmas this brings about. However, we argue for a view that recognizes stability in that those technological affordances tend to reinforce already existing logics and discourses in journalism as well as existing public perceptions concerning the role that news media should play. Such assembling involves increasing dependence on large amounts of data and tools for analysing such data, which transforms not only the ways that news organizations cater to different publics but also the ontology of news and publics. This development questions which news is enhanced by audiences' (hybrid) activities. These audiences influence, contradict, oppose and discursively construct the tales of how citizens stay informed and democratically engage in datafied societies and the role of news in the formation and cultivation of publics. Knowing more about the formation of publics across spheres, we suggest, enables us to understand the multiple realities of datafication, and how these relate and coexist.

Taken together, the chapters offer different versions of how and when datafication matter for public formation and the multiple actors and practices involved in public formation. An important contribution and suggestion in this book is that publics are materialized and constructed over time when people pay attention to the discursive issues and injustices brought to light and represented by the media and direct this attention to engagement, calling for (political) action. In other words, publics are discursive clusters of stratified position takings by citizens (the plural is important here because publics do not always gather as a unit with a common goal) overlapping with clusters of media attention and visibility, legitimizing those position takings to a varying degree. And datafication matters for many of these modes of publicness. In the concluding chapter we revisit these core arguments and suggest that there is a need to blend our understanding of technologies and media with that of audience agency and look at how datafication is bringing about certain forms of power to specific actors, if we are to move beyond the drama and the rise and fall narrative of technologies as being something that is imposed upon us.

References

Anderson, C. (2011) 'Between creative and quantified audiences: Web metrics and changing patterns of newswork in local US newsrooms', *Journalism*, 12(5), pp 550–566. Available at: https://doi.org/10.1177/1464884911402451.

Anderson, C. (2013) 'Towards a sociology of computational and algorithmic journalism', *New Media & Society*, 15(7), pp 1005–1021. Available at: https://doi.org/10.1177/1461444812465137.

Ang, I. (2002) *Desperately Seeking the Audience*, Abingdon: Taylor & Francis.

Aristotle (1996) *Retorik*, Copenhagen: Museum Tusculanum.

Bartlett, J. (2018) *The People vs Tech: How the Internet is Killing Democracy (and How We Can Save It)*, London: Ebury Press.

Beer, D. (2017) 'The social power of algorithms', *Information, Communication & Society*, 20(1), pp 1–13. Available at: https://doi.org/10.1080/1369118X.2016.1216147.

Bolin, G. (2022) 'The value dynamics of data capitalism: Cultural production and consumption in a datafied world', in A. Hepp, J. Jarke and L. Kramp (eds) *New Perspectives in Critical Data Studies*, Cham: Springer International Publishing, pp 167–186. Available at: https://doi.org/10.1007/978-3-030-96180-0_8.

boyd, d. (2008) 'Why youth (heart) social network sites: The role of networked publics in teenage social life', in D. Buckingham (ed) *Youth, Identity, and Digital Media*, Cambridge, MA: MIT Press.

boyd, d. (2010) 'Social network sites as networked publics: Affordances, dynamics, and implications', in Z. Papacharissi (ed) *A Networked Self: Identity, Community, and Culture on Social Network Sites*, Oxford: Routledge, pp 39–58.

Bruns, A. and Burgess, J. (2015) 'Twitter hashtags from ad hoc to calculated publics', in N. Rambukkana (ed) *Hashtag Publics: The Power and Politics of Discursive Networks*, New York: Peter Lang, pp 13–28.

Bucher, T. (2018) *If ... Then: Algorithmic Power and Politics*, New York: Oxford University Press.

Butsch, R. (2008) *The Citizen Audience: Crowds, Publics, and Individuals*, New York: Routledge.

Calhoun, C. (2017) '2 facets of the public sphere: Dewey, Arendt, Habermas', in F. Engelstad, H. Larsen, J. Rogstad and K. Steen-Johnsen (eds) *Institutional Change in the Public Sphere*, Warsaw: De Gruyter Open, pp 23–45. Available at: https://doi.org/10.1515/9783110546330-003.

Chadwick, A. (2011) 'The political information cycle in a hybrid news system: The British prime minister and the "bullygate" affair', *The International Journal of Press/Politics*, 16(1), pp 3–29. Available at: https://doi.org/10.1177/1940161210384730.

Chadwick, A. (2013) *The Hybrid Media System: Politics and Power* (1st edn), Oxford: Oxford University Press. Available at: https://doi.org/10.1093/acprof:oso/9780199759477.001.0001.

Christin, A. (2020) *Metrics at Work: Journalism and the Contested Meaning of Algorithms*, Princeton: Princeton University Press.

Couldry, N. and Powell, A. (2014) 'Big data from the bottom up', *Big Data & Society* 1(2). Available at: https://doi.org/10.1177/2053951714539277.

Couldry, N. and Mejias, U.A. (2019) *The Costs of Connection: How Data is Colonizing Human Life and Appropriating It for Capitalism*, Stanford: Stanford University Press.

Cukier, K. and Mayer-Schönberger, V. (2014) 'The rise of big data: How it's changing the way we think about the world', in M. Pitici (ed) *The Best Writing on Mathematics 2014*, Princeton: Princeton University Press, pp 20–32. Available at: https://doi.org/10.1515/9781400865307-003.

Danske Medier (2021) *Medieudspil*. Available at: https://danskemedier.dk/wp-content/uploads/2021/10/Medieudspil_Danske-Medier.pdf.

Deleuze, G. (1992) 'Postscript on the societies of control', *October*, 59, pp 3–7.

Deuze, M. and Witschge, T. (2018) 'Beyond journalism: Theorizing the transformation of journalism', *Journalism*, 19(2), pp 165–181. Available at: https://doi.org/10.1177/1464884916688550.

Dewey, J.V. (2012 [1927]) *The Public and Its Problems: An Essay in Political Inquiry*, State College: Penn State University Press. Available at: https://doi.org/10.5325/j.ctt7v1gh.

Diakopoulos, N. and Koliska, M. (2017) 'Algorithmic transparency in the news media', *Digital Journalism*, 5(7), pp 809–828. Available at: https://doi.org/10.1080/21670811.2016.1208053.

Dinello, D. (2005) *Technophobia! Science Fiction Visions of Posthuman Technology*, Austin: University of Texas Press.

Domingo, D. (2005) 'The difficult shift from utopia to realism in the Internet era: A decade of online journalism research: theories, methodologies, results and challenges', paper presented at the First European Communication Conference, Amsterdam, 24–26 November 2005.

Dourish, P. and Bell, G. (2013) *Divining a Digital Future*, Cambridge, MA: MIT Press. Available at: https://doi.org/10.7551/mitpress/978026 2015554.001.0001.

Fenton, N. (2010) *New Media, Old News: Journalism & Democracy in the Digital Age*, London: SAGE. Available at: https://doi.org/10.4135/978144 6280010.n1.

Fraser, N. (1990) 'Rethinking the public sphere: A contribution to the critique of actually existing democracy', *Social Text*, 25/26, pp 56–80. Available at: https://doi.org/10.2307/466240.

Gillespie, T. (2014) 'The relevance of algorithms', in T. Gillespie, P.J. Boczkowski and K.A. Foot (eds) *Media Technologies*, Cambridge, MA: MIT Press, pp 167–194. Available at: https://doi.org/10.7551/mitpress/978026 2525374.003.0009.

Habermas, J. (1988) *Theory of Communicative Action*, Boston: Beacon.

Habermas, J. (1989 [1962]) *Structural Transformation of the Public Sphere*, Cambridge, MA: MIT Press.

Habermas, J. (2006 [1989]) 'Political communication in media society: Does democracy still enjoy an epistemic dimension? The impact of normative theory on empirical research', *Communication Theory*, 16(4), pp 411–426. Available at: https://doi.org/10.1111/j.1468-2885.2006.00280.x.

Hall, S. (1980) 'Encoding and decoding in the television discourse', in S. Hall, D. Hobson, A. Lowe and P. Tillis (eds) *Culture, Media, Language: Working Papers in Cultural Studies, 1972–79*, London: Hutchinson, pp 197–208.

Helberger, N. (2019) 'On the democratic role of news recommenders', *Digital Journalism*, 7(8), pp 993–1012. Available at: https://doi.org/10.1080/ 21670811.2019.1623700.

Ingold, T. (2000) *The Perception of the Environment: Essays on Livelihood, Dwelling and Skill*, London: Routledge.

Introna, L. and Nissenbaum, H. (2000) 'Shaping the web: Why the politics of search engines matters', *The Information Society*, 16(3), pp 169–185. Available at: https://doi.org/10.1080/01972240050133634.

Ito, M. (2008) 'Introduction', in K. Varnelis (ed) *Networked Publics*, Cambridge, MA: MIT Press, pp 1–14.

Kaiser, J. and Rauchfleisch, A. (2019) 'Integrating concepts of counterpublics into generalised public sphere frameworks: Contemporary transformations in radical forms', *Javnost–The Public*, 26(3), pp 241–257. Available at: https://doi.org/10.1080/13183222.2018.1558676.

Kennedy, H., Poell, T. and van Dijck, J. (2015) 'Data and agency', *Big Data & Society*, 2(2), pp 1–7. Available at: https://doi.org/10.1177/205395171 5621569.

Korn, M., Reißmann, W., Röhl, T. and Sittler, D. (eds) (2019) *Infrastructuring Publics*, Wiesbaden: Springer Fachmedien. Available at: https://doi.org/ 10.1007/978-3-658-20725-0_2.

Lievrouw, L.A. (2009) 'New media, mediation and communication study', *Information, Communication & Society*, 12(3), pp 303–325. Available at: https://doi.org/10.1080/13691180802660651.

Lippmann, W. (1993 [1925]) *The Phantom Public*, New York: Transaction Publishers.

Livingstone, S. (2007) 'The challenge of engaging youth online: Contrasting producers' and teenagers' interpretations of websites', *European Journal of Communication*, 22(2), pp 165–184. Available at: https://doi.org/10.1177/ 0267323107076768.

Livingstone, S. (2019) 'Audiences in an age of datafication: Critical questions for media research', *Television & New Media*, 20(2), pp 170–183. Available at: https://doi.org/10.1177/1527476418811118.

Marwick, A.E. and boyd, d. (2014) 'Networked privacy: How teenagers negotiate context in social media', *New Media and Society*, 16(7). Available at: https://doi.org/10.1177/1461444814543995.

Mathieu, D. and Pruulmann Vengerfeldt, P. (2020) 'The data loop of media and audience', *MedieKultur: Journal of Media and Communication Research*, 36(69), pp 116–138. Available at: https://doi.org/10.7146/mediekultur. v36i69.121178.

Mejias, U.A. and Couldry, N. (2019) 'Datafication', *Internet Policy Review*, 8(4). Available at: https://policyreview.info/concepts/datafication.

Møller Hartley, J. (2011) *Radikalisering af kampzonen: en analyse af netjournalistisk praksis og selvforståelse i spændingsfeltet mellem idealer og publikum*, PhD thesis, Roskilde University Centre. Available at: https://forskning. ruc.dk/da/publications/radikalisering-af-kampzonen-en-analyse-af-netjo urnalistisk-praksi.

Møller Hartley, J. and Schwartz, S.A. (2020) 'Trust, disconnection, minimizing risk and apathy', *MedieKultur: Journal of Media and Communication Research*, 36(69), pp 011–028. Available at: https://doi.org/10.7146/mediekultur. v36i69.121182.

Møller Hartley, J. Bengtsson, M., Schjøtt Hansen, A. and Fischer Sivertsen, M. (2021) 'Researching publics in datafied societies: Insights from four approaches to the concept of "publics" and a (hybrid) research agenda', *New Media & Society*, 146144482110210. Available at: https://doi.org/ 10.1177/14614448211021045.

Nielsen, R.K. and Ganter, S.A. (2022) *The Power of Platforms: Shaping Media and Society*, Oxford: Oxford University Press.

Noble, S.U. (2018) *Algorithms of Oppression: How Search Engines Reinforce Racism*, New York: New York University Press.

O'Neil, C. (2016) *Weapons of Math Destruction: How Big Data Increases Inequality and Threatens Democracy* (1st edn), New York: Crown.

Papacharissi, Z. (2015) *Affective Publics: Sentiment, Technology, and Politics*, Oxford: Oxford University Press.

Pariser, E. (2011) *The Filter Bubble: How the New Personalized Web is Changing What We Read and How We Think*, New York: Penguin.

Picone, I., Kleut, J., Pavlíčková, T., Romic, B., Møller Hartley, J. and De Ridder, S. (2019) 'Small acts of engagement: Reconnecting productive audience practices with everyday agency', *New Media & Society*, 21(9), pp 2010–2028. Available at: https://doi.org/10.1177/1461444819837569.

Public Service Media Manifesto (2021) *The Public Service Media and Public Service Internet Manifesto*, online report. Available at: https://ia902206.us.archive.org/5/items/psmi_20220127/psmi.pdf.

Quandt, T. (2018) 'Dark participation', *Media and Communication*, 6(4), pp 36–48. Available at: https://doi.org/10.17645/mac.v6i4.1519.

Schjøtt Hansen, A. and Møller Hartley, J. (2021) 'Designing what's news: An ethnography of a personalization algorithm and the data-driven (re)assembling of the news', *Digital Journalism,* DOI: 10.1080/21670811.2021.1988861.

Strömbäck, J. (2005) 'In search of a standard: Four models of democracy and their normative implications for journalism', *Journalism Studies*, 6, pp 331–345. Available at: https://doi.org/10.1080/14616700500131950.

Sunstein, C.R. (2001) *Republic.com*, Princeton: Princeton University Press.

Tandoc, E.C. (2014) 'Journalism is twerking? How web analytics is changing the process of gatekeeping', *New Media & Society*, 16(4), pp 559–575. Available at: https://doi.org/10.1177/1461444814530541.

Treré, E. (2018) 'From digital activism to algorithmic resistance', in M. Graham (ed) *The Routledge Companion to Media and Activism*, Oxford: Routledge Handbooks Online. Available at: https://doi.org/10.4324/9781315475059-39.

Unesco (2022) *UNESCO World Trends in Freedom of Expression and Media Development: Global Report 2021/2022*. Available at: https://www.unesco.org/reports/world-media-trends/2021/en.

Van Dijck, J. (2014) 'Datafication, dataism and dataveillance: Big Data between scientific paradigm and ideology.', *Surveillance & Society*, 12(2), pp 197–208.

Van Dijck, J., Poell, T. and De Waal, M. (2018) *The Platform Society: Public Values in an Online World*, New York: Oxford University Press.

Velkova, J. and Kaun, A. (2019) 'Algorithmic resistance: Media practices and the politics of repair', *Information, Communication & Society*, pp 1–18. Available at: https://doi.org/10.1080/1369118X.2019.1657162.

Vestager, M. (2020) *Building Trust in Technology*, EPC webinar, Digital Clearinghouse, 29 October. Available at: https://ec.europa.eu/commiss ion/commissioners/2019-2024/vestager/announcements/speech-execut ive-vice-president-margrethe-vestager-building-trust-technology_en.

Vincent, J. (2022) *Beyond Measure: The Hidden History of Measurement from Cubits to Quantum Constants*, New York: W.W. Norton.

Vu, H.T. (2014) 'The online audience as gatekeeper: The influence of reader metrics on news editorial selection', *Journalism*, 15(8), pp 1094–1110. Available at: https://doi.org/10.1177/1464884913504259.

Ziewitz, M. (2016) 'Governing algorithms: Myth, mess, and methods', *Science, Technology, & Human Values*, 41(1), pp 3–16. Available at: https://doi.org/10.1177/0162243915608948.

Zuboff, S. (2019) *The Age of Surveillance Capitalism: The Fight for the Human Future at the New Frontier of Power*, London: Profile Books.

Zuiderveen Borgesius, F.J., Trilling, D., Möller, J., Bodó, B., de Vreese, C.H. and Helberger, N. (2016) 'Should we worry about filter bubbles?', *Internet Policy Review*, 5(1), pp 1–16. Available at: https://doi.org/10.14763/2016.1.401.

PART I

Agentic Publics

2

Deconstructing the Notion of Algorithmic Control over Datapublics

David Mathieu

Introduction

Facebook has identified that I am interested in certain genres of music, even certain bands, and that I regularly go to concerts. On that basis, its algorithm puts me in connection with a concert ticket seller for a band I like, and a sponsored ad is shown on my newsfeed. I click on the ad and contact my friend. I buy two tickets.

Algorithms – in this case a recommender model – exert considerable control. They know a lot about me, anticipate my interests, decide what information to show me and even succeed in making me buy concert tickets. In this well-known tale of algorithmic control, however, other accounts go untold.

From my perspective, I had an interest in this band long before Facebook took an interest in me. Had I seen the ad elsewhere, the outcome would have been the same. Had my friend not wanted to join, I would not have bought tickets. It happened that the Facebook algorithm was aligned with my sociocultural practice, though not quite. After purchasing the tickets, I was recommended the same concert the day after. There are still many things the algorithm does not know about me and my reality.

The aim of this chapter is to challenge the myth of algorithmic control from an audience perspective. What I wish to question is whether the intense datafication taking place in media organizations leaves audiences without associated agency. In other words, do audiences have any 'data agency'?[1] To answer this question, I applied an audience and reception perspective to the notion of algorithmic control. My interest lies in the pragmatics of algorithmic control in the same way Stuart Hall (1980) was interested in finding out *how* media effects take place, opening the door for understanding how media control is resisted by audiences.

I see four reasons why the notion of algorithmic control is worth challenging in Media and Communication research. First, the notion reflects considerations for media production more than for media consumption. Second, as Hall (1980) argued, media consumption does not directly follow media production and should be studied in its own right. Third, algorithmic control concerns audiences as *imagined* (at the moment of production) rather than as *actualized* at the moment of consumption.[2] Fourth, audiences tend to be regarded as easily manipulated, vulnerable, gullible, and so on (Livingstone, 2019), especially in the context of emerging technologies. For all these reasons, we need to examine the moment of consumption to explore the relations between agency and algorithmic control.

The chapter first situates the notion of algorithmic control in the broader literature on datafication and algorithms. Claims that user agency has disappeared from media consumption do not have much empirical basis; it is clear, however, that algorithms and data are replacing the agency of media producers. User-centred studies emphasize the everyday experiences of users and underline how the work of algorithms is met by their imaginations and emotional responses.

To advance an audience perspective on the notion of algorithmic control, I present some general evidence that calls into question the dependence of audiences on media. Algorithmic control is not as effective as it is imagined – or wished for – in the moment of production. Rather, data and algorithms need to be inserted in prolongation of the larger history of the audience measurement industry. This industry has attempted to control audiences by producing knowledge about them from what Ang (1991) calls an 'institutional perspective', a perspective that has repeatedly succeeded in creating audience measurements but that has repeatedly failed at understanding them. A distinction between an institutional and a sociocultural perspective on audiences is further elaborated in the context of data by making a distinction between our 'uses of media' – what is essentially captured as data and turned into (limited) knowledge – and our sociocultural practices, which remain to date largely invisible and incomprehensible to the algorithm. I further argue that the gap between uses and practices provides a reflexive space of agency, which I conceptualize in relation to two moments in the data loop (Mathieu and Pruulmann Vengerfeldt, 2020) as inspective and inscriptive agency.

The problems with the notion of algorithmic control

Algorithms provide a radical shift in the way we imagine the formation of publics on contemporary media (Fisher and Mehozay, 2019). Publics were known to be selective (Katz et al, 1974), to form communities of interpretation (Fish, 1980) and to freely give their attention to public issues (Warner, 2002). It would appear that publics are now selected, interpreted, calculated and anticipated by algorithmic media in ways that call into question their agency. There is no industry other than news where these issues are more pressing due to the implications that algorithms may have for democracy (Bozdag and van den Hoven, 2015), for our participation in public life (Gillespie, 2014) and for our individual autonomy (Andrejevic, 2020).

Gillespie (2014) suggests the notion of 'calculated publics' to underline the work of algorithms in anticipating which issues citizens should be exposed to, contributing 'to constitute and codify the publics they claim to measure, publics that would not otherwise exist except that the algorithm called them into existence' (2014, p 23). In other words, algorithms are not so much filtering content as they are filtering and ordering publics (Birkbak and Carlsen, 2016). If publics can be calculated, they become amenable for manipulation and control, and the value of public attention for the functioning of democracy becomes severely impaired. Similarly, if algorithms create regimes of visibility and recognition of public issues (Jacobsen, 2021), those who own algorithms are essentially in control of the digital public sphere. Given that a platform like Facebook had on average 2.9 billion active users per month in 2021,[3] there are reasons to be concerned when publics emerge within its walled gardens.

Thus, it appears that the literature has espoused the notion of algorithmic control. It is said that algorithms have the power to shape our thoughts (Berry, 2014; cited in Beer, 2017), our actions and our identity (Turow, 2011; Cheney-Lippold, 2017) and are therefore viewed as technologies of 'control' or 'soft power' (Karakayali et al, 2018) or manipulation (Tufekci, 2015). Yet, there are several issues with the notion of algorithmic control that I address in this section.

This literature makes implicit claims regarding how data and algorithms shape, control or even produce publics, bringing us back to a new era of effect studies not felt through the power of ideology but through the everyday presence of algorithms and data in our mediated encounters (Lash, 2007; Willson, 2017). There is a soft technological determinism implied in the theorizing of algorithmic control. The concepts of calculated publics or algorithmic publics imply the idea that something is done to these publics, not the other way around. It is not that these concepts were developed with an explicit view of technological determinism, but rather that they convey this assumption by virtue of not paying attention to actual consumption.

To avoid the spectre of technological determinism that hangs over research on algorithmic control, we should look beyond considerations for the production and distribution of content and consider algorithms as part of the broader sociocultural practice of media users. If we do not pay sufficient attention to the difference that consumptive practices bring to the formation of datapublics, we risk seeing these publics as defenceless and easily manipulated or seeing algorithmic power as inevitable (which brings us back to technological determinism).

Another argument in favour of algorithmic control is that algorithms are viewed as possessing agency and therefore have the power to act (on humans). Tufekci (2015) conceptualizes them, with inspiration from Actor-Network Theory, as 'actants'. While authors like Beer point to the 'meshing of human and machine agency' (2017, p 4), others, such as Willson (2017), argue that human agency is delegated to the algorithms as we rely on them to perform tasks once done by humans. Thus, as we increasingly rely on algorithmic media, we are presumedly giving away our agency.

It is however more accurate to state that algorithms replace agency from media producers. Algorithms can perform actions once in the province of media producers. They can filter content for audiences and make predictions about their tastes or interests, actions that newspaper editors and journalists have taken in profusion before the advent of big data. Thus, any agency that is lost seems to be so at the moment of production rather than consumption. There is no evidence that agency is a zero-sum game, so that what is taken by the algorithm at the moment of production does not necessarily mean a loss to users at the moment of consumption.

Because media and platforms are avidly relying on data and algorithms, it is said that algorithms have the power to shape consumption. It is argued that the data profiles constructed about us define our identity (Cheney-Lippold, 2011, 2017) and filter our encounters with media (Pariser, 2012) by 'tailoring the "conditions of possibility"' (Cheney-Lippold, cited in Prey, 2018, p 1097) for our media consumption.

In the context of music listening, for example, algorithms are said to shape musical taste, contexts of consumption and ultimately culture (Hallinan and Striphas, 2016; Prey, 2018). A prominent voice in this context is Robert Prey, who argues that data do not so much mirror users but serve to enact them. Prey argues 'that instead of focusing on the relative accuracy or inaccuracy of one's "data shadow", we need to study the processes of data subject formation and its implications for subject formation' (2018, p 1088).

Using the concept of 'algorithmic individuation', Prey articulates a clear view of algorithmic control, but this view is confined to the moment of production. A data subject is constructed with help of the algorithm, but how does the meeting with actual subjects take place? Similarly, it is said that algorithms shape identity and culture, but what is meant is that algorithms encode our identity and culture. There is decidedly a missing concept of 'decoding' (Hall, 1980) to confirm the effectiveness of algorithmic control in the realm of consumption.

The argument advanced by Prey and others is reminiscent of the 'subject position' in literary theory in which the subject is constructed by the text (now by data). We know from a long tradition of audience research that readers, viewers and listeners do not always endorse the subject position presented to them (see the pioneering work of Radway, 1991)[4] and that the anticipated audience used by media producers to conceive their texts does not always resonate with the actual audience encountering these texts (Livingstone, 2007).

Since Hall's ground-breaking paper 'Encoding and decoding in the television discourse' (1980), we know that media consumption does not follow media production. In 'The problem of ideology', Hall (1986) argues that it is reductionist to believe that changes in technology necessarily result in changes in cultural practices. He argues that the moment of cultural production and its embedding in technology provides determination in the first instance, while consumption provides determination in the last instance.

Another claim advanced by Birkbak and Carlsen (2016) highlights algorithmic filtering as a significant issue because the public is dependent on media to provide orientation in public affairs. Lacking knowledge to make sense of the world, the public is dependent on news. It is this link of dependence that is said to make data and algorithms particularly powerful.

This idea that publics are dependent on news media comes from an old normative understanding of the role of journalism in correcting an inadequate public and filling up empty recipients with the right news for them. As algorithms are replacing important functions incumbent to media production, a crude argument can be made that, in the process, an outdated paternalistic conception of the role of journalism for the public is indiscriminately transferred to the algorithm.[5]

There is also empirical evidence calling into question this dependency of audience on media. Schrøder and Phillips (2007), in a study that exemplifies the gap between media production and consumption, show that the discursive repertoires presented in the news and those held by audiences, while representing the same agendas, have different prominence, leaving us with a classic chicken-and-egg problem. According to Schrøder, 'the theoretical solution to this paradox consists in complexifying the way we conceptualize the notion of discursive power in a mediatized society and leaving open the possibility ... that the power relationship between media and audience-citizens is "complex and bi-directional"' (2017, p 109).

It should be clearer at this point that, as algorithmic control takes place in media production, notions such as calculated publics and algorithmic publics refer to audiences as they are imagined, represented or anticipated by media professionals, now by algorithms. The distinction between imagined and actual audiences is important because it clarifies that algorithmic control is first and foremost a sought-after power, meaning that it is an *attempt* to control the audience (and at times even an illusion of control).

To further illustrate the relative independence of the audience towards this sought-after power of algorithm, let us consider the success rate of Google AdWords,[6] one of the most prevalent algorithms that puts advertisers in contact with consumers in real-time based on principles of algorithmic relevance. As of 2018, the average click-through rate was 3.17 per cent for search and 0.46 per cent for banner display.[7] It is worth noting that for advertisements delivered alongside search results, users are already placed in a relation of relevance towards the advertisements recommended, as these are intended to match their search for information. In other words, in a situation of consumption, highly motivated users are rejecting or ignoring the prospect of 96.84 per cent advertisements aimed at them, testifying to a gap between algorithmic production and consumption that is far too seldom explored and theorized. At the same time, such a high rejection makes sense if we consider that algorithmic recommendations reflect not an effective way to produce attention but rather the desire of an industry in desperate search of audience attention.

Attempts at controlling the audience are not a new concern in media studies (especially regarding the advertising industry); however, the novelty concerns both the means by which this control is attempted and its application to the public sphere. Tufekci, concerned with possible harms to democracies, views algorithms as manipulative in that they are based on user data, allowing for recommendations tailored to individual users. The effect of algorithmic work is 'neither transparent nor obvious' (Tufekci, 2015, p 206) and hence more effective, making it difficult for users to react with their own agency.

And yet, the difficulty for audiences to understand algorithms or their intent should not be equated with audience passivity nor with algorithmic effectivity. User-centric studies argue that, while most users have no insights into the inner workings of algorithms, they rely on their 'imagination' (Bucher, 2017), 'folk theories' (DeVito et al, 2017; Ytre-Arne and Moe, 2020; Büchi et al, 2021) or 'heuristics' (Mathieu and Møller Hartley, 2021) to understand the implications of algorithms and datafication on their mediated experiences. Among these scholars there is a consensus that to properly understand the consequences and implications of algorithmic work, the everyday experiences of ordinary citizens need to be considered (Kennedy, 2018; Lomborg and Kapsch, 2019; Ytre-Arne and Moe, 2020).

Users often notice the workings of algorithms when they make inaccurate predictions, fail to properly capture their identity or when their outcomes are made visible (Buchi et al, 2021). These encounters contribute to a recognition that algorithms are not all-powerful, but also fallible (Buchi et al, 2021). These encounters create strong emotional reactions among users (Bucher, 2017), who are shocked, amused, angered, upset, annoyed, uncomfortable or consternated by the omnipresence of algorithms, especially when data is 'creeping back' to them (Lupton and Michael, 2017; Ruckenstein and Granroth, 2019). These thorny experiences can stimulate reflections (Swart,

2021), which create 'potentials for critical user engagement with algorithmic media' (Ytre-Arne and Moe, 2020, p 820).

In spite of their opacity, there is still room for users to influence the outcomes of algorithms (Lomborg and Kapsch, 2019; Schwartz and Mahnke, 2021). Examining not what algorithms *do to* users but rather what users *do with* algorithms, Karakayali et al argue that users rely on algorithms as companions to actively change aspects of their music listening practices (2018, p 4). In the context of news reading, Min (2019) shows that most US users actively instruct the algorithm in consuming more or less news, or even challenge its logic. Some users react to the very idea of having their news curated by the algorithm 'due to fears of missing out, concerns around surveillance, and because they wanted journalism to contain elements of surprise' (Swart, 2021, p 8).

Algorithmic control as an extension of audience measurement

Most discussions on algorithmic control have their locus on the moment of production, and hence the real target of this notion seems to be, not audiences, but media producers. Audiences come into the picture in their imaginations, often objects to control. Thus, I suggest understanding the use of data and algorithms in prolongation to the audience measurement industry, as this is useful to understand the nature of algorithmic control.[8]

In 'Desperately seeking the audience', Ang (1991) projects the distinction between imagined and actual audiences into a political economy of media. She argues that knowledge produced about audiences by media organizations – the way they imagine audiences – is 'constructed from the vantage point of the institutions, in the interests of the institutions' (Ang, 1991, p 2). She claims the institutional perspective to be rather blind to the sociocultural practices of audiences but useful in producing knowledge that allows organizations to operate and make decisions that are essential to their survival and reproduction.

As Crawford points out, audiences were anticipated long before the advent of algorithms (2016, p 81). Algorithms are comparable to other techniques used to know the audience that focus on behavioural measurements, such as ratings with their measures of attention, or eyeballs. Fisher and Mehozay suggests that 'the algorithmic episteme does not see the audience more accurately, but differently' (2019, p 1) based on its empiricist ideology of 'dataism' (van Dijck, 2014), which primarily considers behavioural traces and relations between them, resulting in a quantification of the lens by which audiences are viewed by the media. Similarly, the control afforded by algorithms, such as providing personalized recommendations, can be assimilated to other strategies used by media companies to anticipate the audience, such as programming and scheduling in flow television.

According to Ang (1991), the power of media to form or control the subject – to borrow the expression used by Prey (2018) – is only discursive in the sense that it rests on the production of knowledge about audiences and not the exercise of coercion. Following Ang's rationale, I contend that algorithmic control rests on the production of knowledge about audiences from the multiple datapoints that are collected about them. Algorithmic control is discursive control.

Media content is now produced and distributed from the knowledge that results from the collection of data on media audiences. Clicks, likes, tags, time spent, time of the day, location and a host of other data are collected from our uses of media. In addition, we are assigned a variety of categories and profiles depending on the characteristics of the content we click on. These attributions are largely the result of second-guessing our interests, preferences, motivations and identities rather than having us voice these in any deliberate way. These meanings are inferred from our uses; they are so-called 'indicators of user engagement' (Napoli, 2011), and they come at the price of insecurity, sometimes inaccuracy and even vagueness towards what is going on in our sociocultural environment.

Information about us is also aggregated with other users and compared to extrapolate from the available information in order to make predictions about future use or looked-for content intended to capture or maintain our attention. These aggregations, computations and recommendations are common tasks performed by a variety of algorithms built by media and cultural institutions.[9]

As long as these categories, attributions and predictions perform their roles in media organizations to provide a non-negligible difference that can be linked to profit, their reliance will be maintained, even perhaps assimilated to the truth or to all there is to know about the audience (what van Dijck [2014] calls the ideology of dataism). This is why it is important to link algorithmic control to the audience measurement industry. This industry has been created for the pursuit of profits, notably by helping media companies fix the price of audience attention they were able to capture, which they then sell to advertisers. The (sometimes inaccurate, surely incomplete and rather ineffective[10]) work of data is only acceptable in a commercial framework that views audiences as profit margins. Algorithmic control appears less acceptable – and relevant – in the context of public formation, which might be linked more to social and cultural practices than the activity of consuming.

The gap between media use and sociocultural practices

Platforms can be seen as a space *in which* communication takes place rather than as something users interact with. Users *google* their questions, *hashtag* an issue, *tweet* their network, *tag* their friends on Facebook, and so on. This may give the impression that today's technology *contains* and thus shapes communication and culture by constraining (enabling and disabling) what users can do with it.

Also considering the sociocultural practices of users allows to relativize this view. The issue with the view of technology as a container is that it primarily attends to the *uses of media*, the behavioural traces that can be observed and surveilled on digital media, but it lacks an appreciation for the sociocultural practices that drive usage. Livingstone urges research to avoid reducing audiences to mere data and confusing the *activities* of platform users with the *work* of the platform in collecting and monetizing those activities (2019, p 285). This has, according to Livingstone, led us to incorrectly assume that technology defines the practices of audiences. Consider this situation discussed by Couldry:

> Watching a football game on television (an apparently simple media 'object') might for one person be best analyzed as part of their practice as a football fan; for another, it may be not their own passion to watch football, but an obligation or pleasure shared with others that explains their watching, for example in a public space as an expression of group solidarity or at home as an expression of family solidarity; another person may simply be filling in time, a practice that like some magazines is instantly 'putdownable' (Hermes 1995) as soon as an interesting interruption occurs. (Couldry, 2011, p 218)

A way of using media such as 'watching television' (or in the context of digital media, clicking, liking, tagging, and so on) can mean different things when inserted in different practices. Clicking on a news item found on social media can be part of the practice of passing time for one, while it can be part of the practice of information-seeking for another. In this respect, clicking on a news item is similar to turning the pages of a newspaper, a rather meaningless activity in itself unless inserted into a practice. While use is necessary to enact practices, it in no way defines these practices. Conversely, a practice can be fulfilled by a variety of uses. For example, the practice of reading news can be fulfilled through a variety of media uses and non-media activities – newspaper, radio, television, social media and conversation – and is in no way dependent on a particular platform, such as Facebook. In fact, the practice of news reading pre-dates Facebook and will surely outlive Facebook.

Usage and practices are two sides of the same coin, but the distinction is nevertheless an important one. As should be obvious at this point, usage is both the object of measurement and something that can be contained by technology. Practices are neither of these things. Practices are shaped by meaning, tradition, habit, culture and identity, and populate the sociocultural everyday life of audiences. Couldry (2004, 2011), a strong advocate of this perspective, defines media practice as 'the mass of things people do and say (and indeed believe) that are oriented to, or related to, media' (2011, p 217). Clicking on a news item is an online behaviour, a way of consuming digital media (just like a newspaper affords the turning of its pages). As a practice, news reading owes more to ideas about democracy, civic engagement and the public sphere than it does to the recommendation algorithm of Facebook.

Practices play a strong role in orienting media use. In my own research, we showed how different practices – the practices of 'public connection', of 'keeping up with family' or of 'engaging in local communities' – provides a system of relevance to organize the activities of scrolling and clicking that characterize the use of the Facebook newsfeed (Mathieu and Pavlíčková, 2017). These practices allow users to parse, select and exclude content and decide what to click on and what not to click. In other words, meaningful practices are what allow users to organize and give meaning to an otherwise monotonous flow of various content suggested by the algorithm, turning the activities of scrolling and clicking on an algorithmically produced list of content into a meaningful and unique experience for users.

However, only clicks and other uses of media that can be encoded are visible to the algorithm, which cannot make a distinction between an accidental click and an intentional click, for example. Algorithms categorize media uses from an institutional perspective and not through the eyes of those who engage in a cultural practice. An examination of the interests that Facebook uses to categorize its users show that these categories reflect more the interest of advertisers than the sociocultural interests of users.[11] Our practices are largely invisible to the algorithm. Instead, algorithms generate a data double as a substitute to these practices that reflects first and foremost the interests of media producers and advertisers.

Because algorithms feed on 'surface' behavioural data (Fisher and Mehozay, 2019), the institutional perspective runs the risk of reducing or misrepresenting the sociocultural practices of users. This gap is intriguing enough to prompt Groot Kormelink and Costera Meijer (2018; see also Steensen et al, 2020) to investigate the misfits between clicking on news (a use) and interest in news (a practice). As they explain:

> [M]aking use of news might not be equivalent to finding it important or even having an interest in it. And vice versa, non-use may not mean people find it unimportant or do not have an interest in it. ... Still, measuring interest or value through usage frequency is a common research practice. (Costera Meijer and Groot Kormelink, 2017, p 346)

What these scholars also show is that clicking on news can mean not one thing but 30 different things to users (Groot Kormelink and Costera Meijer, 2018). There is therefore a reduction in the complexities and variations of our sociocultural practices when it is registered through the measurement of surface behaviours according to an institutional perspective that has an interest not in knowing us but in monetizing content. More clicks simply mean more revenue.

Algorithms can recognize a specific *media use* because it is recognizable as a token, because it is valuable (and not necessarily valuable to the user), or because the use fits a pattern or category that is deemed salient, or it is attributable to some categories already encoded in the system. The reasons are many and commonly opaque to the user, but once the algorithm has recognized a media use that it identifies as salient, it will often repeatedly provide a recommendation of content that is aligned with the usage. This is often noticed by the user when the algorithm continues to show similar content that demands a disproportionate amount of attention not warranted by the user's practice.

There is therefore a quantification at play in misunderstanding sociocultural practices. Once we are being registered by the algorithm as a particular type (for example, organic-friendly mother) or as having a particular interest (for example, in a coming event), we often receive repetitive recommendations that can be considered intrusive (Mollen and Dhaenens, 2018), irritating (Ytre-Arne and Moe, 2020) or even harassing. Our reaction against this insistence of the algorithm to define us in a certain way comes from a fracture felt between our sociocultural reality and its quantification through data. Some media uses can easily be associated with certain aspects of our practices; aspects that become overemphasized by the algorithm, creating a distorted view as we see our practices through the mirror of the algorithm.

We also become aware of the gap between uses and practices when media incorrectly categorize our identity, but the gap between use and practice is there even when the work of data can be said to be correct. Even when it aligns with our sociocultural practice, the work of an algorithm was never intended to represent our practices. Returning to the example provided at the beginning of this chapter, the algorithm does not 'know' why I am interested in music or in that particular band. It does not 'know' that I will refuse to go to this concert alone. It does not 'know' why I might stop taking an interest in this band, or on the contrary, that I am ready to go to all of their concerts. The algorithm only has a surface representation of us based on our previous uses of media, popular uses of other people and uses of people who display similar patterns to us. It was never intended to provide a picture of our sociocultural practices with all that implies of complexity and fluidity.

Reversing the ontology of data

The discursive control afforded by algorithms resides in its capacity to classify users into categories and profiles, which generates certain outputs, such as recommendations of content. These profiles, which Prey (2018) calls data subjects, are enacted in various ways, constraining the uses of different platforms. However, rather than presume that these profiles are imposed on users or simply accepted by them, we can imagine that the audience can become aware of the reflection that datafied media provides to them. 'The media, then, act here not as a camera [recording our every move, cf surveillance (Zuboff, 2020)], but as a mirror, reflecting back the image they capture. This, according to Gillespie, creates a feedback loop by which "the algorithmic presentation of publics back to themselves shape a public's sense of itself"' (in Fisher and Mehozay, 2019, p 13).

These profiles are therefore 'interactive' (Couldry et al, 2016, p 122) and 'sustained in the reflexive activities of the individual' (Giddens, 1991, p 52). Giddens considers identity formation as a 'trajectory' (1991, p 14) rather than as a moment-to-moment creation. Identity has a past and a future, and individuals can call into question the fragmented flow of content recommendations according to these imagined trajectories. Carrigan defines 'technological reflexivity' as 'drawing upon technology in a way that is satisfying and sustainable, consistent with our existing purposes and projects' as something more distinct than 'picking it up and putting it down'.[12]

Hence, it is no surprise to experience gaps between these surface measurements and the practices we engage in. Our practices are informed by our ideals, by our identity – who we are and want to be – and by what we want to get out of media. In this sense, practices are dynamic and fluid and in constant negotiation as they relate to our self under constant construction, not to our data double as fixed by the algorithm.

In behavioural research, it is often argued that behavioural data provide the true picture of a person. What people *say they do* and what they *actually do* are two separate universes, the latter characterized by precision and measurement and the former as vague and unreliable. This belief has regained vigour with the advent of Big Data. There is no longer a need to ask people what they do because we have access to a mass of data on their behaviours.

When compared to interview data (data obtained via a method dedicated to exploring talks and meanings) behavioural data is often given precedence. For example, it is well-known in interview research that social desirability provides a normative bias that can lead participants to overestimate their consumption of news compared to what can be measured by behavioural methods. Audiences overestimate their consumption of news because it is seen as a desirable practice, and conversely, people tend to underestimate their consumption of entertainment because this is socially frowned upon and regarded as a waste of time.

What if we turned this around and argued that people, through their behaviours, under-consumed news compared to the social ideals they live by. In other words, we could say that there is a tension and a constant negotiation between their practices and their actual uses. It is a slippery slope to give behavioural data prominence over practices and meanings because we cannot deny the reality of people having these ideas about what they do. The ideas that lead people to overestimate their behaviours are the same ideas that push people towards those behaviours. Instead of understanding this as a bias, as is often done, we could understand these overestimations as the expression of ideals that people live by, perhaps even as dissatisfaction towards a reality that they themselves suspected ('I should make an effort to read the newspaper more often'). Perhaps we could even push the envelope and say that the behavioural measure of news consumption is simply a bias that misrepresents the ideals by which people live by.

On the one hand, one could argue that it is precisely this lack of attention to practice – this emphasis on behaviours only – that limits the capacity of algorithmic media to fully understand what users are doing on their platforms. On the other hand, it is also this gap that provides an opportunity for audiences to resist the control of algorithms, a control fuelled by uses, not practices.

Communicative agency as mirroring in the data loop

The relation between the institutional and sociocultural perspectives on audiences – or between imagined and actual audiences – is interactive. To properly understand this interaction at the age of data, we need to understand how these two perspectives interact in what we (Mathieu and Pruulmann Vengerfeldt, 2020) have called elsewhere the 'data loop of media and audience'.

This model of the data loop is a suggestion to understand the relation between encoding and decoding (Hall, 1980) in the age of data (given that audiences also encode [Livingstone, 2019, p 174]). We suggest that as data travels back and forth between media production and consumption, the relation between encoding and decoding becomes reciprocal. Hence, data collected at the moment of media consumption inform media production and are then retroacted back to users in the form of datafied mediated experiences, such as algorithmic recommendations.

The data loop we describe not only implies the collecting and analysing of data but also the 'feeding of such data back to users, enabling them to orient themselves in the world' (Kennedy et al, 2015). When personal data deliver algorithmic recommendations, media not only capture the audience but also provide a 'mirror reflecting back the data the media capture' (Fisher and Mehozay, 2019, p 13). This reflexive practice is considered crucial for the development of agency (Couldry, 2014, p 891). In turn, this reflexivity can incite users to modify their use of media to influence subsequent encoding of their data and so forth.

It is the space between the uses of media registered during data collection and the practices of users that permits reflexivity to work. What we suggest with the model of the data loop is that audiences can become aware of these reflections in datafied experiences, and based on this reflexivity, can possibly react to, circumvent or resist how they are imagined by media producers through the datafication of their mediated experiences.

However, the relationship between imagined and actual audiences is clearly asymmetric. It has been argued that data bring another divide between those who have access to data (as well as access to the means by which data are turned into knowledge, such as computation, artificial intelligence, machine learning, algorithms) and those who do not (Zuboff, 2020). Media producers can learn much more about users through data than the opposite. The work of data and algorithms is said to be invisible, automatic, complex, opaque, and so on, making it difficult for users to rely on their agency.

In that connection, Ytre-Arne and Das (2020) argue that there is a need to develop the notion of agency in the specific contexts of communication (how agency is linked to communication processes, such as interaction, engagement, influence, and so on) and datafication (how agency is linked to data, algorithms, infrastructures, and so on). They argue that communicative agency has become increasingly prospective in the face of a complex, widespread, opaque and risk-inducing datafication of media, leaving the audience with no choice but to recourse to their imagination (Bucher, 2017) to navigate these new environments.

There is growing literature showing how users are resisting datafied media, ranging from disconnecting, providing false information about themselves, restricting their uses, gaming the algorithms, and so on (see Lomborg and Kapsch, 2019). When users are engaged in these behaviours, they do so against a set of ideas about themselves, about the significance of their media use or about the assumed workings and effects of algorithms. Knowledge of algorithms is not simply factual or technical but also practical (Cotter, 2022) and is reflected in the ideas that people have about themselves, what they do and why they do it.

In other words, people's ideas about themselves and their mediated experiences are increasingly relevant to understanding agency in the context of the datafication of media. Therefore, I wish to suggest the concept of *inspective agency* to characterize these occasions when our experiences of datafied media resonate with our practices and provoke reflexivity. That is, at the moment of data retroaction, users have the occasion to inspect their uses of media against the ideas that are informing their practices.

In this respect, agency is not only *prospective* (that is, forward-looking) but can equally be *retrospective* (looking at the past), *introspective* (looking at oneself), *respective* (looking at norms) and *suspective* (looking at risks). The word *inspection* originates from the Latin *specere* – to look at – and means to examine something closely.

As they consume media, audiences can adapt their uses of media following their reflections and as such can influence the capturing of audience that media accomplish through data collection. Here, agency is *inscriptive* in the sense that these reflections can be inscribed in the data loop via the encoding of uses on digital infrastructures. In other words, inscriptive agencies are ways for users to inscribe practices into uses, meaning to instruct the algorithms about their practices by controlling the encoding of data in a bid to transform the mediated experiences that result from the travelling of data in the loop.

The word *inscription* has also a rich etymology; it is derived from the Latin *scriber* – to write. Here, the idea is that audiences are inscribing their practices into media use by way of *descriptions* (providing an account of a practice), *prescriptions* (instructing a practice), *transcriptions* (rearranging a practice), *proscriptions* (forbidding access to a practice), *subscriptions* (adhering to a practice), *circumscriptions* (restricting access to a practice) or *ascriptions* (explaining a practice).

I suggest the concepts of *inspection* and *inscription* as sensitizing concepts, as they have a rich etymology meant to inspire empirical research in paying attention to the subtle ways by which agency can be performed in algorithmic-mediated spaces. Given that the working of algorithms is opaque, automatic and even 'obfuscated' (Draper and Turow, 2019), it is important to sharpen our analytical lenses to not lose sight of 'small acts agency' (Picone et al, 2019) in our encounters with algorithmic media. The inspections and inscriptions that audiences can perform are ways to conceptualize the activity involved in the movement from uses to practices and vice versa. While use is ostensive and visible (which is the reason it is measured), practices are not, and hence we need concepts to help us determine not simply how use relates to practices but especially how practices relate to use.

Conclusion

This chapter argues that it is important to think about user agency in datafied societies for at least three reasons. Not only because it is presumed absent, but also because it is not very visible, and especially because user agency is the last line of defence against the control that media may seek using algorithms. Therefore, it is important to deconstruct the narrative of algorithmic control, not by exposing it as a narrative (see instead boyd and Crawford, 2012; Van

Dijck, 2014; Beer, 2017) but by showing its inadequacy when the narrative is inserted in an audience perspective. Then, the very notion of algorithmic control becomes contestable.

I have shown that this narrative falls short when taken into the realm of consumption. The chapter has deconstructed the narrative by arguing that it pertains to media production and how its institutional perspective imagines audiences as an object to be controlled. I have reframed algorithmic control as discursive control, consisting essentially in collecting data about audiences and forming knowledge about them to facilitate audience control. I have also underlined how these attempts at discursive control are limited by the reliance on measurements of surface behaviours collected through our uses of media.

Establishing a distinction between our uses of media and our sociocultural practices, I argue that the gap between them can be a site of agency vis-à-vis forms of algorithmic power. The sociocultural practices of media users, understood as ongoing reflexive constructions, can be used as a lens to question the datafied experiences that are retroacted to us in the data loop and accordingly to instruct the algorithms at the moment of media consumption. Given the opacity and complexity of these experiences, I have suggested a conceptualization based on the etymology of the words *inspect* and *inscribe* to guide our research lens in exploring the subtle ways by which the reflexivity of users can be agentic.

The extent to which users of datafied media can recognize the work of algorithms is yet to be explored by empirical research. With imagination (Bucher, 2017), users can begin to see through the invisible, opaque and complex processes of datafication. Users may not see inside the black box, but through their everyday lives, they can develop an informed relation to datafication and algorithms. In the near future, and pressed by ethical or economic considerations, media may be encouraged to render the work of algorithms more visible and transparent while offering possibilities for users to control the encoding of their data. Whether media stop obfuscating or users start resisting, we need to study both media production and consumption. We need to explore both how production practices are shaping media use, understood as conditions of possibility offered to audiences to sustain their practices, and how agency in the reflexive gaps between use and practices is shaping media consumption.

Notes

[1] I define data agency as agency which relates to the circulation of data in the circuit of media production and consumption, see the data loop (Mathieu and Pruulmann Vengerfeldt, 2020).

[2] That is not to say that these imagined audiences have no effect as they are indeed used to inform many aspects of media production (Christin, 2020) – an aspect I discuss later in this chapter; however, this is not the same as having an effect on actual audiences. In

fact, we need to better understand the relation between imagined and actual audiences in the age of datafication, a project that I initiated (with my colleague Pille Pruulmann Vengerfeldt) in the article 'The data loop of media and audiences' (2020).

[3] Source: investor.fb.com.

[4] The study of romance readers by Radway was the first to openly challenge the idea of a subject position and has come to represent a paradigmatic case in audience research, leading to many more studies observing the same patterns.

[5] There is also a romantic notion involved in understanding the power of algorithms to filter content for audiences as though audiences ever had access to an unfiltered world prior to algorithms. Newspapers have essentially always filtered content for their publics, and newsrooms and news organizations have always represented, to a greater and lesser extent, black boxes for most news readers.

[6] See Zuboff (2019) for an account of Google and its role in surveillance.

[7] Source: www.wordstream.com.

[8] It is true that algorithms and data play many roles in media organizations that go beyond audience measurement. To justify the adoption of algorithms – often in the form of large models, recommender systems and machine learning – tech companies emphasize the abundance of content (hence the need for filtering), the link of relevance established by better knowing the user (hence the need to collect data) and the enhanced user experience that results (hence the need for personalization). Algorithms are now also firmly integrated in the technical infrastructure of digital media and hence are a necessary feature of modern media.

[9] These algorithms are now commonplace in search engines (for example, Google's *PageRank*), news media (for example, the *New York Times'* contextual multi-armed bandits), social media (for example, Facebook's *EdgeRank*) and shopping platforms (for example, Shopify's *Vanilla Pagerank*) as well as music (for example, Spotify's BART algorithm) and film and television distribution (for example, *Netflix Recommendation Engine*).

[10] Keeping in mind the example from Google AdWords presented before.

[11] This observation is based on an ongoing research project asking students to validate the interests attributed to them by Facebook based on their uses of the platform.

[12] Cited from https://markcarrigan.net/2021/01/26/the-missing-skill-of-technological-refl exivity/.

References

Andrejevic, M. (2020) *Automated Media*, London and New York: Routledge.

Ang, I. (1991) *Desperately Seeking the Audience*, London and New York: Routledge.

Beer, D. (2017) 'The social power of algorithms', *Information, Communication & Society*, 20(1), pp 1–13. Available at: https://doi.org/10.1080/13691 18X.2016.1216147.

Birkbak, A. and Carlsen, H.B. (2016) 'The public and its algorithms: Comparing and experimenting with calculated publics', in L. Amoore and V. Piotukh (eds) *Algorithmic Life: Calculative Devices in the Age of Big Data*, London and New York: Routledge, pp 21–34.

boyd, d. and Crawford, K. (2012) 'Critical questions for big data: Provocations for a cultural, technological, and scholarly phenomenon', *Information, Communication & Society*, 15(5), pp 662–679. Available at: https://doi.org/ 10.1080/1369118X.2012.678878.

Bozdag, E. and van den Hoven, J. (2015) 'Breaking the filter bubble: Democracy and design', *Ethics and Information Technology*, 17(4), pp 249–265. Available at: https://doi.org/10.1007/s10676-015-9380-y.

Bucher, T. (2017) 'The algorithmic imaginary: Exploring the ordinary affects of Facebook algorithms', *Information, Communication & Society*, 20(1), pp 30–44. Available at: https://doi.org/10.1080/1369118X.2016.1154086.

Büchi, M., Fosch-Villaronga, E., Lutz, C., Tamò-Larrieux, A. and Velidi, S. (2021) 'Making sense of algorithmic profiling: User perceptions on Facebook', *Information, Communication & Society*, pp 1–17. Available at: https://doi.org/10.1080/1369118X.2021.1989011.

Cheney-Lippold, J. (2011) 'A new algorithmic identity: Soft biopolitics and the modulation of control', *Theory, Culture & Society*, 28(6), pp 164–181. Available at: https://doi.org/10.1177/0263276411424420.

Cheney-Lippold, J. (2017) *We Are Data: Algorithms and the Making of Our Digital Selves*, New York: New York University Press. Available at: https://doi.org/10.2307/j.ctt1gk0941.

Christin, A. (2020) *Metrics at Work: Journalism and the Contested Meaning of Algorithms*, Princeton: Princeton University Press.

Costera Meijer, I. and Groot Kormelink, T. (2017) 'Revisiting the audience turn in journalism: How a user-based approach changes the meaning of clicks, transparency and citizen participation', in B. Franklin and S.A. Eldridge (eds) *The Routledge Companion to Digital Journalism Studies*, London and New York: Routledge, pp 345–353.

Cotter, K. (2022) 'Practical knowledge of algorithms: The case of BreadTube', *New Media & Society*, 146144482210818. Available at: https://doi.org/10.1177/14614448221081802.

Couldry, N. (2004) 'Theorising media as practice', *Social Semiotics*, 14(2), pp 115–132. Available at: https://doi.org/10.1080/1035033042000238295.

Couldry, N. (2011) 'The necessary future of the audience … and how to research it', in V. Nightingale (ed) *The Handbook of Media Audiences*, Malden: Wiley-Blackwell, pp 213–229. Available at: http://onlinelibrary.wiley.com.molly.ruc.dk/doi/10.1002/9781444340525.ch10/summary.

Couldry, N. (2014) 'Inaugural: A necessary disenchantment: myth, agency and injustice in a digital world', *The Sociological Review*, 62(4), pp 880–897. Available at: https://doi.org/10.1111/1467-954X.12158

Couldry, N., Fotopoulou, A. and Dickens, L. (2016) 'Real social analytics: A contribution towards a phenomenology of a digital world', *The British Journal of Sociology*, 67(1), pp 118–137. Available at: https://doi.org/10.1111/1468-4446.12183.

Crawford, K. (2016) 'Can an algorithm be agonistic? Ten scenes from life in calculated publics', *Science, Technology & Human Values*, 41(1), pp 77–92. Available at: https://doi.org/10.1177/0162243915589635.

DeVito, M.A., Gergle, D. and Birnholtz, J. (2017) '"Algorithms ruin everything": #RIPTwitter, folk theories, and resistance to algorithmic change in social media', in *Proceedings of the 2017 CHI Conference on Human Factors in Computing Systems*, Denver: ACM, pp 3163–3174. Available at: https://doi.org/10.1145/3025453.3025659.

Draper, N.A. and Turow, J. (2019) 'The corporate cultivation of digital resignation', *New Media & Society*, 21(8), pp 1824–1839. Available at: https://doi.org/10.1177/1461444819833331.

Fish, S.E. (1980) *Is There a Text in this Class? The Authority of Interpretive Communities*, Cambridge, MA: Harvard University Press.

Fisher, E. and Mehozay, Y. (2019) 'How algorithms see their audience: Media epistemes and the changing conception of the individual', *Media, Culture & Society*, 41(8), pp 1176–1191. Available at: https://doi.org/10.1177/0163443719831598.

Giddens, A. (1991) *Modernity and Self-identity: Self and Society in the Late Modern Age*, Stanford: Stanford University Press.

Gillespie, T. (2014) 'The relevance of algorithms', in T. Gillespie, P.J. Boczkowski and K.A. Foot (eds) *Media Technologies*, Cambridge, MA: MIT Press, pp 167–194. Available at: https://doi.org/10.7551/mitpress/978026 2525374.003.0009.

Groot Kormelink, T. and Costera Meijer, I. (2018) 'What clicks actually mean: Exploring digital news user practices', *Journalism*, 19(5), pp 668–683. Available at: https://doi.org/10.1177/1464884916688290.

Hall, S. (1980) 'Encoding and decoding in the television discourse', in S. Hall, D. Hobson, A. Low and P. Willis (eds) *Culture, Media, Language: Working Papers in Cultural Studies, 1972–79*, London: Hutchinson, pp 197–208.

Hall, S. (1986) 'The problem of ideology-Marxism without guarantees', *Journal of Communication Inquiry*, 10(2), pp 28–44. Available at: https://doi.org/10.1177/019685998601000203.

Hallinan, B. and Striphas, T. (2016) 'Recommended for you: The Netflix Prize and the production of algorithmic culture', *New Media & Society*, 18(1), pp 117–137. Available at: https://doi.org/10.1177/1461444814538646.

Jacobsen, B.N. (2021) 'Regimes of recognition on algorithmic media', *New Media & Society*, 146144482110535. Available at: https://doi.org/10.1177/1461444821105355.

Karakayali, N., Kostem, B. and Galip, I. (2018) 'Recommendation systems as technologies of the self: Algorithmic control and the formation of music taste', *Theory, Culture & Society*, 35(2), pp 3–24. Available at: https://doi.org/10.1177/0263276417722391.

Katz, E., Blumler, J.G. and Gurevitch, M. (1974) 'Utilization of mass communication by the individual', in J.G. Blumler and E. Katz (eds) *The Uses of Mass Communications: Current Perspectives on Gratifications Research*, Beverly Hills: SAGE, pp 19–32.

Kennedy, H. (2018) 'Living with data: Aligning data studies and data activism through a focus on everyday experiences of datafication.', *Krisis: Journal for Contemporary Philosophy*, 1, pp 18–30.

Kennedy, H., Poell, T. and van Dijck, J. (2015) 'Data and agency', *Big Data & Society*, 2(2), 205395171562156. Available at: https://doi.org/10.1177/2053951715621569.

Lash, S. (2007) 'Power after hegemony: Cultural studies in mutation?', *Theory, Culture & Society*, 24(3), pp 55–78. Available at: https://doi.org/10.1177/0263276407075956.

Livingstone, S. (2007) 'The challenge of engaging youth online: Contrasting producers' and teenagers' interpretations of websites', *European Journal of Communication*, 22(2), pp 165–184. Available at: https://doi.org/10.1177/0267323107076768.

Livingstone, S. (2019) 'Audiences in an age of datafication: Critical questions for media research', *Television & New Media*, 20(2), pp 170–183. Available at: https://doi.org/10.1177/1527476418811118.

Lomborg, S. and Kapsch, P.H. (2019) 'Decoding algorithms', *Media, Culture & Society*, 42(5), pp 745–761. Available at: https://doi.org/10.1177/0163443719855301.

Lupton, D. and Michael, M. (2017) ' "Depends on who's got the data": Public understandings of personal digital dataveillance', *Surveillance & Society*, 15(2), pp 254–268.

Mathieu, D. and Pavlíčková, T. (2017) 'Cross-media *within* the Facebook newsfeed: The role of the reader in cross-media uses', *Convergence: The International Journal of Research into New Media Technologies*, 23(4), pp 425–438. Available at: https://doi.org/10.1177/1354856517700383.

Mathieu, D. and Pruulmann Vengerfeldt, P. (2020) 'The data loop of media and audience', *MedieKultur: Journal of Media and Communication Research*, 36(69), pp 116–138. Available at: https://doi.org/10.7146/mediekultur.v36i69.121178.

Mathieu, D. and Møller Hartley, J. (2021) 'Low on trust, high on use: Datafied media, trust and everyday life', *Big Data & Society*, 8(2), 205395172110594. Available at: https://doi.org/10.1177/20539517211059480.

Min, S.J. (2019) 'From algorithmic disengagement to algorithmic activism: Charting social media users' responses to news filtering algorithms', *Telematics and Informatics*, 43, 101251. Available at: https://doi.org/10.1016/j.tele.2019.101251.

Mollen, A. and Dhaenens, F. (2018) 'Audiences' coping practices with intrusive interfaces: Researching audiences in algorithmic, datafied, platform societies', in R. Das and B. Ytre-Arne (eds) *The Future of Audiences: A Foresight Analysis of Interfaces and Engagement*, Cham: Springer International, pp 43–60. Available at: https://search.ebscohost.com/login.aspx?direct=true&scope=site&db=nlebk&db=nlabk&AN=1775642.

Napoli, P.M. (2011) *Audience Evolution: New Technologies and the Transformation of Media Audiences*, New York: Columbia University Press.

Pariser, E. (2012) *The Filter Bubble: How the New Personalized Web is Changing What We Read and How We Think*, London: Penguin Books.

Picone, I., Kleut, J., Pavlíčková, T., Romic, B., Møller Hartley, J. and De Ridder, S. (2019) 'Small acts of engagement: Reconnecting productive audience practices with everyday agency', *New Media & Society*, 21(9), pp 2010–2028. Available at: https://doi.org/10.1177/1461444819837569.

Prey, R. (2018) 'Nothing personal: Algorithmic individuation on music streaming platforms', *Media, Culture & Society*, 40(7), pp 1086–1100. Available at: https://doi.org/10.1177/0163443717745147.

Radway, J.A. (1991) *Reading the Romance: Women, Patriarchy, and Popular Literature*, Chapel Hill: University of North Carolina Press.

Ruckenstein, M. and Granroth, J. (2019) 'Algorithms, advertising and the intimacy of surveillance', *Journal of Cultural Economy*, 13(1), pp 12–24. Available at: https://doi.org/10.1080/17530350.2019.1574866.

Schrøder, K.C. (2017) 'Towards the "audiencization" of mediatization research? Audience dynamics as co-constitutive of mediatization processes', in O. Driessens, G. Bolin, A. Hepp and S. Hjarvard (eds) *Dynamics of Mediatization*, Cham: Springer International, pp 85–115. Available at: https://doi.org/10.1007/978-3-319-62983-4_5.

Schrøder, K.C. and Phillips, L. (2007) 'Complexifying media power: A study of the interplay between media and audience discourses on politics', *Media, Culture & Society*, 29(6), pp 890–915. Available at: https://doi.org/10.1177/0163443707081693.

Schwartz, S.A. and Mahnke, M.S. (2021) 'Facebook use as a communicative relation: Exploring the relation between Facebook users and the algorithmic news feed', *Information, Communication & Society*, 24(7), pp 1041–1056. Available at: https://doi.org/10.1080/1369118X.2020.1718179.

Steensen, S., Ferrer-Conill, R. and Peters, C. (2020) '(Against a) theory of audience engagement with news', *Journalism Studies*, 21(12), pp 1662–1680. Available at: https://doi.org/10.1080/1461670X.2020.1788414.

Swart, J. (2021) 'Experiencing algorithms: How young people understand, feel about, and engage with algorithmic news selection on social media', *Social Media + Society*, 7(2), 205630512110088. Available at: https://doi.org/10.1177/20563051211008828.

Tufekci, Z. (2015) 'Algorithmic harms beyond Facebook and Google: Emergent challenges of computational agency', *Colorado Technology Law Journal*, 13, pp 203–218.

Turow, J. (2011) *The Daily You: How the New Advertising Industry is Defining Your Identity and Your Worth*, New Haven: Yale University Press.

Van Dijck, J. (2014) 'Datafication, dataism and dataveillance: Big Data between scientific paradigm and ideology', *Surveillance & Society*, 12(2), pp 197–208.

Warner, M. (2002) 'Publics and counterpublics (abbreviated version)', *Quarterly Journal of Speech*, 88(4), pp 413–425. Available at: https://doi.org/10.1080/00335630209384388.

Willson, M. (2017) 'Algorithms (and the) everyday', *Information, Communication & Society*, 20(1), pp 137–150. Available at: https://doi.org/10.1080/1369118X.2016.1200645.

Ytre-Arne, B. and Das, R. (2020) 'Audiences' communicative agency in a datafied age: Interpretative, relational and increasingly prospective', *Communication Theory*, pp 779–797. Available at: https://doi.org/10.1093/ct/qtaa018.

Ytre-Arne, B. and Moe, H. (2020) 'Folk theories of algorithms: Understanding digital irritation', *Media, Culture & Society*, 016344372097231. Available at: https://doi.org/10.1177/0163443720972314.

Zuboff, S. (2019) '"We make them dance": Surveillance capitalism, the rise of instrumentarian power, and the threat to human rights', in R.F. Jørgensen (ed) *Human Rights in the Age of Platforms*, Cambridge, MA: MIT Press, pp 3–51. Available at: https://doi.org/10.7551/mitpress/11304.001.0001.

Zuboff, S. (2020) *The Age of Surveillance Capitalism: The Fight for a Human Future at the New Frontier of Power*, London: Profile Books.

3

Counterpublicness and Hybrid Tactics across Physical and Mediated Spaces

Mette Bengtsson and Anna Schjøtt

Arriving at the Christiansborg Palace Square, I[1] spot Catherine, a COVID-19 sceptic and protester who I met at another protest organized by Men in Black a few weeks back, at the large statue of King Frederik VII in the middle of the square. She is unpacking metal trays from her backpack to prepare for the protest. As I follow many of the Facebook groups, including one whose purpose is to provide an overview of the coming demonstrations, I know that today's protest is a 'klinky klonky' protest – a protest where participators try to make as much noise as possible by, for example, banging pot lids together, which originates from protests in Iceland.

I greet Catherine and explain that I am again out to observe the protests. She points to a woman with long dark hair named Marie, who is the organizer of today's protest and leader of the 'Freedom Movements Council', another subgroup among the sceptics. I recognize her from one of the Facebook groups, where she was live-streaming from her car on the way here, urging people to join today's protest. As I approach her, she steps up onto the stairs of the statue and says, 'The plan is to make as much noise as we can, so they [the politicians in parliament] can hear we are dissatisfied'. She further explains that the time of the protest was chosen because the new 'safety legislation', which among other things gives the police more authority to disperse protests that are demonstrating unsafe behaviour. It is number 44 on the agenda in parliament today. The plan is to make noise throughout the entire session, but she emphasizes that it will be important to save energy for the moment when it is being deliberated. She points to a spot underneath the window on the left side of the building, explaining that it is right underneath the room where parliament will be deliberating, so that is where they will place themselves during the protest.

She ends by saying that during the deliberation of the 'safety legislation', she and a few others will enter the parliament hall and hopefully get on live TV stating their dissatisfaction. ... After a while, all the protesters gather back at the statue. Marie explains that they were now at number 38, so it was almost time for the safety legislation. 'I think it is so great. Like the epidemic legislation, we are going to knock them over with noise. Let's all go under the window and give it our all!' she says to the crowd of about 20 or 30 people. The intensity of the noise increases from a slow rhythmic klonk, klonk, klonk, to fast constant strokes, making it impossible to hear anything else – many of the protesters look towards the window. (Excerpt from fieldnotes, 1 June 2021)

Introduction

At the turn of the millennium, a general concern among many scholars was a decline in public engagement; Robert Putnam argued that the reduction of in-person activities in the US since the 1950s might result in an undermining of active civic engagement and thereby a less strong democracy (Putnam, 1995, 2000), and a few years later, Nick Couldry, Sonia Livingstone and Tim Markham worried about UK citizens' weakened 'public connection', especially among younger people (Couldry et al, 2007). However, more recently, solid instances of civic engagement have played out, not only during the COVID-19 pandemic with anti-vaxxers and similar groups, as we will explore here, but also with protest movements like Fridays for Future, Black Lives Matter and MeToo. Common to all these groups is that they must navigate a highly datafied, hybrid media setting where collective formation and action happen across different spaces – not only between old and new mediated spaces but also between mediated and physical spaces. This is also clear in the vignette, where Facebook streaming and event sharing were used to create awareness, while physical presence in front of parliament and noisemaking were chosen to make a statement that could not be ignored. Puncturing the idea of audience as passive victims of datafication, we in this chapter pick up on Sonia Livingstone's suggestion that 'the audience project ... seemingly must be reasserted for each generation of scholarship, rearticulating their role in relation to each new phase of sociotechnological change' (2015, p 439). By following how the COVID-19 sceptics work with and against the datafication processes, we empirically show how these groups actively used different tactics across physical and mediated spaces to manifest themselves through acts of counterpublicness. We offer a typology of the hybrid public formation tactics that we saw used in these processes, focusing particularly on how datafication materializes in the processes and argue that the ways people act is sometimes with the purpose of becoming datafied.

As a way of explaining how datafication is central in the public formation processes, we highlight how the tactics seem to be driven by an underlying logic, which we conceptualize as a 'hybrid quantification logic'. The importance of quantification is nothing new; strength in numbers has always been considered key for the legitimization of publics and their issues (Biggs, 2018). However, as many of the activities of publicness, particularly in the forming stages, take place on social media platforms today, we see how these traditional quantification logics are becoming intensified and take new datafied forms that complement existing measures of public presence. The fact that numbers materialize on social media through listed group sizes and engagement metrics, rather than being fleeting during a physical protest, produces new tactics by those who attempt to make themselves count in the public debate. Here, we use the term 'count' deliberately to connote the quantification element we see as essential in public formation processes, but which can take many forms, such as noise, numbers present and comments posted, and to highlight the struggle implicit in this process, where publics must convince society, media and politicians about the legitimacy of their issue.

This fight for legitimacy is further intensified when the moments of publicness are related to issues and viewpoints considered to be outside what is generally accepted. This is also the reason why we chose this case, as these sceptics, often labelled and degraded as 'tin foil hats', start from a marginalized position and must use all tactics available to them to make themselves count. Thus, the guiding question for this chapter is: how do marginalized groups attempt to make themselves count as legitimate instants of publicness in a society characterized by a highly datafied and hybridized media environment? With this question, we are less interested in whether these groups of people manage to make themselves and their issues legitimate in the wider public sphere; rather, we are interested in how they concretely try to get there and the tools and tactics they employ. We explore this by following online and physical activities and interviewing the sceptics, which proves to be a messy affair with many factions, internal squabbles and competition, but also one in which significant coordinated efforts take place.[2]

In the following, we first outline how publics have been researched as both physical and online phenomena. Then, we move on to describing how we engage with publicness across offline and online spaces, focusing on dissolving the often-upheld dichotomies between online/offline and new/old media. In the analysis, we first present a typology of public formation tactics that we distilled based on the empirical material, then provide an in-depth analysis of core examples of these tactics and their use. We conclude by discussing how datafication reconfigures the ways in which these groups engage in public formation processes and legitimation practices.

Theoretical backdrop: researching publics and public formation

Over the years, multiple scholars have engaged in the study of publics and their formation, but even so, the concept of publics has remained elusive, and the approaches to studying it multiple. Modern theories of publics have, to some extent, been developed from or in response to classic understandings of the formation of publics developed throughout the 19th century, going back to the Dewey–Lippmann debate and Habermas (see Habermas, 1991; Lippmann, 1993; Dewey, 2012 for a good overview over the first conceptualizations and how they differ; for shared characteristics, see Calhoun, 2017). In this chapter, we primarily focus on discussions with newer conceptualizations of publics that specifically deal with the question of how publics form and how that formation has changed with the changing media landscape (for a full review of the approaches, see Hartley et al [2021] and Chapter 1 in this volume). However, before immersing ourselves in the rich qualitative case study, we will elaborate upon some of the current conceptualizations of publics and conditions for public formation that are important for the understanding of current public formation processes, namely *hybridity*, *datafication* and *normativity*.

The hybrid nature of the public formation processes

With the rise of social media, many scholars have turned their attention towards public formation processes and the new possibilities that came with these spaces, bringing forward concepts such as 'networked publics' or 'hashtag publics' (see, for example, boyd, 2008; Ito, 2008; Bruns and Burgess, 2015). These concepts have been influential in highlighting how specific dynamics or affordances on particular social media platforms allow publics to emerge in new ways – ways that circumvent the traditional gatekeepers. The openness of Twitter, for example, allows new possibilities for politicians, journalists and citizens to control the flow of the information they receive, while trending hashtags can also induce new actors to join a certain public by gaining awareness of it on Twitter.

However, as publics typically develop and act across different platforms and online and physical spaces, we need conceptualizations that consider this. To fully understand the dynamics, we argue that we must investigate the affordances of specific social media platforms, the interplay between these platforms, the constraints that come with these spaces and the movements across spaces, digitally as well as physically. Through a range of case studies,

Andrew Chadwick (2013) showed how new and old media hybridize, meaning that there is an increasing interplay and adaptation as stories from social media move into mainstream media and vice versa. Chadwick was not interested in public formation processes as such but studied political communication and how specific actors gained power and agency in the hybrid media system. Nonetheless, his fundamental insights provide a good foundation for this context and many others. Another work that can serve as an inspiration for conceptualizing public formation is Wendy Willems (2019), who emphasized the interplay between physical (material and spatial) and online strategies: 'Sites of publicness may shift from digital spaces to a physical location or vice versa because of particular constraints in circulation associated with either domain' (2019, p 194). Bridging these insights and using them when theorizing public formation processes helps us capture and describe the movements back and forth between different spaces and the hybridity between them.

Algorithms, information and datafication in the public formation processes

Another dynamic that provides both opportunities and limitations in relation to public formation processes is algorithms and the way they take part in organizing the flow of information (Gillespie, 2014; Bruns and Burgess, 2015). This has produced extensive scholarship on the power dynamics of algorithms, which both take part in sorting social life (Beer, 2013; Pasquale, 2015) and in moderating and censoring public debate (Gillespie, 2020; Cobbe, 2021). Studies using the term 'algorithmic resistance' show how users engage to either avoid or game the algorithmic dynamics, with users attempting to appropriate algorithmic dynamics to gain more visibility or to correct what is perceived as injustice or shortcoming in the algorithmic systems (Treré, 2018; Velkova and Kaun, 2021). Due to the opacity of the concrete workings of these systems, both for sorting and moderating algorithmic systems, users utilize what they know and experience in practice – their developed 'folk theories' of algorithms – in these acts of resistance (Ytre-Arne and Moe, 2021). In conceptualizing public formation processes, examining these dynamics and their interplay with each other is necessary for understanding how and why these groups act the way they do, based on the affordances and constraints of both spaces. However, while the conceptualizations of publics have developed to encompass digital and algorithmic considerations, the way the dynamics of datafication also intervene and influence how acts of publicness occur still has to be more thoroughly explored. One explanation may be that datafication is rather difficult to grasp and describe because it is everywhere but invisible at the same time. Others have described datafication as something that permeates and fundamentally changes our everyday life, framing it as 'a form of colonization' (Couldry and Mejias, 2019) or 'pervasive ideology' (van Dijck, 2014). Rather than try to conceptualize what datafication is, we in our work give attention to the role of datafication and attempt to describe its concrete manifestations. As a result, we consider datafication to be a general constraint for the formation of publics that can both hinder and enable the development of new, powerful actors and larger groups of people in the process. This provides new insights into how agency is negotiated in the datafied societies, by illustrating how datafication is both resisted and utilized via different tactics in the processes of public formation.

The good, the bad and what comes in between

Finally, the normative considerations that have characterized both previous and recent research are also relevant to address when researching 'publics' or what is maybe more precisely in this case described as 'contentious publicness' because of its highly controversial, dynamic and fleeting character (Kavada and Poell, 2021). In the 1990s, scholars building on Habermas' initial work began to conceptualize publics that were engaging with topics and causes outside the mainstream public debate. Here, Oskar Negt and Alexander Kluge (1993) and Nancy Fraser (1990) argued for a focus on the many unheard and often subordinate voices in the debate, theorizing respectively the concepts of 'counterpublics' and 'subaltern counterpublics', which represented publics that would form in response to the exclusion from and in contrast to hegemonic constructions of dominant publics. In her work, Fraser highlighted marginalized groups, such as women, the working class and racial or sexual minorities, as the social groups that become part of these counterpublics, 'where members of subordinated social groups invent and circulate counterdiscourses, which in turn permit them to formulate oppositional interpretations of their identities, interests, and needs' (1990, p 67). She uses the example of the late-20th century US feminist subaltern counterpublic as one of the clearest and most far-reaching examples, where a group of feminists invented new terms to describe the social realities, such as 'sexism' and 'acquaintance rape', which helped to recast the identities and needs of women.

Ultimately, Fraser offered a new language that, while not eliminating the disadvantages of the official public sphere, at least began to reduce these advantages by offering an alternative framing. While Fraser acknowledged that such progressive counterpublics were not the only type out there, referencing the republican counterpublic to the feminist movement that aimed at retaining women in traditional values, the concept was ultimately tied to a normativity of progressiveness and important fights from the margins. There is also evidence in how she countered it with the republican example that some counterpublics are normatively judged as better than others. Interestingly, in the last couple of years, a range of new concepts addressing the opposite, namely 'bad' or antagonistic publics, has emerged, framed as 'dark participation' (Quandt, 2018) and 'uncivil participation' (Frischlich et al, 2021). These concepts are connected to the openness that the internet has offered and some of the same affordances as addressed earlier but focuses on how these affordances are utilized to spread misinformation and act in hateful and offensive ways towards others in these spaces. We find this normative turn interesting but also problematic, as it leads to an exclusion of what can be considered acts of publicness. While some acts of publicness are against the common norms of how to act in society (for example, violence) these negative framings of publicness also move into discussions of the cause, and what is a worthy cause to support. In our study of the COVID-19 sceptics, we saw that many of them were frustrated with their marginalization because it was based on the topic, not their actions, and some of them were highly oriented towards deliberation. In this chapter, we also discuss this 'dismissal' of certain modes of publicness by illustrating how the attempt to marginalize them in some instances fuelled their actions and in-group dynamics and for some of them this resulted in harm to democracy.

A hybrid ethnographic approach

In our approach to studying the public formation processes, we attempt to avoid the traditional dichotomies that have been dominant in studies of publics and strive to explore the formations across the different spaces in which the formations take place. We also discuss the different functions of these spaces. As a result, we do not follow the sceptics' activities on one specific platform, but a range of activities across several platforms and both online and offline activities, which can be termed 'hybrid ethnography' (Przybylski, 2021).

This overarching approach led us to collect several forms of empirical data.

As primary material, we conducted 12 in-depth interviews, including think-aloud elements, with COVID-19 sceptics who were engaged in the protests for different reasons (for example, anti-vax or anti-control) and who varied in their subgroup involvement (Kvale and Brinkmann, 2015; Bengtsson, 2018).

We also carried out a digital ethnographic enquiry into selected open Facebook groups in Denmark, whose members were sceptical about the handling of COVID-19 in Denmark (including both thematic groups and organization-oriented groups) (Postill and Pink, 2012; Markham, 2013). The groups were chosen based on their differences in their wider focus and their significant size.

Finally, we conducted ethnographic observations at three physical protests in Copenhagen (Geertz, 1973; Emerson et al, 2011).

The fieldwork (both digital and physical) and interviews started in the spring of 2021, when the protests reached new heights again, spurred on by a violent protest by one of the critical sceptic groups called Men in Black in January 2021. It continued until the COVID-19 pandemic was declared over in Denmark in February 2022.[3] Many of the interviewees were recruited during observations at protests, through the social media groups or through the interviews themselves, where participants sometimes connected us with other relevant sceptics to talk to. In the choice of interviewees, we also focused on talking to sceptics from different subgroups who had varying reasons for participating in the protests. As this is vast material, in this chapter, we predominantly focus on the interviews and relate what was said to the concrete actions observed online and during the protests to qualify the findings.

We understand the sceptics as both an 'extreme/deviant' and a 'paradigmatic' case (Flyvbjerg, 2006, pp 229–233). It is deviant because it is an extreme case of counterpublicness since the sceptics were highly marginalized and occupied a negative normative position from the beginning. As a group, the sceptics were widely considered 'nut cases', outsiders, and as having no right to protest due to the special circumstances of the pandemic; rather, they were considered a threat to democracy. However, it is also paradigmatic, as it allows us to speak more generally about how the conditions of public formation processes in society have changed. The extremeness allows us to see some of these dynamics more clearly, but we argue that the dynamics would, in most cases, apply to other forms of counterpublicness as well. This is not to say that the identified tactics would be the same if we had explored other cases, but rather that the underlying logics and ways of engaging with the physical and mediated environment would be.

Analytical framework: (media) logics and related tactics

As an analytical framework, we draw on the theory of 'media logics' (Altheide and Snow, 1979; Altheide, 2016), including 'social media logics' (van Dijck and Poell, 2013), 'network media logics' (Klinger and Svensson, 2018) and 'algorithmic logics' (Gaw, 2022). In our observations during the pandemic, we noticed how public formation processes characterized by counterpublicness were permeated by several underlying logics, such as the ones mentioned earlier, that the sceptics reacted to with rather advanced tactics that transgressed the classical divides between old and new media and physical and online settings. The theory of 'media logics' is a well-established tradition described by Altheide and Snow (1979). The theory of media logics originates from a traditional mass media setting studying processes of how news content is selected, produced and consumed. Altheide described media logics as a 'general framework for understanding the nature, impact and relevance of media and information technologies for social life, as well as its use and appropriateness for investigating political communication' (2016, p 1). Furthermore, he underlined that 'media logic does not refer to just one logic for one medium, for example, television, but is a conceptual model of mediation' (Altheide, 2016, p 1).

In his work, Chadwick (2013) highlights how new and old media logics do not replace each other but hybridize. This is also why he argues that 'media logic provides a useful approach to understanding the power of media and the power relations within media' (Chadwick, 2013, p 23). In this chapter, we analyse how the sceptics engage with different media logics through their actions to make themselves count, but also critically discuss how mass media logics remain at the centre of their efforts as these are still key to becoming legitimized as a public (see also Chapter 6 in this book for an alternative analysis of logics, where the focus is on the power relations within media organizations rather than between different forms of media).

To operationalize our study of media logics, we combine it with the notion of tactics. Here, we draw on de Certeau (1988), who understood tactics as everyday life, bottom-up ways to deal with the 'strategies' of the system, strategies being ways for the (media) system to organize itself. In the analysis, we point to the logics as inherent or built-in rules and the tactics that we see as ways of responding to the logics. To conclude, we introduce and develop our own concept, namely, the concept of 'hybrid quantification logic', as a way of pointing to what we consider a transgressing, dominating logic in a hybrid setting across old and new media. Holding on to the concept of logics implies that we believe that some human agency is still at stake and that algorithms have not triumphed over human interaction.

A typology of formation tactics and the hybrid quantification logics

In the following, we present a typology entailing some of the most prominent formation tactics we observed when following the sceptics and their attempts to make themselves 'count' as an act of counterpublicness. Presenting the tactics in chronological order, we start by analysing the *mobilization tactics* in the initial phase of the public formation processes, in which the mobilization of fellow supporters seemed to be the initial imminent challenge. In our study, gathering as a critical opposition to the government's handling of the pandemic seems to be the common cause, but other causes, values and interests coalesced in a sometimes-blurred picture. Hereafter, we point to some of the *counter-tactics* that we saw later, when the emerging counterpublic – what in practice was an intermingle of diverse groups and people who tried to manifest themselves as a counterpublic – tried to navigate constraints in the different spaces, digitally and physically, by shifting from one space to the other. We conclude by describing how all respondents, without exception, talked about how they struggled being recognized by traditional mainstream media, which we have labelled *publicity tactics*. Having followed the scholarly discussions praising the democratic potential of the internet and social media, it is striking how the recognition from traditional mainstream media of the counterpublic still is a cardinal point for the citizens in the public formation process. When describing these three types of tactics in depth, we move from an inward to an outward perspective (see Table 3.1).

Mobilization tactics

When following the sceptics, we saw a wide range of mobilization tactics – in the digital space, in the physical space, and in the intersections between them. Some of these tactics are similar to those existing in the non-digital era, but we describe them as they unfold across digital and physical spaces, emphasizing their relation to the underlying logics within this new hybrid setting. Social media was a highly important digital space for the sceptics, who would utilize the affordances of, for example, Facebook to make groups, share events, post information on their profiles or post comments to, for example, posts made by Danish politicians. In the Facebook groups, users would sometimes post calls to go and post comments on a specific post by a politician or to share events (interview, 2021). They also had a Facebook group dedicated to collecting all the upcoming protests around the country. As an interviewee explained, it was very much a shared and organized effort, where the network was mobilized with the aim of illustrating the size or to mobilize new interests in the cause:

'Well, it is about really collaborating on Facebook and the groups we have and try to promote each other content and spread the message. We have people who sit and comment on *Ekstra Bladet* [Danish tabloid] and DR [the Danish public broadcaster] site. They take the fight in there and try to recruit new people. ... Then there are people like me who do physical protests. There are some that do live videos aimed to get people to participate in the protests and some who do the comments and share posts on Facebook. There are many ways to do it.' (Interview, 2021)

This quote helps illustrate how the different physical and mediated spaces each were important for the mobilization tactics. During physical protest the participants always referenced the importance of easily finding the events on social media, but they also expressed how the mediated spaces had certain constraints. Some of the constraints that the sceptics pointed to

Table 3.1: Public formation tactics

Mobilization tactics *Inwardly* →	Counter-tactics	Publicity tactics *Outwardly* →
Consolidate main arguments Sharing content and ideas (expert statements/ explanations and investigative material) in and across Facebook groups and Messenger to consolidate main arguments.	**Secure knowledge spread before deletion** Attempting to ensure reach of content before deletion by using intros such as 'SHARE SHARE SHARE' in Facebook posts that encourage others to spread the message.	**Make the cause relevant** Organizing protests across Danish cities and in front of the Danish parliament to illustrate the size of the group of sceptics.
Join us! Inviting personal Facebook network to join Facebook groups and attend protests as well as inviting bypassers at physical demonstrations to join physically or in Facebook groups.	**Cheat the 'Facebook police'** Avoid using words that it is believed the Facebook algorithm will react to, like 'fascist' or 'nazi' and using intentional misspellings (for example, 'måderna' or '🦠rona') as well as doing live–streams to give visibility to banned users.	**Comments on posts from mainstream actors** Commenting on Facebook posts by mainstream actors, such as politicians or journalists, to get their attention.
Share and RSVP Sharing and pressing attend to events in and across Facebook groups and producing overviews of activities (for example, a specific Facebook group for that purpose alone).	**Save the network** Making backup Facebook groups and Facebook profiles as well as fake profiles to ensure networks remain in case of quarantine and banning.	**Invite for deliberation** Extending invitations to politicians to be present during protests or debates via email or Facebook comments.
Make it Instagrammable Using attention-grabbing means both *physically* (visual and auditory elements in protests, for example, making noise, shouting repetitive slogans, 'klinky klonky', fireworks, coloured smoke, soap bubbles, drawing with chalk, sitting in circles) and use these and other measures *digitally* to create support for future activities (for example, photos of protests, selfies, lives).	**Consider the channel** Considering the affordances of the different channels, for example, using Messenger instead of posting in the Facebook group when discussing potentially sensitive topics or doing stories or using lives or stories instead of permanent posts because stories and lives are ephemeral (typically 24 hours), whereas posts are permanent (at least until manual deletion) as well as avoiding sharing of specific content, especially videos; only watching.	**Force the political agenda** Formulating citizens' proposals, which are a Danish democratic tool where citizens can write proposals for changes in, for example, legislation and if the proposal gets 50,000 signatures, then it will be deliberated by the Danish parliament.

(continued)

Table 3.1: Public formation tactics (continued)

Mobilization tactics *Inwardly* ←	Counter-tactics	Publicity tactics *Outwardly* →
Call the comment army Asking people to comment on Facebook posts by politicians, news outlets, journalists and other mainstream actors and on the news sites' comment sections.	**Ditch the Facebook police** Moving conversations and groups to uncensored physical locations or alternative platforms, for example, Telegram.	**Seek press support** Pitching stories to Danish journalists (for example, about upcoming protests) or providing quotes to national or international media.
Advertise future protests Doing pre- and post-protest videos on Facebook to ensure visibility in the network and attendance during protests.	**Keep the groups tidy** Tidying by deleting posts not addressing what the administrator regards as the group's central issue – the logic being that the higher the number of posts, the higher the risk of something problematic happening and consequent banning.	**If you can't beat them, join them** Making new political parties (for example, The Freedom Party), who will have the right to deliberate.

were the unconstructive, person-oriented quarrels, the difficulties in getting in contact with strangers and the algorithms and perceived censorship. As a common way to solve these issues, the sceptics moved to physical locations. As one interviewee said: "I quickly went out to do something active and visual instead of just sitting and shouting on Facebook because with all these algorithms running, it can soon become the same people you reach, and you do not reach any new people, any strangers" (interview, 2021). Another said:

'To create something in the streets that people can look further into, read about, or ask questions about, was crucial because digitalization is everywhere today, but it has limitations regarding algorithms or stuff that get deleted or censored. You can't censor people who walk the streets in the thousands. You just can't.' (Interview, 2021)

In the movement back and forth between the digital and physical spaces, the sceptics seemed rather aware of the importance of making people present in both spaces – to make them count in both spaces. For example, one respondent talked about the enrolment of bypassers at physical demonstrations: "Every time I meet someone that I talk to during demonstrations, rallies, or events, we also 'connect' on Facebook" (interview, 2021). Another respondent talked about doing 'lives' on Facebook before, during and after a demonstration to encourage people to come to the specific event, but also to future activities.

In both the digital and physical realms, documenting the growth and consolidation of the group along the way seemed important as a way of archiving or materializing the messy and diverse actions in the forming collective. One interviewee described how he had several times commented on posts made by the Danish prime minister, but she had yet to reply to any of them, which he related to the size of the group: "She is yet to reply, and we are more than 100,000 people on social media who are against this. I know this because there are statistics about how many we know and stuff, and we have calculated that we are about 80–100,000 people" (interview, 2021).

Here, we see the importance of mobilizing numbers (illustrated via collected data by Facebook) only to legitimize the cause. The physical spaces also played a hugely important role in the aim of mobilizing more people on social media, as activities in the physical realm that could subsequently be used to create attention in the digital realm. We labelled this tactic 'make it Instagrammable'. One interviewee described her female group in contrast to the Danish Men in Black protesters, who self-identified as a 'protest movement' and demonstrated in the streets wearing black clothes, hoodies and masks to cover their faces (not COVID-19 face masks!), carrying roman candles, torches and playing loud music. She says:

'We make anti-propaganda, as we call it. We sensed that in the Men in Black protests, the press only took pictures of the hard stuff, so we went and took pictures of all the other stuff. We take pictures of people blowing soap bubbles and children writing with coloured chalk on the ground. You know – all the positive things instead of violence.' (Interview, 2021)

This respondent continued to talk about using colourful smoke and how this made people stop in the street, as well as how pictures of it were attention-grabbing online and supported a wider circulation – and, through that, mobilization. From these different examples of mobilization tactics, we can see how constraints in different spaces produce certain actions that are aimed at specific media logics and ideas of how content will circulate better. These ideas of circulation and mobilization are tightly interwoven with data, as physical spaces enable the illustration of size, but so does the number of group members and commenters. We, therefore, see how both old and new forms of quantification logics are at play in the tactics. What we also found interesting was the relationship between the physical and digital spaces, as well as the battle with the established media, which we will come back to when talking about 'publicity tactics', which are also related to mobilization tactics.

Counter-tactics

A common position among the sceptics was to understand themselves and act in opposition to, for example, fact-checkers, Big Tech and the algorithms used by these actors. An important part of their public formation process was also to resist and navigate these structures to secure their continued opportunities to deliberate the issues on their minds. Everyone we talked to had either themselves experienced, or heard of others who had experienced, censorship online, such as total or time-limited bannings on Facebook as well as loss of functions, such as the ability to comment. Many were unsure of the exact workings of the censoring mechanisms and tried to make sense of them via inferences of how the system worked and how to avoid future consequences. In the Facebook groups they would even engage in shared speculation over how the systems worked and share 'tips' for how to avoid being caught by the 'Facebook police', as they often referred to it, or, if penalized, the 'Facebook jail', as one sceptic framed his banning: "Many of the people I know get their Facebook profiles closed or restricted, and, every day I'll have someone go: 'Yay, I'm out of Facebook jail again, I got 30 days this time, next time I'll probably get 60 days'" (interview, 2021).

Other respondents reflected on the experience of suddenly being restricted in receiving and posting comments, and the possibility that the lack of comments and notifications was also part of a penalty, referring to concepts like 'ghosting' and 'shadow banning' (interview, 2021). One interviewee said: "Look, no one has commented. I think it has to do with the algorithms" (interview, 2021). Another reflected on the connection between the promotion of an event and the inability to comment:

> 'I think it was just around May 1st when I started promoting the event a lot, and then, all of a sudden, Facebook restricted my account. But I did not get a "You have done this and that and therefore you have limited activities during the next three days" kind of message. I could not comment on anything!' (Interview, 2021)

As a countermeasure to avoid banning or other types of restrictions, the sceptics developed a wide range of 'counter-tactics', including local practices on specific platforms and moving across different digital platforms and from digital to physical spaces. In the following, we summarize some of these counter-tactics.

A widespread tactic was the encouragement of fellow sceptics to share and reinforce the circulation of specific content before it is deleted. Across several groups, variations of the same phrasing were used in many posts, often with capital letters to separate the metatext and the post, for example, 'SHARE, SHARE, SHARE', 'COPY PASTE', 'SHARE BEFORE DELETION', and so forth. Evidently, the sceptics worked with a range of imagined constraints in the digital space. They envisioned a fight played out in the digital realm against some controlling elite actors who prevented them from sharing important content and arguments. Who these elite actors are and what they do was not transparent to the sceptics, but because of earlier experiences with deleted material, they assumed that this might happen again. Therefore, they acted with constant fear of being suppressed. Pace became a key tactic to ensure they spread their content to as many users as possible before deletion.

Another tactic was 'cheat the Facebook police' where the sceptics used intentional misspellings or specific language to avoid triggering censoring mechanisms. One example of this was using emojis instead of words, such as using the cow emoji to write Covid, which makes sense in Danish, as cow is 'ko', which mimics the 'co' sound in 'Covid'. The tactic also includes more general considerations of what language to use, which we see in this quote by one of the interviewees, who describes how she uses certain references but leaves out specific words. As she explained: "I sometimes reference the Second World War, but I would never dream of writing, for example, 'Nazi' in a post. I think those who do are also the ones who get quarantined or stuff like that" (interview, 2021). As with the first tactic, the actors are acting against these hidden mechanisms of censorship controlled by Big Tech, which they can only speculate about. Since the algorithms employed by, for example, Facebook constantly evolve and learn to detect these adversarial tactics, the concrete manifestations of this tactic constantly changed throughout the pandemic, based on ideas developed in the sceptics' group of what work best to escape the systems.

A third counter-tactic was the creation of backup or alternative profiles and groups. One interviewee described being banned completely from Facebook and how he created a new profile shortly afterwards using the fake name 'Frank Sølyst' (interview, 2021). The interviewee explained how he was also restricted in doing 'lives' from this new account and that he therefore arranged a demonstration in front of the Facebook headquarters in Copenhagen and would do lives via another sceptic's Facebook account on a regular basis. This is a good example of a cross-cutting activity; when constrained in the digital space, he first tried to navigate this space but moved to the physical space when it proved impossible. Other interviewees described preparing backup profiles on Facebook to ensure they would not disappear if banned completely. This was an important precaution as they strongly believed that it would be necessary; it was just a matter of time, as they knew banning was a widespread phenomenon among all sceptics (interview, 2021). One interviewee was amused when talking about one of her female friends, who operated from a new profile, taking the male name 'Claus' (interview, 2021). The same was the case with groups, where they would also make backup groups and have the members of the existing groups also join there to ensure the network was not lost in case their group got deleted.

A fourth tactic involved moving to uncensored physical locations, other platforms such as Twitter or LinkedIn, or 'alternative' platforms such as Telegram. While the former tactic was about 'cheating', this was a more bombastic act that we call 'ditch the Facebook police'. Again, the sceptics were aware of the constraints in the digital space and the audience in these different spaces. One interviewee talked about how he was able to share everything on his Telegram account without being censored but that he was 'preaching to the choir' and did not reach new people there, as Telegram is a less used platform in Denmark. Surprisingly, he also mentioned LinkedIn as an operating platform, and said that he had never been banned on either LinkedIn or Twitter (interview, 2021). Several of the interviewees also mentioned Messenger as a way of sharing content that they were unsure of because they experienced less censoring there. So, they would often discuss phrases with fellow sceptics before sharing it more widely (interview, 2021). Sometimes, this platform was also used for practical or organizing purposes not relevant for the entire Facebook group and was afforded smaller group conversations. In a Facebook post from the Facebook group 'We are the people! We have had it!', a member encourages fellow sceptics to follow the group on Telegram if they want 'the newest, uncensored and fact-checked stories'.

Two of the interviewees were not only members of the Facebook groups but also administrators. They both expressed that they felt a certain responsibility for acting in hyper-strict ways so that their actions or the actions of others in the group would not cause trouble for the group, and as a result they would enforce strict regulation of the groups in terms of which posts were approved or not. They were both convinced that Facebook paid attention to them as administrators and to their compliance with Facebook's community standards. To counter this, they both used a range of tactics to avoid being censored or closed. One example was the continuous tidying of the digital space by deleting posts that did not address what they regarded as the group's main issue(s). The logic behind this is that the higher the number of posts, the higher the risk of something potentially problematic leading to consequent banning. Likewise, one of the administrators said that she sometimes passed on the warnings she received from Facebook about the circulation of the information shared in the group that the fact-checkers perceived as misinformation, showing us a concrete formulation of a heads-up: "Please, take it easy with the discussion about vaccines, because if you continue, we will be shut down" (interview, 2021). This mimics the tactics of language use discussed earlier. Here, we saw how the tactics used are responses to constraints in the digital space and all engage in forms of 'algorithmic resistance' (Velkova and Kaun, 2021), but based on self-developed ideas of what the system does.

Publicity tactics

Going into the streets was not just a way for the sceptics to avoid the Facebook police; it was also a way of showing 'outsiders' that they were a 'real public' with numbers, not just a small group online. The move to the physical realm was, therefore, not only a counter-tactic but also a publicity tactic oriented towards gaining recognition in the wider society. Moving to the streets was part of a tactic that we call 'make the cause relevant' because this tactic aimed at both rallying support among existing and new members and gaining recognition of the cause and its relevance by systemic actors. The move to the physical space was, therefore, partly a response to the constraints in the digital space, but also a way to engage with mass media logics. In this way, physical protests were also a means to demand attention from legacy media. In the following, we go through some of the publicity tactics used by the sceptics with the aim of being recognized by institutional actors, especially the media and politicians. The fact that so much effort was put into creating this connection implies that the constitution of counterpublics is still very much dependent on the recognition of elite actors and that to gain influence, the counterpublics believed they had to contact the traditional system. One respondent spoke quite definitively: "We will not break through until we get broadcasted by DR1 or TV 2 and on the radio. They are the ones who are in power" (interview, 2021).

Besides demonstrating, which is one of the primary ways of getting media attention (especially if the demonstrations include violent episodes and confrontation with the police or if they involve many participants), a widely used tactic for getting in contact with systemic actors is commenting on their social media posts. As one respondent explained: "If I see that they [my Facebook friends] are on Mette Frederiksen's page [the prime minister], I check their comments, and then I also write some myself, and then there are several who see that I write, and then it rolls" (interview, 2021). The implicit logic here is that connecting to a politician is a way of contacting important elite actors as well as starting a deluge of comments that make them visible as a counterpublic. Similar tactics include inviting politicians to debates and actively seeking press support, especially before going to demonstrations (interview, 2021). One interviewee was amazed that the newspaper *The Guardian* had cited a fellow protester and referred to the number of followers on Facebook:

'Then there was this journalist from *The Guardian* who had quoted her by name and the whole shebang in *The Guardian*. And I said to her, "*The Guardian*, Stephanie, do you know what this means …". And then, I had to show her that they have 8.5 million followers on Facebook.' (Interview, 2021)

The citation by a large, well-renowned media outlet was for the sceptics like borrowing a catapult of agency. This reminds us that agency is relational. Agency is not something that you just have; it is something that you are awarded by others. Two other system-embracing tactics are making citizen proposals and creating political parties. The respondents do not necessarily believe that they will succeed in this, but it will certainly lead to increased attention, particularly from the press (interview, 2021). What characterizes the publicity tactics is an outward-facing focus on connecting with rather than resisting the system (as with counter-tactics). They also help to illustrate the different ways the spaces afford agency differently, as social media, while giving easy access, do not give access to the right mechanisms of power. On the other hand, the mass media and politicians would not engage in deliberation, therefore, the agency to act with these systems was limited.

When going through the tactics – mobilization tactics, counter-tactics and publicity tactics – a unifying component seems to be an orientation towards quantification (via data). To put it another way, the quantification logic seems to permeate all the tactics in the hybrid media system. All interviewees talked about likes and shares and attached great importance to high numbers. As one respondent said:

'If you take TV 2 [Danish national broadcasting], for example, and the posts they make on Twitter, they get 50–100 likes. If they make a post on Facebook, they get around 1,000, 10,000 or 50,000 likes. Depending on the kind of post. Magnus Heunicke [Danish politician] is both on Twitter and on Facebook, and he might get something like 20–40 likes [on Twitter], but on Facebook, he can get 15,000.' (Interview, 2021)

That numbers were crucial for the agency can be seen in the negotiation of group sizes. Several respondents mentioned that the media always underestimated how many of them there were, which they saw as an attack on their legitimacy as a public, thereby limiting the effect their presence in the physical space could have on the wider society as reached through mass media: "We were around 3–4,000 people, but they wrote that we were only 400 people" (interview, 2021). Furthermore, some of the groups also collaborated in a common group to gain more visibility and power (interview, 2021). This was again driven by an underlying quantification logic of 'the bigger, the better'. One respondent ended by saying, "It is of no use if there are five people shouting. It is the number of people that is crucial for someone to bother to listen" (interview, 2021).

Conclusion

In this case, we see how agency is constantly at stake and fought for in the processes of public formation and how data becomes an integrated part of these processes. At the end of the COVID-19 pandemic, the administrators of some of the now-large Facebook groups experienced that other people were highly interested in taking over the groups that had been central during the pandemic and using these to forward their agendas. The negotiations over such 'takeovers' were highlighted by the administrator of one of the largest Facebook groups for sceptics, who was worried about what the members would feel. The allure of the group was, of course, its metrics – its size, its frequency of posts and interactions, and its reach – all datafied proofs of the groups' societal relevance and ability to bring forward a legitimate issue. Our study shows how important the materialization and datafication of the activities were for the people involved; data of their numbers and activities were seen as a resource. The focus on datafication was part of the way they planned their activities, where they would leave data traces through photos of physical events and store event lists. They aimed to produce data traces in the way they commented and became part of multiple groups as a way for the group of sceptics to seem larger than it was. They attempted to quantify their physical protests to counter the numbers presented in the press.

An overall (bridging) goal seemed to be the struggle for demonstrating a certain volume, showing that they were a larger group and should therefore be taken seriously, which is what we illustrated with the concept of hybrid quantification logic. This, however, raises an important discussion on how the agency of publics is intimately interlinked with data production, both as a resource and a danger, which was evident in the counter-tactics aimed at algorithmic and human moderators, where aims to leave limited or the right data traces became a concern and where agency manifested itself through resistance (see also Treré, 2018; Velkova and Kaun, 2021).

Christina Neumayer and David Struthers (2018) recently highlighted the role of social media as 'activist archives', but in a critical way, as the data processes of these 'archives' were not in the hands of the activists but controlled by social media logics. In this chapter, we showed how these logics become a resource for the counterpublics in formation, but also that much agency is tied up in this relationship. More research is needed to fully understand the implications of this highly datafied dance of publicness and counterpublicness, how the inherent logics of the platforms that collect data change the practices of publics, and how that data might be used in other ways than intended by the publics.

Notes

[1] Observations were carried out by the second author, Anna Schjøtt.

[2] We choose the framing 'sceptics' as a broad term for all people who act against the government's handling of the COVID-19 pandemic. 'Sceptics' emphasizes their common attitude but does not entail a positive or negative interpretation on their actions. In this way, we avoid taking a normative stance towards the people and their actions. Furthermore, this framing leaves room for discussing the activities as part of a formation process in which the people, their activities and incipient formations do not necessarily yet take shape as a 'counterpublic', 'public' or 'movement', but are in process and might (or might not) develop as such.

[3] As part of another project, we also did historic scrapes in three of the open Facebook groups explored in this case study. The Facebook posts shared in these groups were collected during four two-week periods with three months between them (1–14 May 2020, only two months after the official lockdown of Denmark on 11 March 2020; 1–14 September 2020; 1–14 January 2021; and 1–14 May 2021) (see Bengtsson et al [2021] for details on the study). Therefore, we had some insights into how these groups had developed over time before the period of ethnographic enquiry.

References

Altheide, D.L. (2016) 'Media logic', in G. Mazzoleni, K.G. Barnhurst, K.I. Ikeda, H. Wessler and R.C. Maia (eds) *The International Encyclopedia of Political Communication*, Hoboken: John Wiley and Sons. Available at: https://doi.org/10.1002/9781118541555.wbiepc088.

Altheide, D.L. and Snow, R.P. (1979) *Media Logic*, Beverly Hills: SAGE.

Beer, D. (2013) *Popular Culture and New Media*, London: Palgrave Macmillan.

Bengtsson, M. (2018) 'Think-aloud reading: Selected audiences' concurrent reaction to the implied audience in political commentary', in J.E. Kjeldsen (ed) *Rhetorical Audience Studies and Reception of Rhetoric: Exploring Audiences Empirically*, Cham: Palgrave Macmillan, pp 161–183.

Bengtsson, M., Hansen, A.S., Hartley, J.M., Kristensen, J.B., Mayerhöffer, E. and Ramsland, T.G.B. (2021) 'Conspiracy theories during the Covid-19 pandemic: The case of Denmark', *Zenodo*. Available at: https://zenodo.org/record/5556012#.Y7bXtuKZO-E.

Biggs, M. (2018) 'Size matters: Quantifying protest by counting participants', *Sociological Methods & Research*, 47(3), pp 351–383.

boyd, D. (2008) 'Why youth ♥ social network sites: The role of networked publics in teenage social life', in D. Buckingham (ed) *Youth, Identity, and Digital Media*, Cambridge, MA: MIT Press, pp 119–142.

Bruns, A. and Burgess, J. (2015) 'Twitter hashtags from ad hoc to calculated publics', *6th European Consortium for Political Research General Conference*. Available at: https://snurb.info/files/2015/Twitter%20Hashtags%20from%20Ad%20Hoc%20to%20Calculated%20Publics.pdf.

Calhoun, C. (2017) 'Facets of the public sphere: Dewey, Arendt, Habermas', in F. Engelstad, H. Larsen, J. Rogstad and K. Steen-Johnsen (eds) *Institutional Change in the Public Sphere: Views on the Nordic Model*, Warsaw: De Gruyter Open Poland, pp 23–45.

Chadwick, A. (2013) *The Hybrid Media System: Politics and Power*, Oxford: Oxford University Press.

Cobbe, J. (2021) 'Algorithmic censorship by social platforms: Power and resistance', *Philosophy & Technology*, 34(4), pp 739–766.

Couldry, N. and Mejias, U.A. (2019) 'Data colonialism: Rethinking big data's relation to the contemporary subject', *Television & New Media*, 20(4), pp 336–349.

Couldry, N., Livingstone, S. and Markham, T. (2007) *Media Consumption and Public Engagement: Beyond the Presumption of Attention*, Basingstoke: Palgrave Macmillan.

de Certeau, M. (1988) *The Practice of Everyday Life*, translated by S. Rendall, Berkeley and Los Angeles: University of California Press.

Dewey, J. (2012) *The Public and Its Problems: An Essay in Political Inquiry*, edited by M.L. Rogers, State College: Penn State University Press.

Emerson, R.M., Fretz, R.I. and Shaw, L.L. (2011) *Writing Ethnographic Fieldnotes* (2nd edn), Chicago: University of Chicago Press.

Flyvbjerg, B. (2006) 'Five misunderstandings about case-study research', *Qualitative Inquiry*, 12(2), pp 219–245.

Fraser, N. (1990) 'Rethinking the public sphere: A contribution to the critique of actually existing democracy', *Social Text*, 25/26, pp 56–80.

Frischlich, L., Schatto-Eckrodt, T., Boberg, S. and Wintterlin, F. (2021) 'Roots of incivility: How personality, media use, and online experiences shape uncivil participation', *Media and Communication*, 9(1), pp 195–208.

Gaw, F. (2022) 'Algorithmic logics and the construction of cultural taste of the Netflix Recommender System', *Media, Culture & Society*, 44(4), pp 706–725.

Geertz, C. (1973) *The Interpretation of Cultures*, New York: Basic Books.

Gillespie, T. (2014) 'The relevance of algorithms', in T. Gillespie, P.J. Boczkowski and K.A. Foot (eds) *Media Technologies: Essays on Communication, Materiality, and Society*, Cambridge, MA: MIT Press Scholarship Online, pp 167–193.

Gillespie, T. (2020) 'Content moderation, AI, and the question of scale', *Big Data & Society*, 7(2). Available at: https://doi.org/10.1177/205395172 0943234.

Habermas, J. (1991) 'The public sphere', in C. Mukerji and M. Schudson (eds) *Rethinking Popular Culture: Contemporary Perspectives in Cultural Studies*, Berkeley: University of California Press, pp 398–404.

Hartley, J.M., Bengtsson, M., Hansen, A.S. and Sivertsen, M.F. (2021) 'Researching publics in datafied societies: Insights from four approaches to the concept of "publics" and a (hybrid) research agenda', *New Media & Society*. Available at: https://doi.org/10.1177/14614448211021045.

Ito, M. (2008) 'Introduction', in K. Varnelis (ed) *Networked Publics*, Cambridge, MA: MIT Press, pp 1–14.

Kavada, A. and Poell, T. (2021) 'From counterpublics to contentious publicness: Tracing the temporal, spatial, and material articulations of popular protest through social media', *Communication Theory*, 31(2), pp 190–208.

Klinger, U. and Svensson, J. (2018) 'The end of media logics? On algorithms and agency', *New Media & Society*, 20(12), pp 4653–4670.

Kvale, S. and Brinkmann, S. (2015) *Interview: Det kvalitative forskningsinterview som håndværk* (3rd edn), Copenhagen: Hans Reitzels Forlag.

Lippmann, W. (1993) *The Phantom Public*, New Brunswick and London: Transaction Publishers.

Livingstone, S. (2015) 'Active audiences? The debate progresses but it is far from resolved', *Communication Theory*, 25(4), pp 439–446.

Markham, A.N. (2013) 'Fieldwork in social media: What would Malinowski do?', *Qualitative Communication Research*, 2(4), pp 434–446.

Negt, O. and Kluge, A. (1993) *Public Sphere and Experience: Toward an Analysis of the Bourgeois and Proletarian Public Sphere*, Minnesota: University of Minnesota Press.

Neumayer, C. and Struthers, D.M. (2018) 'Social media as activist archives', in M. Mortensen, C. Neumayer and T. Poell (eds) *Social Media Materialities and Protest: Critical Reflections*, London: Routledge, pp 86–98.

Pasquale, F. (2015) *The Black Box Society: The Secret Algorithms that Control Money and Information*, Cambridge, MA and London: Harvard University Press.

Postill, J. and Pink, S. (2012) 'Social media ethnography: The digital researcher in a messy web', *Media International Australia*, 145(1), pp 123–134.

Przybylski, L. (2021) *Hybrid Ethnography: Online, Offline, and In Between*. Thousand Oaks: SAGE.

Putnam, R.D. (1995) 'Bowling alone: America's declining social capital', *Journal of Democracy*, 6(1), pp 65–78.

Putnam, R.D. (2000) *Bowling Alone: The Collapse and Revival of American Community*, New York: Simon & Schuster.

Quandt, T. (2018) 'Dark participation', *Media and Communication*, 6(4), pp 36–48.

Treré, E. (2018) 'From digital activism to algorithmic resistance', in M. Graham (ed) *The Routledge Companion to Media and Activism*, London: Routledge, pp 367–375.

van Dijck, J. (2014) 'Datafication, dataism and dataveillance: Big data between scientific paradigm and ideology', *Surveillance & Society*, 12(2), pp 197–208.

van Dijck, J. and Poell, T. (2013) 'Understanding social media logic', *Media and Communication*, 1(1), pp 2–14.

Velkova, J. and Kaun, A. (2021) 'Algorithmic resistance: Media practices and the politics of repair', *Information, Communication & Society*, 24(4), pp 523–540.

Willems, W. (2019) '"The politics of things": Digital media, urban space, and the materiality of publics', *Media, Culture & Society*, 41(8), pp 1192–1209.

Ytre-Arne, B. and Moe, H. (2021) 'Folk theories of algorithms: Understanding digital irritation', *Media, Culture & Society*, 43(5), pp 807–824.

4

Stratified Public Formation
in Mundane Settings

Morten Fischer Sivertsen and Mikkeline Sofie Skjerning Thomsen

Introduction

Post:	My newest creation for teaching my sex education class (★presents crotched female genitalia★). Women also come in many colours and sizes.
Respondent 1:	Why can't you open Facebook without getting that sort of content stuck in your face. Vaginas in the morning coffee – thanks, but no thanks.
Respondent 2:	Do you also find all the needlework portraying penises offensive? Or is it just female private parts you don't like?
Respondent 3:	My thoughts exactly. Of course, we need to shame the private parts of women and not the crocheted penis-creations we see here every day, which are oh so funny.
Respondent 1:	Alright, radical feminist alert. I never said that I prefer the genitals of men.
Respondent 2:	No, you just said that you are disgusted by the genitals of women ;) [+ 45 comments]. (Excerpt from a crochet group on Facebook)

The distinction between the public and the private has a long intellectual history. Whether the empirical example from the Facebook crochet group adds to this history is open to debate, but it does convey one of our primary messages through the colourful imagery of crotched genitalia in a telling way; if there ever was a line between the public and the private, this line is increasingly hard to spot in digital and datafied societies.

72

Used in relation to politics, 'public' in a conventional sense predominantly refers to matters of formal government and acts of citizenship in the public sphere characterized by participation, deliberation and collective decision-making; it thus relates to matters of the collective in contrast to matters of private and personal interest. The classical notion of 'public' reverberates in canonical studies, for example, in the work of Dewey (2012), Arendt (2018) and Habermas (1991), but also holds ground in more recent studies and literature. For instance, Couldry et al developed their concept of public connection, referring to the mediated orientations of citizens towards a public world of matters beyond 'purely private concerns' (2010, p 65). Their analytical work builds on Habermas and the idea of 'one' public sphere, which citizens connect to through news consumption, political interest and formal public engagement (Couldry et al, 2010, pp 40, 188). Thus, the authors operate with a clear distinction between public and collective versus private and personal interests, which, as they admit, is not without analytical difficulties. For example, while initially acknowledging how public connection can take many forms, they primarily evaluate their findings through news consumption, political interest and formal public engagement (Couldry et al, 2010, pp 40, 188), expressing distinct concern for the disengaged and disconnected strata.

Thus, while seminal contributions to the study of the public sphere, of both classical and more recent origin, seem to uphold the classical distinction between the private and the public, the rendezvous with the empirical reality of modern societies seemingly puts us in a conceptual rut; how can we, for example, meaningfully categorize the excerpt on crotched private parts and broader discourses on gender and equality between sexes – does it adhere to the private or the public domain? Are publics formed only when citizens discuss matters of so-called shared concern? Who might decide what such matters of shared concern are? And what constitute legitimate ways of connecting to and engaging in them?

To us, such an approach faces at least two problems. First, the fact that citizens in contemporary societies are simultaneously present in both digital and non-digital arenas and have a multitude of ways to enact their relations to the public world. Scholarly efforts therefore need to be observant not to dismiss newer forms of public engagement, which differ from the canonized units of measure, such as voting, volunteering or watching 'hard' news. One such example of newer forms of public formation processes is the activities within citizen-led Facebook groups, which are scrutinized in this chapter.

Second, we need to pay attention to how patterns of social stratification play a principal role in how citizens monitor and engage in the public sphere. Drawing on insights from the sociology of Pierre Bourdieu (for example, 1984) and Bourdieusian scholars, such as Jan Fredrik Hovden (2022), we argue that what constitutes legitimate public sphere activities in society are not evenly accessible to all. On the contrary, it is a matter of social class, where the less affluent tend to be labelled as disengaged and disconnected when they might lack the social resources to engage as 'informed' citizens (Moe et al, 2019). Considering the social reasons behind the public sphere activities of citizens paves the way for a sociological critique of the private/ public distinction: namely, that it is normative and seemingly unconcerned with the constitutive patterns of social inequality.

To summarize, this chapter argues for viewing the public sphere as a patchwork of stratified publics, which form across and beyond both traditional and newer forms of media. Rather than focusing on how legacy media (especially the news) connects citizens to matters of allegedly shared concern (Couldry et al, 2010), we see public formation as sustained by both digital, legacy and non-mediated practices. Furthermore, such practices can only be understood in the context of the socio-hierarchical patterns they are situated in. Our main empirical ambition thus revolves around a two-step analysis; first, through quantitative analysis of representative survey data, we scrutinize how the resources (or capital) of agents influence respondents' habitual way of relating to the public sphere, denoted as their public lifestyle (Hovden, 2022). Public lifestyles, however, vary, and do not enjoy equal social recognition. Interest in politics, for instance, is something that is reserved for the privileged groups in society, while the socially disadvantaged appear disengaged when viewing their responses in the survey questionnaire. Though this pattern is evident in their relations to the public sphere, their actions differ, as we explore in the second part of the chapter. Using the format of Facebook groups as our object of study, we provide empirical evidence through netnographic field studies that even the most politically disinterested citizens actually partake in deliberation and discussions on matters of shared concern. In doing so we emphasize how the private and public blur in the concrete everyday, mundane engagement in these groups. We also argue that the groups function as a training ground (Dahlgren, 2006) for more formal public formation.

Our use and understanding of the word 'publics' refers to spaces of public formation, which in our view can occur on multiple levels. A Facebook group about cats can be seen as a public (albeit a smaller one), if deliberation of matters of shared concern occurs among the members. Being a member of a Facebook group is thus one modality of a given public lifestyle, which may in this case also include reading magazines about animals, demonstrating for animal rights or being vegan. In this way, multiple public lifestyle preferences bind people together in larger publics across different formats in both the online and offline world. As will become evident later in the multiple correspondence analysis (MCA) (Roux and Rouanet, 2004), Facebook groups about pets are located in a larger public, which we have called the *mundane/digital public*, because such pet group preferences correlate with preferences for, for example, using Snapchat, celebrity online culture and less social resources (such as income and education). Thus, analogous to the image of the Russian doll, we believe that 'publics' is a relevant term to describe the reciprocal processes of public formation on both the micro and macro level.

The chapter will progress through the following steps: first, we briefly present our methodological design. Second, we review key perceptions of the private/public distinction in both conventional and more recent scholarly work and introduce the notion of public lifestyle, developed by Jan Fredrik Hovden (2022). Third, we present our combined analysis; we perform MCA on the survey data, construct the space of public lifestyle patterns in Denmark and show how they are linked to patterns of social inequality and dominance of certain publics over others. From this overview, we zoom in on findings from the mapping and netnographic analysis of the Danish Facebook group landscape. Finally, we discuss how public formation can be seen as stratified and symbolically misrecognized and consider how such a perspective can help us understand public formation in the datafied era.

A mixed-methods design

The analysis of the chapter is based on a mixed-methods design combining MCA (Roux and Rouanet, 2004) of a representative sample of Danish citizens (N=5,660, collected in the first quarter of 2021) with quantitative mapping, qualitative categorization and netnographic fieldwork (Kozinets, 2010) within a large sample of Facebook groups.

First, the MCA constructs a space of public lifestyles in which we combine a rich body of variables on media usage (including newspaper and magazine reading, television, radio, social media usage and streaming services) and broader public lifestyle patterns (cultural interests, leisure time activities, civic engagement such as voluntary work) in both online and offline settings.[1] In addition to this, we include variables relating to social stratification (income, wealth, education, social background, social network, and so on). The survey also contains a range of variables on membership in Facebook groups, which were specifically designed to link the survey study with the Facebook study. The MCA in this way facilitates a general overview and analysis of how people monitor and engage in the public sphere in Denmark through digital, legacy and unmediated practices, with a relational emphasis on how these practices link to patterns of social stratification.

From here, we take a deep dive into one particular and popular arena of public formation; the landscape and activities of Danish Facebook groups, which have only recently gained the attention of the scholarly community. This second section builds on two previous publications by one of the authors and her team (Thomsen, 2020; Thomsen et al, 2022), which represent the first attempt at a comprehensive mapping of a national Facebook group landscape numbering 5,249 groups.[2] While the empirical material and the scholarly analysis are too extensive to include in their entirety here, we have focused our work in two directions for the present chapter. First, we have assigned each of the 5,249 Facebook groups one of 24 group topics (for example, local communities, pets, environment, family) based on the name of the group and the group description. Respondents of the survey were asked about their membership in Facebook groups related to the same 24 topics, which allowed us to visualize the group landscape through a stratificational lens using the MCA. Second, we have performed extensive netnography (Kozinets, 1998) within more than 400 out of the 5,249 groups since 2016. Netnography is a method used to investigate specific instances in which a community is produced through computer-mediated communication. Kozinets (1998) states that the method 'can be important not only for understanding what these new "villages" and "communities" are but, equally important, for imagining the kinds of publics that human groups can create with the help of emerging technologies' (p 1). The method of netnography includes joining the groups, making observations, producing fieldnotes and collecting examples of discourse from within. Over the years we have gained a thorough understanding of the debates and discussions taking place inside this particular yet widely used digital infrastructure. The netnographic approach can help us uncover the more qualitative aspects of how Facebook groups facilitate public formation, even among those who do not understand themselves as particularly interested in politics and deliberative practices (as will be shown in our analysis).

Public formation in mundane settings

While many established studies maintain the distinction between the private and the public (for example, Habermas, 1991) and some critique it (for example, Fraser, 1990), several contemporary scholars underline how this distinction seems especially elusive in the present day. A crucial point is how digital media enable citizens to be highly creative and personal regarding public sphere activities and citizenship practices (Friedland and Wells, 2018), as exemplified in Thorson's (2014) 'do-it-yourself' citizenship or Hartley's (2010) account of how political participation is expressed through playful activities and performances in YouTube dance videos. Along the same lines, Wahl-Jorgensen notes how social media 'challenges conventional divides between the private and the public, the individual and the collective, and the personal and the political' (2019, p 151). Similarly, Picone et al (2019) elaborate on how billions of 'small acts of engagement' every second in the digital sphere blur the dividing line between the public and the private domain. As portrayed in the broad category of ubiquitous citizenship in audience research (Schrøder, 2013), and as also Wright et al (2015) suggest, 'political talk' and public deliberation is not reserved for the arenas of politicians or social movements; it also happens in non-political everyday life settings, in 'third spaces' that are 'not intended for political purposes, but rather – during the course of everyday talk – become political through the connections people make between their everyday lives and the political/social issues of the day' (Wright et al, 2015, p 1). Although studied in the format of television, Graham and Harju (2011) exemplify such rationale by showing how political talk not only emerges from news journalism, but also thrives in forums dedicated to popular reality TV programmes such as 'Wife Swap' and 'Big Brother' in a British context. In our view, such forms of everyday, informal practices, that nonetheless 'may provoke the citizen in us' (Graham and Harju, 2011, p 1), can be thought of as mundane citizenship; a perspective 'that place civic participation deep into the heart of everyday life' (Bakardjieva, 2012, p 1356). To Bakardjieva (2009), mundane citizenship is exercised through practices described as acts of subactivism; small-scale, often individual and private decisions or actions that 'have either a political or ethical frame of reference and never appear on the stage of social design, but on the contrary, remain submerged in everyday life' (Bakardjieva, 2009, p 96) According to Bakardjieva (2012), everyday talk not only has the potential to shift the individual's values and political positions but may also motivate the individual to further political commitment. The exercise of mundane citizenship is an important foundation for more active political mobilization, without, however, necessarily leading to it. Summing up, the perspectives presented in this paragraph underline the need for studying public formation outside the world of hard news and formal politics.

A Bordieusian approach to publics

In this chapter, we take a sociocultural approach and apply the notion of *public lifestyles* (Hovden and Moe, 2017; Hovden, 2022; Moe et al, 2019) to understand processes of public formation across social strata. In the view of Hovden and Moe (2017), mediated public connection needs to be broadened out and acknowledge how 'cultural works outside the media and engagement in political and civic organisations' (p 392) may constitute a valid way of relating to the public sphere. The word 'lifestyles' might have an odd ring to some, but it has a specific connotation within the Bordieusian literature. The key insight to build upon here, is Bourdieu's idea of the double nature of social reality, which refers to the homology between social positions, capital (or resources) and placement within the hierarchy of society on the one hand, and the stratified distribution of preferences, classifications and interpretations of agents in the social space on the other (Bourdieu and Wacquant, 1992), the latter often denoted as their lifestyle. In one of his most famous books, *Distinction*, Bourdieu (1984) shows how social positions with different compositions of cultural and economic capital (for example, teachers, business leaders, manual workers) tend to choose differently in life with regards to the culture they consume, the food they eat and the political attitudes they express. In other words, Bourdieu's argument is that the 'space of lifestyles' is situated homologically in relation to the space of social positions. Inspired by this, Hovden's aim is 'to map the main divisions in people's public lifestyles in Norway' and take note of 'the role of social differences, in particular class differences, for structuring such public lifestyles' (2022, p 6).

Hovden's empirical investigations thus highlight how people's relation to politics and broader debate 'are structured stably along class lines while also emphasising, as others have done, the need to look at the intersection between class and generational cleavages' (Hovden, 2022, p 18). In this regard, Hovden gives special attention to the structuring factor of the former and discusses how 'normative democratic theory' provides an unrealistic framework for understanding how lower-strata groups engage in the public sphere. The result being, he argues, that working-class people are seen as disengaged and, to some extent, pathological in a democratic sense. Such an argument is also supported in the work by Butsch (2008), who shows how audiences historically have been characterized as either crowds or as isolated individuals in a mass (both considered as examples of poor citizenship) versus the images of democratically legitimate publics. These images were, according to Butsch (2008), clearly linked to social hierarchies and class, even though they at times were contested by the groups, who were stigmatized.

In general, we are very inspired by the work of Hovden. Our analytical design, however, allows us to take a step further than Hovden, who, with a quasi-fatalistic tone, finishes his study with these words: 'The adage that politics is "the art of the possible" is not only true for politicians; it also contains a hard truth about the realities of the social world and its limitations for the political engagement of ordinary citizens' (Hovden, 2022, p 19). While this conclusion is appealing and the analysis is sound, we also believe that it highlights the limitations of using survey data. Thus, even if lower-strata respondents might answer in a certain way when filling in a survey questionnaire (for example, 'politics is not for me'), their actions may differ. The second part of our chapter thus shifts focus from studying how people on a general level view themselves in relation to the public sphere to focusing on how people actually act, deliberate and discuss, in this case in the context of Facebook groups. Because we specifically ask about Facebook groups in the questionnaire, we can locate these Facebook groups in the social space and focus on the lower-strata groups that seem broadly disengaged from public sphere activities.

Thus, located far away from news media and expert discourses, Facebook groups about needlework (as exemplified in the beginning), pets, family, local life and gardening may not exactly be places where one would normally expect to find citizens engaging and deliberating. We deliberately write 'expect' to emphasize how certain spaces or types of activities in society have symbolic legitimacy as places nurturing proper public lifestyle practices, while others seemingly only have relevance in the private sphere (Couldry et al, 2010). In our view, however, the Facebook groups transcend this distinction. Constantly fluctuating between the seemingly private and public, we observe in the Facebook groups how everyday life interaction more than often involves deliberation of matters of public interest, and how engagement through Facebook groups constitutes a basic mobilization of people who are ready to rise to more political formal action if, for example, their local communities, family lives or rights within the healthcare system are threatened. In the larger context of understanding public connection and participation in modern societies, the mapping and analysis of Facebook groups provide unique insight into the nature and extent of how publics are shaped in digital spaces.

Public lifestyles across social strata

We now turn to the task of analysing the two-dimensional space of public lifestyles, produced by the statistical operations of the MCA (for further information, see Sivertsen, forthcoming). First, we turn to the so-called active variables, consisting of 51 different types of media usage, which construct the dimensions of the space. The first axis, the horizontal, constitutes the primal dimension and can be interpreted as the difference between preferring traditional and legacy media such as public and commercial television and radio while having a distaste for social media, as opposed to more modern and digital forms of media usage, for example, using streaming services, social media, podcasts and eBooks. We thus interpret this axis as the relative differences between traditional and digital media users, which clearly correlate with respondent age. The second axis, the vertical, is interpreted as the difference between different forms of media taste in terms of content; at the top, respondents prefer printed newspapers, hard news programmes, non-music radio providing public information, and reading fictional and non-fictional literature and magazines. The bottom prefers commercial and public entertainment TV, soft news such as 'Good Morning, Denmark' and Friday night television shows such as 'Dancing with the Stars', Snapchat, commercial hit music radio and reality series, such as 'Paradise Hotel'. We thus interpret this axis as depicting the differences between varying degrees of elite media usage and more mundane and entertainment-based media

Figure 4.1: Four different types of publics

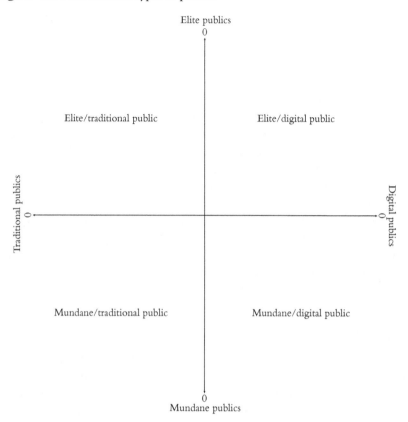

usage, backed by how this correlates with overall capital volume (which we will exemplify in the following).

This essentially provides us with a crude, but useful, overview of four different types of publics, who differ in terms of the public lifestyle patterns of the respondents; the elite/traditional, the elite/digital, the mundane/traditional and the mundane/digital public as portrayed in Figure 4.1.

Constructing a space using these two dimensions and subsequently projecting the supplementary variables of interests – public lifestyle patterns (including membership in Facebook groups), demography and measurements of different forms of social stratification – we can examine an overall space of public lifestyles across social strata as portrayed in Figure 4.2.

The *elite/traditional public*, located in the upper left quadrant, are distinctively older (around 60 and up), read a lot of conservative printed newspapers, listen to public information and perspectives on public radio channel P1, expand their horizons through evening classes and attend lectures as a part of their public lifestyle, which contrasts with their disinterest in pop and

Figure 4.2: Space of public connections and lifestyles

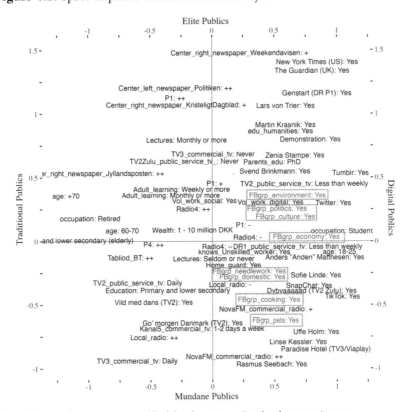

Note: Diagram shows a map of public lifestyle patterns. Facebook groups in grey.

rock music and television in general. Differing from the mundane publics, they partake in activities such as ballet, art galleries, theatre and concerts, preferring intricate styles of classical music and jazz. In terms of political participation, they exert strong influence in local communities, do charity work, and, in general, belong to social circles where politics and debate are a natural part of their everyday life.

In the upper right corner of the map, the *elite/digital public* distinctively uses social media to follow political actors such as Greta Thunberg or Zenia Stampe (a politician from the Danish Social Liberal Party [Radikale Venstre], whose electoral base is mainly highly educated big city residents). They also follow chief editor Martin Krasnik of *Weekendavisen*, a newspaper for the accomplished bourgeoisie prioritizing analysis, debate and reflection about national and international events (in the sections 'Society', 'Culture', 'Books' and 'Ideas') over daily news updates and have a good laugh at the acclaimed political satire of the fictional online news site, *Rokokoposten*. These distinctive preferences are also reflected in the Facebook groups they are members of, which revolve around issues of climate and sustainability, politics and debate, culture and religion (for a more detailed view on the placement of the Facebook groups, see Figure 4.4). Coming from the humanities and social sciences, their educational backgrounds and social upbringings are distinctively academic, and they occupy positions such as researchers and lawyers, earning the highest incomes among respondents and socializing with prestigious people such as journalists and politicians.

The *mundane/traditional public*, located in the lower left quadrant of the map, can be viewed as twofold: The upper part likes tabloid newspapers and watches TV 2 and TV 2 News daily. They like to read magazines about domestic life and keep up with what happens in the world of handball, swimming, ice hockey and dance. The lower part is more attracted to commercial and entertainment television, local radio and gossip magazines. They distinctively do not trust other people and have no interest in issues of climate, politics or culture. In general, the whole quadrant tends to have vocational education or very little education (primary schooling and, for some, upper secondary), works with skilled or unskilled manual work in the production sector and tends to come from homes with low educational capital as well.

The *mundane/digital public* is very much attracted to the digital world of entertainment and personal and domestic life, mostly on Facebook, Snapchat and TikTok. They tend to follow people such as celebrity pastry chef Mette Blomsterberg, from the Danish equivalent of 'The Great British Bake Off', and former tennis athlete Caroline Wozniacki. In the right part of this public, the younger groups follow a range of celebrity figures, such as influencer Anders Hemmingsen, the comedic duo of Adam and Noah and stand-up comedian Uffe Holm. These preferences are also resembled in the Facebook groups they participate in, which revolve around matters of domestic and family life, entertainment (chats, jokes, memes, quotes), cooking, baking and grilling, cars, pets, local issues, COVID-19 and health (and sickness). Outside the world of social media, they occasionally watch public television, listen to commercial hit music radio and frequent events with stand-up comedy. They primarily work in the hospitality or retail sectors, have relatively little education (if any) and earn relatively low incomes.

While distinctively not spending much time with the world of politics online, they do follow the politician, Inger Støjberg. Though a part of the representative political system in Denmark (at that time), Støjberg arguably differs from most other politicians. Her distinctly critical attitudes towards Middle Eastern immigrants and her talent for communicating this very effectively on social media has gained her many followers, who, according to this data, resemble a public lifestyle that in every other aspect is not attracted to the world of politics.

So far, this first part of our mixed-methods study has established an overview of how people monitor and participate in different publics related to their public lifestyles. The initial impression seems to suggest that the overall public sphere in Denmark is divided similarly to the findings of Couldry et al (2010), who contrasted traditional and issue connectors (the publicly connected) with the 'celebrity cluster' and the 'low interest' cluster (the publicly disconnected). However, we do notice certain results that mandate further and deeper scrutiny. For instance, we saw from the survey how the mundane publics seemingly have a clear distaste or disinterest towards the world of politics, but still follow a politician such as Inger Støjberg, distrust key democratic institutions (the prime example being the Danish Health Authority in the context of the COVID-19 pandemic). This does seem to imply some form of political awareness and will, although it may differ from the political taste of the most affluent. In a digital and datafied world where 'almost everybody can choose to be politically active about anything at any moment in time' (van Deth, 2016, p 5), but only some apparently understand themselves as actually being politically engaged, it seems appropriate to supplement our survey findings with an analysis of actual public formation practices. We thus argue that public formation cannot be seen as a distinction between the political and the non-political, but as differentiations in *how* citizens are political and how such political engagement differ in terms of symbolic value. The less renowned forms of being political are explored in the following in the context of Facebook groups.

Facebook groups as small-scale digital publics

Post:	I've never even considered not following the national vaccination programme, since I've never suffered any side effects from my own vaccinations. But recent posts in this group have made me question. Please help. Don't comment your opinions. I want facts.
Respondent 1:	Noooo. Please, please, please don't doubt science. Why would you rather believe the anecdotes of strangers in here?
Respondent 2:	You won't find many facts in here. Most of the evidence of the failure of vaccines has been concealed by big pharma.
Respondent 3:	I feel you, Mama. I don't doubt vaccines in general though, but I have a bad feeling about this hasty COVID vaccine.
Respondent 1:	*Tagging a moderator*: you might want to follow this. Misinformation will spread fast.

Respondent 4:   I'm a doctor (when I'm not on maternity leave) and you are welcome to write me a private message with questions and concerns. (Extract from a debate within a Facebook group for new mothers)

This example is just one from the extensive mapping and analysis of 5,249 Danish and predominantly citizen-led Facebook groups. In our view, this excerpt exemplifies how most of the groups represent publics forming around topics traditionally considered private: social and family relations, interests and local community are more popular than the explicitly political. The netnographic field study, however, shows how even the most seemingly private and non-political Facebook groups are homes to public deliberation of matters of shared concern. They thus function as civic spaces of engagement and deliberation, even among citizens in mundane publics who tend to be understood (and understand themselves) as disengaged from the political realm.

As a result of the *quantitative mapping*, we found 5,249 Danish Facebook groups, with 23 million accumulated memberships. The average member count of a group being 4,541 members (the smallest group within the dataset having 31 members and the largest just above 500,000 members). Over the course of nine months an estimated 3.3 million unique Danish Facebook users were actively engaging in at least one – and often more – groups (Thomsen et al, 2022).[3]

After identifying them we analysed them through *manual qualitative categorization*. Each group was assigned a topic based on its name and public group description. The purpose was to answer the question of around what topics and purposes citizens form digital publics on their own initiative. One overarching observation we have made based on reading through the names and descriptions of the groups is that identification and common denominators are at the basis of group formation. They are often explicitly called things such as 'We who love Sæby' (a Danish town), 'For all of us who have lost someone', 'We who visit the national archives' and 'All of us with beards, tattoos and humour', or they elaborate on the common denominator in the group description. Another overarching observation we have made about the group landscape is that, no matter where you live and what interests or issues you have, there is a group for you: woodturning, infertility, classic motorcycles, camping, silver heirlooms, hair extensions, plastic surgery, polyamory, board games, nursing, permaculture, being young in the city of Nyborg in the 1980s, welcoming immigrants and refugees, opposing immigrants and refugees, LGBTQIA+ support groups, knowledge-sharing for clairvoyants or dating for people with early retirement benefits. And the list continues. However, for the purpose of this chapter we confined ourselves to classify the groups based on 24 categories that were also put forth in the survey. Figure 4.3 shows the most popular main topics of the groups Danes are members of.

Figure 4.3: The main topics of Danish Facebook groups

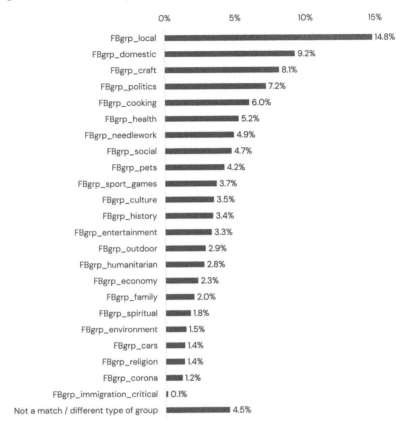

Although the digitization of public formation has removed physical barriers and made it possible for us to find like-minded people based on many factors other than geographic affiliation, it turns out that the most popular topic or common denominator is where we live.[4] Most users participate in groups formed around their local community, and almost every Danish town will have at least one (and sometimes multiple) Facebook groups formed around them. In the local groups, we observe that people come to share local news, complain and vent their feelings, gossip, applaud local initiatives, recommend or warn against local businesses and services, look for help, offer help and, last but not least, maintain a local spirit and consubstantiality. These groups contain the smallest and largest of debates – from the best day-cares to whether the local authorities are trustworthy and the plans for future urban planning. Apart from their local communities, the most prominent topics of the groups are associated with the private sphere: domestic life, health, cooking, needlework (and creativity), pets, sports and games, and social relations (around 50 per cent of the total number of group memberships).

Figure 4.4: Space of Facebook groups and civic engagement

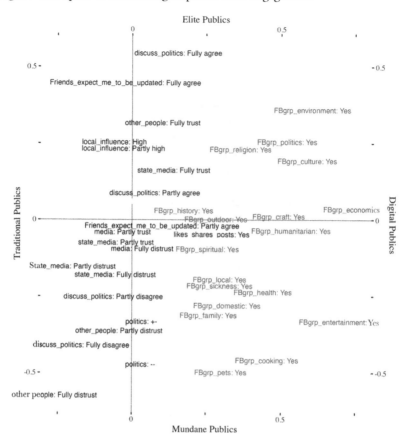

Note: Diagram shows a map of public lifestyle patterns. Facebook groups in grey.

Considering the relative popularity of such groups, there seems to be a demand for participation in digital publics centred around topics around which traditional news media don't offer forums for public conversation. Where do we go and debate domestic life and family? Where can we get day-to-day updates on small events in our local community? How can I connect with others with the same creative interests? The groups we form emphasize the need for a space of vernacular conversations. Overall, the share of groups established around topics traditionally considered political (politics, the environment, religion, COVID-19) is small compared to groups centred around the local community, hobbies (cars, needlework, the outdoors, pets, cooking, and so on) and domestic affairs. Thus, if we look at the groups merely based on their assigned topics, it seems that most groups are formed under headlines typically associated with the private sphere.

As portrayed in Figure 4.4, the *elite/digital public* engage in groups formed around public agendas, traditionally including politics, the environment, religion and culture, while the *mundane/digital public* is engaged in groups formed around domestic life, family, pets, cooking and entertainment. However, the netnographic field study of the Danish landscape of Facebook groups suggests that the widely used Facebook groups are blurring the lines between the public and the private along with the political and the non-political: deliberation of issues of public concern seeps in, even within communities formed around pets and domestic life, disproving their members to be disengaged, even if they self-identify as such. In the next section we will elaborate further on the netnographic fieldwork we have done within the Danish Facebook group landscape.

The political within the seemingly mundane

While the exchanges of some groups are fairly limited to the overall topic of the group (in some, political debate is not even allowed), most groups do contain political conversations, which expands as the confidentiality between its members grows stronger. Our analysis shows that even though we might not primarily gather in groups under the headline of fighting climate change, the debate on climate change and environmental issues is present within many groups; what green dinner options do kids like (cooking group)? What great books or movies do we know that address climate change (a group for kindergarten teachers)? What are tips for minimalism and recycling on a daily basis (family and domestic groups)? These are selected and illustrative examples, yet we observe that matters of shared concern permeate any apparently 'private' discussion within communities formed around 'private' issues. The starting point of a debate is often a citizen's personal experience, but personal experiences and dilemmas often act as proxies for debating what is in general right, reasonable, relevant and constructive as regards family, gender, climate, religion, science, education, physical and mental welfare, human nature, and so on. In other words – the analysis of the groups based on their names and descriptions doesn't do justice to the civic engagement within. Most groups, we argue, are versatile forums where 'people like us' gather. They can be centred around any interest, hobby, identity, sexuality, life circumstance, family structure, illness, profession, religious affiliation, geographical affiliation or other topic. And the debate within the groups often has personal or local experiences and dilemmas as the point of departure, but the conversations often touch upon or expand into issues of current affairs and shared concerns, be it with regard to crocheted genitalia, vaccinations, sustainability, gender roles, immigration, racism, work/life balance, and so on. What most groups have in common is that they have developed into forums serving multiple functions for the members: debate, knowledge sharing, socializing, counselling, coordinating actions or events, emotional and practical support, or sharing of news and inspiration.

In forums related to family, children and parenthood, there is a lot of talk about sleep patterns, pacifiers and the best diaper brands, but just as often, members will discuss the distribution of housework, gender roles, the ideal upbringing of children, the political conditions of day-care institutions and whether to adhere to the national vaccination programme. In most health groups, members will debate the public healthcare system, issues around pharmaceutical companies and the legitimacy of alternative treatment options. As shown in Figure 4.4 in the map produced by the MCA in our survey data, groups centred around family and cooking were preferred by the somewhat 'disengaged' *mundane/digital publics*, who were not into politics. Still, many of the groups assigned a hobby-related topic – such as cars, pets, sports and games, the outdoors and needlework – comprise publics that are often deliberating matters of shared concern. In one home decoration group, members debated the morality of dogmatic life quotes people had put on their walls. Is it damaging to our mental health to be encouraged to make lemonade every time life gives us lemons? In groups for people into motoring they will discuss whether manufacturers or customers should be the main drivers of the green transition of motoring. We observed this tendency within all of the groups, yet naturally to a different degree. Some groups stick more rigorously to one purpose: sharing photos or giving away free stuff. But even here, people will discuss whether the giver of a free couch should donate to the person first in line or choose between beneficiaries. Subsequently they will also debate how racial discrimination potentially affects who gets more stuff. Suddenly, when looking at the discourse within these digital small-scale publics, very few of them seem to represent political disconnection.

Some groups (7 per cent) have political campaigning or mobilization for a political cause as their main topic, which shows that even though political issues are not the most popular to form groups around, the group format is being put to use for formal political engagement. The political groups are used to recruit supporters, organize protests and make a case visible to politicians and mainstream media by, for example, producing debate pieces or citizen bills or organizing demonstrations. These types of groups are often referred to as 'issue publics' (Marres, 2005) because they arise as a response to a public issue. It seems that some of these groups are indeed making themselves heard by formal public agents, such as politicians and mainstream media.[5] Engagement in political Facebook groups is located within the upper right quadrant of the *elite/digital public* (see Figure 4.4). Yet here again we observe some discrepancy when looking into the group data. Many of the explicitly political Facebook groups are formed around low trust in authorities or supporting right-wing politicians such as Inger Støjberg, or right-wing political agendas such as anti-immigration – all variables located in the quadrant of the *mundane/digital public*. And while some political groups are formed around issues which are also driven by news or legacy media (for example, climate change, immigration and gender) other large political groups are formed around issues that would traditionally be considered 'private' and which the members explicitly consider to be overlooked by mainstream media; for example, groups fighting for healthcare for people giving birth, protesting the low funding and quality within public day-care centres, or fighting for the rights of people on social welfare. In these cases, groups seem like drivers of change, since their issue was not very visible within news media prior to their engagement. One example is the group 'Friends of Amager Fælled' (*Amager Fælleds Venner*), which has engaged thousands of locals (politicians and citizens alike) and played an important role in repeatedly thwarting and delaying housing development projects in Amager Fælled, a large nature reserve in the south of Copenhagen (similar instances include the parent movement #wherearethegrownups? (*#hvorerderenvoksen?*) who swiftly mobilized in local and national campaign groups, or the group 'TAAGF Total abolition of mutual support obligations' ('*TAAGF Total afskaffelse af gensidig forsørgelsespligt*'), which was thanked by the Socialist People's Party of Denmark for its political efforts to push for a change in the law (the law will be changed by January 2023). However, based on our research, we argue that even the seemingly non-political Facebook groups organized around topics traditionally considered 'private' are also to be regarded as important public powerhouses, even when they are not involved with formal political protest. As our netnographic studies show, nearly all the groups we have looked into are forums of debate and negotiation of matters of shared concern and thus function as places of public formation.

A digital training ground for publicness

Similar to the studies by Bakardjieva (2012) on mundane (digital) citizenship in Bulgaria, we observe a high degree of trust in the groups, which is expressed through members sharing personal stories, dilemmas, opinions, or asking for advice and guidance in relation to both technical and social issues. As windows of attitudinal change are opened through identification and trust, the groups preserve a simmering political potential among citizens. For one, citizens are practising public debate and disagreement in a more comfortable setting, because the groups encompass both the social, practical and political conversation. Thus, their democratic skills are enhanced through participation analogues to the comment by Dahlgren (2006), who writes that civil society 'can serve as a training ground that "grooms" citizens, preparing them for civic participation and political engagement' (p 272). Second, the organization of 3.3 million citizens in different Facebook groups ensures a basic mobilization of the respective members of a group and ensures that more people will know or become aware of the political threats to the community (as in the case of TAAGF, Friends of Fælleds Venner, or the parent movement #wherearethegrownups). These are the cases where we observe how non-political groups become recruitment grounds for groups that are more dedicated to political mobilization. A third political and democratic quality of the Facebook groups is how non-political common denominators pave the way for demographic bridging. While some groups are mostly either for people with high education or low education (groups about climate change and sustainability issues versus groups about pets), Facebook groups about local communities or family attract the same percentage of people across differing levels of education, indicating that these groups indeed can be seen as meeting points between different social classes. And living in the same local area or expecting a baby in May does not guarantee political consensus. Thus, the groups provide an opportunity for being exposed to different opinions from people with different backgrounds.

While the Facebook groups in this way show great potential in facilitating civic engagement among Danish citizens, we also feel the need to put forward some critical considerations as we draw to the close of this chapter. First, it is important to remember the normative structures by which these groups and their members are surrounded. In some cases, it is likely that the arguments and knowledge of the group members are influenced by social movements, professional political actors and legacy media. Such a linkage is especially evident in our empirical data in the discourses about gender politics, which has (in our view, rightfully so) gained more and more focus over the last few years in the established media. In Bordieusian terms, the symbolic power of certain discourses will influence and, to some extent, frame how certain debates within these groups unfold. This questions to what degree the agenda setting within the groups is really citizen-led. Second, we should also emphasize how the debates within the groups are also necessarily influenced by social differences among members. This concerns what members are attracted to, how they perform in discussing certain points and the extent to which their efforts are supported or rejected by the rest of the community. In addition, the administrators and moderators of the groups arguably have more power than the average member. For all their potential, which we will still argue for, Facebook groups should not be seen as postcard-perfect spaces of civic engagement and deliberation, as they do not reside in a social vacuum. We do, however, regard them as a very promising example of how public formation is sustained through digital practices in seemingly 'private', mundane and non-political settings.

Conclusion

In this chapter, we set out to explore the public lifestyles of Danish citizens through a mixed-methods approach combining survey research and digital methods. We initially grounded our work in the private and public distinction and argued, like other contemporary scholars, that this distinction seems increasingly hard to uphold in modern societies. With inspiration from the Bordieusian tradition of thought, we emphasized that publics can also form outside legacy media, as broader unmediated practices or in the context of digital and datafied everyday life. Furthermore, we argued for the importance of being attentive to the socio-hierarchical context within which these public formation processes are situated.

Our results initially indicated that the Danish public sphere can be roughly divided between those who are attracted to politics and those who are not. The public 'taste' of the elite public is firmly tied to the world of formal politics (Hovden, 2022); in the words of Couldry et al (2010), these citizens are very well publicly connected as opposed those in the mundane publics.

Upon further scrutiny, however, we found several political preferences expressed by those who in the survey data say that they have no interest in politics. This puzzle becomes easier to solve if we apply the notion of symbolic violence (Bourdieu, 1993) as a possible theoretical interpretation. Bourdieu's argument goes as follows: When capital and those who possess it are deemed worthy (enough), they obtain symbolic value, which can be used as 'a power of constituting the given through utterances, of making people see and believe, of confirming or transforming the vision of the world, and thereby, action on the world and the world itself' (Bourdieu, 1989, p 179). Consequently, the symbolic dominance of one stratum is often accompanied by symbolic violence imposed upon another, in which the practices of some strata (normally the most underprivileged) are deemed less valuable – in this case, by stipulating strict criteria for what constitute legitimate public lifestyles and instilling this social construct as normal and natural for both the dominant and the dominated (Bourdieu and Wacquant, 1992). In our analysis, the symbolic violence thus manifests in how mundane public citizens explicitly express political stances (through, for example, right-wing populist sentiments or COVID-19 scepticism) but at the same time express distaste towards politics; seemingly, they have internalized the symbolic misrecognition of the social space with regard to their own preferences and see formal politics as something which is not for them, thus refusing 'what they are refused' (Bourdieu, 1984, p 471). Consequently, the space of public lifestyles does not depict the difference between essentially non-political and the political citizens in our view, but rather presents the differences between symbolically legitimate and illegitimate ways of relating to public life.

In fact, when examining political talk and deliberation in even the most allegedly politically disinterested Facebook groups, we find reasons to be rather optimistic. The examined groups largely enable citizen-led digital publics of varying sizes, which seems to appeal to those who may not self-identify as politically engaged. We see how they obligingly and passionately engage in the negotiation and maintenance of common values and beliefs within these groups – sometimes in relation to trending issues (for example, gender, climate) and sometimes related to issues they consider not to be trending enough (for example, child care and social benefits). Public formation through citizen-led groups is blurring the lines between the private and public, as the everyday lives of citizens, their personal and private interests, are constantly linked to larger political issues.

On the basis of these points, we argue for the need to update and broaden the analytical scope to seriously examine the multiple ways that public formation processes may occur in modern societies, thus agreeing with Zizi Papacharissi in this insightful comment: 'It is also possible that our quest for civic behaviours has not produced the desired results because we have not been looking at places that civic behaviours now inhabit: spaces that are friendlier to the development of contemporary civic behaviours' (2010, p 78). Spurred on by our empirical work, we too believe that civic engagement exists as a ubiquitous human potentiality that can and will manifest in myriads of social settings. Each setting, however, still does not enjoy equal social recognition as we may evaluate publics very differently according to the symbolic order of a given context; politics is everywhere, but so are inequalities and symbolic hierarchies.

Notes

[1] In sum, 51 variables on media usage were used as active variables to construct the space, while variables on public lifestyles and measurements of social stratification was projected as supplementary variables to further characterize the structures of the space. This analysis – and the statistical operations underlining it – is presented in further detail in Sivertsen (forthcoming).

[2] The groups were identified and collected using a webscraper through the method of network sampling (Lavrakas, 2008, p 507). For thorough methodological elaboration of this process see the works of Analyse & Tal (Thomsen et al, 2022).

[3] *Active engagement* is defined as: making a post in a group, commenting on a post in a group, or reacting to a post or comment in a group using the 'like', 'wow', 'haha', 'love', 'angry' or 'care' reaction buttons.

[4] The digitization of these publics paves the way for participation by people who are physically or mentally challenged by physical presence. We have observed how people with, for instance, social anxiety, chronic illnesses and physical immobility have prospered within the groups where their knowledge and guidance are sought and acknowledged. The drawback is that the groups favour proficiency in the written language and technology.

[5] A search within Infomedia, a Danish media monitoring service, shows that in ten years (4 June 2010 to 4 June 2020), 60,672 articles within mainstream media mention a Facebook group. The query contained the following word pairs (translated from Danish): 'Facebook-group', 'Facebookgroup' or 'group on Facebook'.

References

Arendt, H. (2018) *The Human Condition* (2nd edn), Chicago: University of Chicago Press. Available at: https://press.uchicago.edu/ucp/books/book/chicago/H/bo29137972.html.

Bakardjieva, M. (2009) 'Subactivism: Lifeworld and politics in the age of the internet', *The Information Society*, 25(2), pp 91–104. Available at: https://doi.org/10.1080/01972240802701627.

Bakardjieva, M. (2012) 'Mundane citizenship: New media and civil society in Bulgaria', *Europe-Asia Studies*, 64(8), pp 1356–1374. Available at: https://doi.org/10.1080/09668136.2012.712247.

Bourdieu, P. (1984) *Distinction: A Social Critique of the Judgement of Taste*, Cambridge, MA: Harvard University Press.

Bourdieu, P. (1989) 'Social space and symbolic power', *Sociological Theory*, 7(1), pp 14–25. Available at: https://doi.org/10.2307/202060.

Bourdieu, P. (1993) *The Field of Cultural Production: Essays on Art and Literature*, New York: Columbia University Press.

Bourdieu, P. and Wacquant, L.J.D. (1992) *An Invitation to Reflexive Sociology*, Chicago: University of Chicago Press.

Butsch, R. (2008) *The Citizen Audience: Crowds, Publics, and Individuals*, New York: Routledge. Available at: https://doi.org/10.4324/9780203929032.

Couldry, N., Livingstone, S. and Markham, T. (2010) *Media Consumption and Public Engagement: Beyond the Presumption of Attention*, New York: Springer.

Dahlgren, P. (2006) 'Doing citizenship: The cultural origins of civic agency in the public sphere', *European Journal of Cultural Studies*, 9(3), pp 267–286. Available at: https://doi.org/10.1177/1367549406066073.

Dewey, J.V. (2012) *The Public and Its Problems: An Essay in Political Inquiry*, State College: Penn State University Press. Available at: https://doi.org/10.5325/j.ctt7v1gh.

Fraser, N. (1990) 'Rethinking the public sphere: A contribution to the critique of actually existing democracy', *Social Text*, 25/26, pp 56–80.

Friedland, L. and Wells, C. (2018) 'Media and civic engagement', in P.M. Napoli (ed) *Mediated Communication*, Berlin: De Gruyter, pp 411–430. Available at: https://doi.org/10.1515/9783110481129-023.

Graham, T. and Harju, A. (2011) 'Reality TV as a trigger of everyday political talk in the net-based public sphere', *European Journal of Communication*, 26(1), pp 18–32. Available at: https://doi.org/10.1177/0267323110394858.

Habermas, J. (1991) *The Structural Transformation of the Public Sphere: An Inquiry Into a Category of Bourgeois Society*, Cambridge, MA: MIT Press.

Hartley, J. (2010) 'Silly citizenship', *Critical Discourse Studies*, 7(4), pp 233–248. Available at: https://doi.org/10.1080/17405904.2010.511826.

Hovden, J. (2022) 'Worlds apart: On class structuration of citizens' political and public attention and engagement in an egalitarian society', *European Journal of Cultural and Political Sociology*. Available at: https://doi.org/10.1080/23254823.2022.2090401.

Hovden, J. and Moe, H. (2017) 'A sociocultural approach to study public connection across and beyond media: The example of Norway', *Convergence*, 23(4), pp 391–408.

Kozinets, R. (1998) 'On netnography: Initial reflections on consumer research investigations of cyberculture', *Advances in Consumer Research*, 25, pp 366–371.

Kozinets, R.V. (2010) *Netnography: Ethnographic Research in the Age of the Internet* (1st edn), Thousand Oaks: SAGE.

Lavrakas, P. (2008) *Encyclopedia of Survey Research Methods*, Thousand Oaks: SAGE.

Marres, N. (2005) *No Issue, No Public: Democratic Deficits after the Displacement of Politics*, PhD thesis, University of Amsterdam. Available at: https://pure.uva.nl/ws/files/3890776/38026_thesis_nm_final.pdf.

Moe, H., Hovden, J., Ytre-Arne, B., Figenschou, T., Nærland, T., Sakariassen, H. and Thorbjørnsrud, K. (2019) *Informerte borgere? Offentlig tilknytning, mediebruk og demokrati*, Oslo: Universitetsforlaget.

Papacharissi, Z. (2010) *A Private Sphere: Democracy in a Digital Age*, Cambridge: Polity.

Picone, I., Kleut, J., Pavlíčková, T., Romic, B., Møller Hartley, J. and De Ridder, S. (2019) 'Small acts of engagement: Reconnecting productive audience practices with everyday agency', *New Media & Society*, 21(9), pp 2010–2028. Available at: https://doi.org/10.1177/1461444819837569.

Roux, B.L. and Rouanet, H. (2004) *Geometric Data Analysis: From Correspondence Analysis to Structured Data Analysis*, New York: Springer Science & Business Media.

Schrøder, K.C. (2013) 'Audiences as citizens: Insights from three decades of reception research', in R. Parameswaran and A.N. Valdivia (eds) *The International Encyclopedia of Media Studies*, Oxford: Wiley-Blackwell, pp 510–534. Available at: https://doi.org/10.1002/9781444361506.wbiems103.

Sivertsen, M. (Forthcoming) 'Stratified public connections: Beyond the taste of news?', *Journalism Studies* [Preprint].

Thomsen, M. (2020) *Danmarks Digitale Medborgerhuse: Facebookgrupper som fora for digitalt retorisk medborgerskab*, Københavns Universitet, Det Humanistiske Fakultet.

Thomsen, M., Steinitz, S., Neesgaard A., Ikanovic, E., Kristensen, J., Taarnborg, R. and Bornakke, T. (2022) *Danmarks Digitale Medborgerhuse*, Copenhagen: Analyse & Tal. Available at: https://ogtal.dk/publication/danmarks-digitale-medborgerhuse.

Thorson, K. (2014) 'Sampling from the civic buffet: youth, new media and do-it-yourself citizenship', in H.G. de Zuniga Navajas (ed) *New Technologies and Civic Engagement: New Agendas in Communication*. London: Routledge. Available at: www.taylorfrancis.com/chapters/edit/10.4324/9781315750927-2/sampling-civic-buffet-youth-new-media-citizenship-kjerstin-thorson.

van Deth, J.W. (2016) 'What is political participation?', in *Oxford Research Encyclopedia of Politics*. Available at: https://doi.org/10.1093/acrefore/9780190228637.013.68.

Wahl-Jorgensen, K. (2019) *Emotions, Media and Politics* (1st edn), Cambridge: Polity.

Wright, S., Graham, T. and Jackson, D. (2015) 'Third space, social media and everyday political talk', in *The Routledge Companion to Social Media and Politics*, London: Routledge, pp 74–88. Available at: https://doi.org/10.4324/9781315716299-6.

PART II

Cultivated Publics

5

Imagining Publics through Emerging Technologies

Jannie Møller Hartley and Anna Schjøtt

Introduction

When first announcing the new personalization feature in 2011, Denise Warren, senior vice president and chief advertising officer at the New York Times Media Group and general manager at NYTimes.com, stated in a press release: 'With a Web site as broad and deep as NYTimes.com, we are always looking for new ways to help our readers find news of interest beyond the sections they read most' (The New York Times Company, 2011). This initial problem framing shows how the *New York Times* (*NYT*) is setting the stage for personalization, with references to both a problem – the ever-growing web – and a beneficiary – the reader. The solution, of course, was the personalization of the online news site. In short, personalization is an umbrella term that describes the use of a range of algorithmic systems to provide individual recommendations to readers based on their past reading behaviour, thus producing a personalized news feed (see also Chapter 6). We argue in this chapter that personalization represents another evolutionary step in the use of audience measurement technologies, as these projects are founded in a desire to better utilize existing audience data to serve the public (see, for example, Bodó, 2019).

From 2017 and onwards the *NYT* took several steps to increase the use of recommender systems and personalization algorithms. The increasing introduction of more personalized features on the site would, according to the *NYT* publics editor at the time, Elisabeth Spayd, make the *NYT* move away from the news as a monolithic entity towards being something more 'bespoke' and 'responsive' to its audiences. Spayd explained her position to the readers of the *NYT* in an article on the public editor site:

Picture a home page where the dominant spots on the screen show the big news and feature stories, but much of the surrounding content is tailored to your own interests.

More limited experiments are already underway. News alerts, among the primary uses of personalization right now, may be different depending on a particular reader's location. On the home page, there's a customized box called 'Recommended for You' that lists articles Times data shows you haven't yet read.

But these are small lab tests compared with the plans editors have for a next-generation New York Times, one that shifts from monolithic to something more bespoke. (Spayd, 2017)

Since then, the *NYT* has continued describing the development and increasing implementation of new features in blog posts, on the public editor site, on its help page on personalization and via interviews featured in articles published on other news sites. In these different statements, the *NYT* highlights the role and benefits of these algorithmic technologies. Personalization was believed to be on one side the solution to ever growing amounts of content online, while on the other side also a way to increase or at least not challenge the democratic role of news. Interestingly, the personalization efforts of the *NYT* happened in dialogue with readers and many of these comments displayed a rather different opinion and interpretation of the value of personalization. Several of the articles published by the *NYT* regarding personalization received highly negative responses from their readers in the form of 422 replies posted in the comments sections of these articles, with the majority being posted in relation to the one written by Spayd. With her supportive stand for the idea of personalization, she was perceived as betraying her role of holding the publication responsible for conducting itself in the proper (democratic) way as a news organization. In these comments, the idea of personalization was completely rejected, seen as inappropriate and even dangerous for democracy – a rather different story than the one of a brighter personalized future for news. Many of these comments expressed this sentiment through rather colourful language, such as the one posted by an anonymous reader in response to Spayd's article:

'Personalized' news? What a dreadful idea! I already assiduously avoid reading the 'Recommended for You' articles the Times suggests because I resent the implication that I do not know enough to select articles I want to read. Am I now to be forced to stop reading the Times altogether in order to avoid its pre-digested pablum? I'm elderly, but I can still chew my own mental food! (Spayd, 2017)

This comment and Spayd's vision of a brighter personalized future help to highlight the conjunctures of what we argue is a discursive battle of legitimation: a battle over the future of news, its democratic role and the publics it serves.

In this chapter, we use the *NYT* as an illustrative case to demonstrate how emerging technologies, in this case personalization, serve as catalysts in the (re)imagining of the audience and the role of the press, as cultivators of publics – and vice versa how (re)imagined audiences are used to legitimize the need for technological change. To advance this argument, we draw on Bryan Pfaffenberger's (1992) concept of 'technological drama', to frame the discursive battle that unfolded between the *NYT* and its readers, where both attempt to define the meaning and implications of the technology. By analysing the drama over the personalization of *NYT* we illustrate the relations between the imaginaries of publics, the role of the press and emerging technologies. This allows us to take a step back and historize the relation between the imaginaries of audience and technologies as well as critically discuss how newsrooms in their attempts to define and legitimize their use of emerging technologies engage in processes of reinventing themselves discursively and in turn re-constructing publics as personalized.

In the following, we first expand on the theoretical framework, presenting the concept of technological drama in more detail and discussing how following such dramas in the news context allows us to bridge two previously separated perspectives on imaginaries: literature on audience construction through imaginaries and technological/sociotechnical imaginaries. In doing so, we illustrate the dialectical relationship between these imaginaries, in which technological imaginaries work as 'communicative drivers of transformation' (Møller Hartley et al, 2021) inducing the (re)imagination of the audience or public (including their relation to the press) and vice versa. Following this, we outline the relevance of the *NYT* as a case and our methodological choices. With this foundation in place, we venture into the midst of the unfolding technological drama and explore the countering imaginaries of the publics and press and how these imaginaries are discursively produced. The chapter then proceeds to historize this argument by dissecting existing literature on audience imaginaries and constructions. From this, we distil three phases, where publics and the role of the press have been imagined differently on the basis of the audience measurement technologies of the time. Hence, the overall argument of the chapter is that the (re)imagining of publics happens in tandem with the imaginaries of emerging technologies such as measurement systems and currently personalization algorithms. Thus publics are and have been constructed in a constant interplay with technologies, the social imaginaries of the role of the press and the datafied realities of the press system.

Conceptual frame: (re)imagining publics and technologies

The notion of 'imaginaries' is often traced back to the work of Charles Taylor (2004) and his concept of 'social imaginaries'. He defines these as the way ordinary people engage in imaginaries of their social surroundings, producing 'common understanding that makes possible common practices and a widely shared sense of legitimacy' (Taylor, 2004, p 106). As such, imaginaries are the 'background understandings' that guide our everyday actions and common practices (Taylor, 2004). Over the years, this concept has also been used to explore the imaginaries related to audiences of news and technologies. Thus, multiple scholars have explored how journalists and editors have historically imagined different 'audiences' or 'publics' and defined the role of the media in relation to these imagined audiences (Gitlin, 1980; Ang, 2002; Coddington, 2018; Nelson, 2021). Furthermore, scholars have explored how journalists and editors negotiate newsworthiness in relation to specific idealized imaginaries of the audience (see, for example, Ang, 2002; Willig, 2010; Anderson, 2011; Møller Hartley, 2011). As Schudson (2011) argued, 'the news media do not find and respond to an existing audience; they create one' (p 168). Similarly, Ien Ang (2002) has highlighted that audiences are discursive constructs, neither predefined nor static.

Scholars (predominately from the field of Science and Technology Studies) have equally explored the imaginaries of technologies or sociotechnical systems. The concept of imaginaries has, for example, recently been utilized in the analysis of the everyday imaginaries that users of social media have of algorithms (Bucher, 2017), or to explore the counterimaginaries of datafication produced by those who are critically affected by datafication processes (for example, the fear of surveillance) (Kazansky and Milan, 2021). Patrice Flichy defined technological imaginaries as 'the collective, shared visions about technology, which amalgamate intentions and projects as well as utopias and ideologies' (2007, p 366). Later, Sheila Jasanoff (2015) also highlighted the need to understand 'how, through the imaginative work of varied social actors, science and technology become enmeshed in performing and producing diverse visions of the collective good' (2015, p 11). The last part of the quote highlights the connection between technological imaginaries and what in our case is the normative understanding of 'good' journalism, which includes imaginaries of who the public is and the responsibility of the press towards them. Therefore, we use the term 'imaginaries' as an overarching heuristic to describe both the ways in which technologies and publics and their relation to the press are discursively constructed by different actors.

In this chapter we apply Bryan Pfaffenberger's (1992) notion of a 'technological drama' to structure our initial analysis of the introduction of personalization at the *NYT*. Pfaffeberger uses this notion to describe how 'design contitutents' (in our case the *NYT*) must engage in 'technological regularisation' which is the process of discursively constructing a social context for the technology. The 'impact constituents' (in our case the commenters) who become (re)constructed via such discourses can resist this construction via countersiginification processes, as they provide an alternative interpretation of the technology. The technological drama in its essence is, therefore, comprised of a series of 'statements' and 'counterstatements' in which this discursive battle unfolds, where both parties attempt to persuade each other about a particular way of 'reading' the technology (Pfaffenberger, 1992, p 285). While Pfaffenberger does not link the drama to the notion of imaginaries, we argue such dramas are occasions where these imaginaries become more clearly outlined in discourse.

Analysing the technological drama over the personalization of the *NYT* allows us to see how the *NYT* via public statements constructs a social context for personalization, by drawing on certain imaginaries of the technology, the landscape it is part of and the intended audience. By engaging with the counterstatements offered in the comment section, we can explore how different and countering imaginaries guide how the readers in turn interpret the technology. By exploring both, rather than simply one side of the drama, we highlight the political nature of such discourse. In discursively constructing the technology, these actors shape how the technology is more widely understood and legitimized. In taking this perspective, we highlight how the imaginaries of technologies and the construction of publics are deeply intertwined and should be analysed not separately but together, paying attention to their dialectic relationship.

The *NYT* is a good case for explicating this dialectic relationship because it has long been considered one of the most prestigious and well-respected news outlets producing quality journalism and it is a stronghold for journalistic integrity. Further, the *NYT* was one of the first to embark on and experiment with personalization of news on its sites, which meant it was among the first to define how personalization could be beneficial for news.

The *NYT* was also one of the very few media organizations that have been as open in explaining and communicating to the users, which makes it ideal for this empirical illustrative case study. The drama also becomes particularly interesting here, as the readers of the *NYT* are known to be some of the most elitist readers in the world and a global readership, who also, as previously shown, take upon themselves the role of 'press critics' when they comment, particularly on pieces by the public editor (Craft et al, 2016).

The concrete empirical material is comprised of published articles by the *NYT* regarding its efforts to personalize the site (articles, info sites, blog posts and articles by the public editor, a role that no longer exists) as well as articles in which employees at the *NYT* have spoken about these initiatives in other media outlets (in this case, Nieman Lab). A total of 9 documents have been included in this part of the analysis (Garber, 2011a, 2011b; The New York Times Company, 2011; Spangher, 2015; Bilton, 2017; Spayd, 2017; Hassan, 2018; Coenen, 2019). All comments posted in relation to articles directly published by the *NYT* (comments were present on four articles) make up the other part of the empirical foundation, which in total, amounts to 422 comments. Both articles and comments were identified and downloaded in the spring of 2020 and have been inductively and iteratively analysed, with a focus on identifying the underlying imaginaries of the audience and technology of personalization and how this in turn constructs the public and the role of the press.

A technological drama unfolds: personalizing the *New York Times*

In the introduction of this chapter, we already highlighted how the *NYT* presented personalization as the solution to what is refered to as a 'real-estate' problem (Coenen, 2019). As Senior Data Scientist at the *NYT*, Anna Coenen, writes in a blog post: 'The New York Times will publish around 250 articles today, but most readers will only see a fraction of them' (Coenen, 2019). Personalization is presented as a solution to this information overflow as it can support *NYT* readers by 'refining the path our readers take through this content' (Spangher, 2015). We see here how the technology is imagined in relation to the current mode of distribution – the online news format – which does not have the same restrictions as its predecessor, the printed paper. This mode of distribution is imagined to be problematic for the user as they are now tasked with navigating much larger amounts of content than in the past. Thereby, they construct the problem to be solved as one of technological catch up, where personalization is simply a way to adapt to a new mode of distribution. Implied in this definition of the problem and solution is also a construction of the audience as needing help with this task, as being unable to navigate this amount of content by itself.

The value of personalization is also placed in relation to a changing media environment and more directly in relation to the changing behaviour and expectations of the audiences. As Spayd (2017) stated in her article: 'Americans are used to their world being customised around their needs.' She emphasizes how the newspaper, therefore, must become an organization that 'treats readers like individuals, with unique habits and preferences' (Spayd, 2017). Here personalization becomes imagined, not only in relation to the current mode of distribution by the *NYT* but also in relation to how other actors in the media landscape, such as Netflix or

Facebook, who are distributing their content in personalized ways. This further adds to the construction of personalization as a technology aimed to catch up with distributional trends in the media landscape. Beyond this, personalization is also imagined through a specific imaginary of the audiences, namely as individuals who, through their media consumption, have become accustomed to customization. The imaginary emerging through these statements then, on one side, constructs a user/public in need of curating assistance, but on the other constructs the audiences as being composed of individuals who have unique preferences. Personalization is, via this discourse, constructed as a technology able to deliver the solution to both these changes.

More so, it can enable readers to become acting subjects who, as product design director Norel Hassan (2018) wrote in a blog post, gain 'more control over their experience with The Times'. Personalization is, through this imaginary of technological empowerment, also challenging the historic role of the media as paternalistic (see, for example, Anderson, 2011), by handing more control and choice back to the users. By constructing an autonomous and competent patient through the act of choosing, the press mimics the liberal ideal of choice as a democratic act, similar to what Anne Marie Mol has shown to occur in the health system (Mol, 2008). Interestingly, this liberal idea was strongly connected to the idea of the omnibus press, where part of the task of the reader was to navigate their own way through the paper (see, for example, Tuchman, 1978; Schudson, 2011). Fred Turner (2015) has described how in the post-Second World War period, this type and ideal of individual choice and navigation was deeply intertwined with ideas of the competent and democratically minded citizen. The imaginary of personalization as enabling control, via ease of navigating the news, both utilizes this idea of choice as something valuable, but also stands in contrast to how choice has been connected to ideals of the democratic citizen of the past. Personalization is imagined to make choices easier, rather than forcing the users to navigate the ever-growing amounts of content, which induces a (re)imagining of the audience, who are constructed ever more as media consumers (with preferences, expectations and needs) (see, for example, Ang 2002; Willig, 2010).

This construction becomes even more apparent when looking at how this user control is enabled by personalization and how user activity is framed by the *NYT*. In an interview relating to the initial launch, Marc Frons, the Times' chief technology officer for digital operations, told Nieman Lab: 'To me, no matter what the model, the more people who read and are engaged with your website or your digital products, the better. ... So, the recommendation engine just fits into our overall strategy of increasing user engagement' (Garber, 2011b). In this statement, Frons highlights how the technological solution does not matter as long as it can produce engagement.

The quote further illustrates another imaginary of what personalization is to solve, namely, continued user engagement at a time when many news outlets are struggling to introduce sustainable business models in the online news landscape. The users are imagined as being 'knowable' via their data and as calculable subjects whose preferences can be calculated, as data engineer at the *NYT*, Alexander Spangher, describes: 'we were able to calculate preferences in less than one millisecond per reader, enabling us to scale to all registered users' (Spangher, 2015). This imaginary of the audiences as knowable through data and calculated preferences produces a different construction of the audience – namely as aggregated data point optimized towards producing engagement. In Chapter 6 we further explore this datafied and personalized construction of publics in the process of developing these personalized systems.

While the audiences' preferences have taken centre stage in the public statements by the *NYT*, there is also an emphasis on how the new vision of personalized news will not make the editor obsolete, but rather will 'complement' their practices (Coenen, 2019) and remain 'supplements to major events and stories' (Spangher, 2015). Hence, the imaginaries of the personalized news system entails a doubleness, similarly to that pointed out by Ang (2002), as the *NYT* is both imagining the audience-as-market (aggregated data to produce engagement) and the audience-as-publics (citizens to be informed). Personalization is seen as complementary of an orientation towards 'the public' rather than as mutually exclusive. This complementary nature was highlighted by Anna Coenen, who stated that personalization would only be used 'to select content where manual curation would be inefficient or difficult' (Coenen, 2019). Again, personalization is presented – not as interfering – but as supplementing the current practice of news distribution. Also exemplified in this quote by Spayd (2017): 'The goal, in other words, is to surface subjects tailored to the individual readers, without depriving them of a sense of a shared experience. Or without the readers feeling they aren't receiving the same hierarchy of news values as they once did' (Spayd, 2017). We therefore see how the press' relationship to the public is imagined to be 'both and', being both true to the more classic notions of news as producing a shared public sphere and being democratic in new ways, namely by giving the users more choice.

In the remaining part of the chapter we return to characteristics of this reimagined audience and role of the press, which emerges through the imaginaries of personalization, and how this has changed over time. What we want to highlight with this short analysis is how the *NYT* as 'design constituents' of personalization through its statements draws on certain imaginaries of the technology and the intended audience to legitimize personalization. Pfaffenberger (1992) argues the design constituents will often create myths to support this legitimation, and here these myths are present in the concrete imaginaries of personalization as relieving users of having to deal with 'information overload' and better catering for this new breed of users whose expectations are radically different than in the past. In these statements, the dynamic relation between audience and technological imaginaries in constituting each other emerges, as imagined technological and audience changes are foundational for legitimizing this transformation of the news. In dissecting these imaginaries, we also see how the *NYT*, in drawing on these imaginaries, is essentially reconstructing the audience and the role of media in society, as the audience becomes constructed as individuals 'knowable' and 'engagable' via data and empowered via choice and control, while the media becomes constructed as remaining a democratic institution through its ability to balance individual choice and provide a shared experience.

The users: printed utopias and personalized dystopias

We now turn to the 'counterstatements' offered by the 'impact constituencies' – the comments and the users – which are aimed to delegitimize the technology via providing alternative interpretations of the technology. In many of the 422 comments posted by the readers, personalization is immediately dismissed as a solution, as it threatens to impoverish the *NYT* to a degree that, as highlighted by O'Donnel, might mean the beginning of the end for news as something of value in society:

> My subscription and interest in the *NYT* is not about what I want to hear but about what you have to say. I find it increasingly challenging to get a full perspective on an issue in our upside down media culture and *NYT* had been a valued resource. Your plans to filter content to what you think I want to see and hear is a very very, and very, bad decision and perhaps the beginning of the end of a great newspaper. (Comment by O'Donnel, Spayd, 2017)

O'Donnel and many other readers find it important to know what other *NYT* readers know – to have a form of shared knowledge and to be addressed as a collective. In their responses, the commenters offer a counterimaginary of what the press system should do and in turn construct themselves as '(democratic) publics' as opposed to '(personalized) individuals'.

When analysing the comments, it stands out that the printed paper as a curated product remains the measuring stick, and that according to the readers of *NYT*, the publics traditionally served by the physical printed newspaper cannot be cultivated by personalization algorithms. As commenter Donovan from New York City writes, 'This sounds awful! Please *NYT* also give online readers the option of seeing a digital copy of the printed paper. Call it "*NYT* Classic View"' (Spayd, 2017). This counterimaginary is expressed by many commenters through the plea for an 'opt-out' solution that will, as Donovan highlights, allow them to view the paper in its original (printed) form. Tom Rieke from New Zealand writes, 'No thanks. For five or six months each year, I am far away from a shop that sells the printed New York Times, so I read the "paper" on the web with an online subscription. Real news from real writers and editors' (Spayd, 2017). He uses quotation marks to illustrate the lesser quality of online news as a representative of the printed news. But his comment also makes a differentiation between 'real' writers and editors in opposition to algorithmic editors. Here, the printed paper is imagined as inhabiting the 'real' and 'human' in opposition to the personalized site, which places the human and machine as ultimate opposites. As such they almost reintroduce the myth of the editor as the ultimate democratic taste-maker, which over the years has been highly nuanced in research with studies of the importance of routines (Tuchman, 1978) or the spatial layout (Gans, 1979) in deciding the news flow. Personalization is imagined as opposing this ideal as an agent that unpleasantly removes the magic of the editorially curated and democratically oriented printed paper. The tension between news as profitable business and cultivator of democratic publics has always been present, but here we see how the counterimaginary among the *NYT* users draws heavily on an understanding of news as democratic. Unlike in the statements from *NYT*, where this tension could be relieved by the technological design of the algorithm, they are by users imagined as incompatible.

The importance and almost nostalgic imaginary of the editor stands out in the way commenters see personalization as a betrayal of the editors and the newspaper. JB from San Francisco writes:

> The editors are abnegating their most trusted task – curating the news to focus on what is most important in the world. I read the Times because I believe that its editors bring me the news of the day – not the news that an algorithm thinks that I would like to see. (Spayd, 2017)

Others describe how they subscribe because they 'trust the Times editors to decide what is important' (Spayd, 2017) or how they 'use the institution [ie the *NYT*] as a filter of the world's noise' (Spayd, 2017). The commenters' wording choices of 'trust', 'abnegation' and 'institution' reveal how editorial selection is highly intertwined with a certain imaginary news through this editorial selection having a unique role in the media landscape. This unique role is highlighted by several commenters who fear that personalization will ultimately change the identity and role of news. 'I pay for a subscription for a reason: the judgement and experience of the editors and writers that make this paper great. Don't try to be Facebook or Twitter. Be the New York Times and do it right', writes Chris G from New Haven (Spayd, 2017). As with the statements by the *NYT* we see how the relating media landscape is used to support the technological imaginary, but here to the opposite effect – namely to express the need to stay distinct rather than mimic other (social media) actors by introducing personalized distribution. The danger of personalization is further imagined via continued references to the almost mythical tale of 'filter bubbles', which became part of the public debate after the introduction of the concept by Eli Pariser in 2011 who directly connected it to the personalized feeds on social media. Nancy Lederman from New York comments, for example, that 'Isolating Times readers in individual interest bubbles surely rates as the most regressive idea ever' (Spayd, 2017).

The counterimaginary of personalization is also tied to a differently imagined audience of news, which can be detected in the fear of filter bubbles and individualization. The public for the commenters remain a shared collective and news a 'communal experience', as one commenter notes (Spayd, 2017). It also becomes apparent in the way the commenters feel insulted by the proposition of needing help navigating. As Bruce Kaplan from Portland writes, '[w]e are capable of reading and finding and understanding the news that they present without it being pre-chewed for us' (Spayd, 2017). The imagery of having food 'chewed' emphasizes patronization and is seen as an attack on the readers' competence, as Elb from New York emphasizes: 'it's counter-productive to insult the intelligence of your readers' (Spayd, 2017). What comes to the foreground in these comments is an imagined audience that is much closer to the post-Second World War ideals of the independent citizen of liberal democracies connected to the omnibus press, as previously described. Here the part of being a 'reader' is the ability and competence to navigate and choose – and if this is taken away, what is left is not really a news reader. Rather you will end up with a radically different reader, as an anonymous commenter writes: 'If you spoon feed your articles to lazy readers like pablum to an infant you end up with an ill-informed, ignorant and docile populace' (Spayd, 2017).

To return to Pfaffenberger's (1992) argument, this reinterpretation of what audience is produced by the different modes of distribution becomes an example of 'countersignification', in which the commenters who feel their competence as readers is under attack provide an alternative frame to understand the technology in which their understanding of themselves as audiences of *NYT* is not harmed. This alternative frame is not taken out of thin air, rather the image of readers turning into herded sheep who are unable to make up their own minds on important matters is also reminiscent of the narrative that emerged with broadcast TV, where the fear of producing 'couch potatoes' was a key part of the debate (Bolin and Forsman, 2002). As a result, they reinterpret the concept of the control offered by personalization, changing it to a narrative of being *more* controlled rather than *in* control. This they view as a threat to democracy through the control gained by evil social media algorithms and bots, who will result in readers being 'herded like on Facebook or Twitter and the bots that control them' (Spayd, 2017).

Via this countersignification, they also construct an imaginary of the public as composed of democratic citizens who should be educated by the news rather than 'just' engaged by content. Democratic responsibility is placed on the shoulders of the reader, who should and do make an effort to read things they do not normally have an interest in (see also Møller Hartley and Pedersen, 2019), as for example illustrated by this quote by Paul Rosovsky from Queens:

> Whenever I travel to another city, the first thing I do in the morning is buy a copy of the city's local paper, to review it cover to cover, to get a sense of what they consider important and how they cover it. (Even sports, which I could not care less about). (Spayd, 2017)

By placing emphasis on individual competence and responsibility rather than preferences, the imaginary of the public bears a closer resemblance to the traditional construction of the audience-as-publics (Ang, 2002; Willig, 2010). What is interesting is the strong ties between the audience construction and the mode of distribution, namely the printed paper.

As also illustrated in the previous sections, we see how the imaginaries of technologies and audiences are tightly interlinked. Commenters construct themselves as democratic collectives and personalization as the antithesis of these ideals. This counterimaginary is, interestingly, also produced by relating personalization to the transformations of the broader media landscape. However, here the imaginaries draw on the dystopian tales of personalization (for example, filter bubbles and uninformed audience) and the distinction between news and these other media actors in the landscape. We included this alternative interpretation of personalization to both illustrate how dialectical relations between technological and audience imaginaries can be detected on both sides of the drama, but also to highlight the political nature of such discourses of legitimation. The counterimaginary that emerges via the comments illustrate how the *NYT* is carefully crafting a story of personalization that enables it to maintain its identity and purpose of news, which the users fear being destroyed by the same technology.

In the following, we use the *NYT* case as a springboard, to explore how this dual construction of audiences and technologies can be traced back to different technologically enabled modes of distribution.

Historization of the technology–audience constructions

Unfolding the technological drama helps to immediately connect specific technological and audience imaginaries with certain constructions of the public. Further we see how new technologies require the renegotiation and, to some extent, replacement of existing audience constructions; replacements that are contested by employing existing, almost nostalgic, ideals of the press as cultivators of those publics and its distribution technologies, such as the printed newspaper format. Interestingly, we can observe that such nostalgic imaginaries have been present throughout history, often situated between dystopian and utopian tales of emergent technologies highlighting the discursive battles around the introduction of new technologies, in general, and measurement technologies, in particular.

The printed press: publics constructed as unknown democratic collectives

The interplay between media professionals' imaginaries of their audiences and the measured behaviour of those audiences is nothing new, and can be traced back to the first wave of newsroom ethnographies from the 1950s to the 1970s (Breed, 1955; Tuchman, 1978; Gans, 1979). However, much of the early work on audience imaginaries has, with a few exceptions, been largely understood in the literature as independent of the emergent technologies and from the production side of journalism (audiences imagined by media professionals). This, of course, is because as ethnographers observed the everyday routines of the newsrooms, the measurement tools and analytics of the time were not seen as important in many of these newsroom studies; they were seen as tools of marketing with a marginal effect on editorial policies. However, as discussed, other technologies were seen as guiding routines of newsmaking (for example, the telephone or limited format of printed paper).

As Gans (1979) highlighted in his seminal work, the journalists at the time had very little actual information about their readers or viewers and tended to reject feedback from the audience, but there still was a constant awareness of this imagined audience, which influenced the daily work in the newsroom. The journalists and editors, for example, had a tendency to 'overestimate' their imagined audience and attempt to avoid the risk of 'writing down' to them, which the journalists assumed the audience would recognize and be upset by (Gans, 1979, p 239). Warren Breed, in his study of social control in the newsroom, conceptualized these imaginaries of the audience as a 'policy', which he described as 'being in the walls': 'Every newspaper has a policy, admitted or not' (Breed, 1955, p 179). Thus, how the media imagine their 'publics' is a silent part of the (unwritten) policies in a given organization and tied to constructed ideals of the audience, not always representative of the 'actual' public (Gans, 1979). In Todd Gitlin's newsroom ethnography, he, in opposition to Gans, notes that the journalists tended to have 'a low opinion of the audience's knowledge and attention span' (1980, p 267). These low opinions of the audience 'usually derive from editors' and reporters' immediate work and social circles', thus giving little explanatory power to the audience images of the marketing departments (Gitlin, 1980, p 267).

What we can derive from this previous literature is that publics in the era of the printed paper are imagined via the ideals of the printed paper as a democratic product, but also that these imaginaries were highly based on the editors and journalists' own ideas (for example, people they knew) of their audience. These imaginaries included both over- and underestimations of the audience capabilities and their need or want to be informed, and were less tied to concrete measurement technologies but rather to more implicit policies or ideals. This era was a time when the ideal of the omnibus press was strong (Schultz, 2007), an ideal that strived to provide the readers with many different and balanced, neutral viewpoints. The ideal was originally aimed at enlarging the audience of newspapers and increasing advertising revenue, but, as discussed earlier, also resembled the ideals of an appropriate citizen in liberal democracy (Turner, 2015).

Ida Willig (2010), via a detailed analysis of these policy papers, showed how audience constructions had changed over time, particularly as a result of marketing departments gaining more power in the newsrooms and implementing more explicit policies to guide the production and distribution of news. A prominent tool was reader profiles, which directly outlined who the audience was via personas. While still 'low tech', these reader profiles were based on new forms of audience analytics, new technology that entered the newsroom, and while not replacing existing imaginaries, at least helped induce new understandings of who the audience was and what it wanted (Willig, 2010). In her analysis she observes a shift in the audience construction where a new construction was emerging, namely the audience-as-consumer, which was placed in opposition to the audience-as-citizen (drawing on the previous work of Ang, 2002). From this, she concluded that there was the beginning stages in a shift from the omnibus press system that was based on an (implicit) imaginary of the readers as democratic citizens to be informed, to a segmented press system, where the reader was (explicitly) imagined as a consumer, who needed to be satisfied and whose needs and preferences matter (see Table 5.1). As one imaginary of the audience did not simply replace the other, this produced new tensions, as journalists and editors now had to balance these different imaginaries of the audience. A tension that only became even more apparent as newsrooms digitalized in the 1990s and onward, which changed the format of the news to digital formats and made even more granular knowledge of audiences available through the introduction of metrics. This development also became the specific object of ethnographic scrutiny of what this meant for newsrooms and news work, which we now turn to as we describe how this led to a construction of audience as segmented.

Table 5.1: Three phases of the press

	The omnibus printed press	The digital press	The algorithmic press
Public construction	Constructed as democratic collectives	Constructed as segments	Constructed as aggregated datapoints
Measurement technologies	Unknown audiences (sporadic surveys know to marketing)	Metrics and analytics	Artificial intelligence, personalization, machine learning and Natural Language Processing
Business model transformation	Text-based to audience-based model	Audience-based to service-based model	Service-based to performance model

Source: Own model, inspiration from Willig (2010)

The digital press: publics constructed as segmented

In the next phase of newsroom ethnographies, following the digitalization of news, scholars increasingly focused on how audience metrics influenced editorial choices and gatekeeping processes inside the newsroom, and how new tensions arose in relation to how they catered to both what the audience wanted to know (represented in metrics) and what the journalists thought they should know (Anderson, 2011; Møller Hartley, 2013; Tandoc, 2014; Ali and Hassoun, 2019; Christin, 2020). They highlight how journalists are increasingly confronted by audiences, both in metrics and through new interactive features, such as comment sections and direct email, showing how audiences have moved into the newsroom, visible on screens across the newsroom (Møller Hartley, 2013). The introduction of interactive technologies increased the possibilities of engaging with audiences and also meant that the imaginaries of the public changed to an active, contributing one.

In a historical overview and critique of the 'death of the mass audience' argument, Bolin (2014) usefully linked audience imaginings to both the technological developments and changing business models that followed the technological changes. He argued that the printed press replaced the previous *text-based model*, leading to an *audience-based business model* (Bolin, 2014, p 164). Introduced by large advertising agencies, print, TV and radio worked by 'selling audiences' slots of commercials, and an interest in knowing not only how many copies were sold but also who was actually watching, reading or listening grew (Bolin, 2014). We see here how the audience became increasingly a commercialized and segmented construct. This new audience-based model came with certain promises of what new media would mean and a new imagined role for the audience. For example, the promise of turning audiences into 'produsers', a collapsing of the words 'producer' and 'user' (Bruns, 2008), essentially collapsing the boundary between media producers and media audiences. This later proved to be somewhat of a digital utopia (Domingo, 2005; Møller Hartley, 2011).

Offering a similar criticism of such a numeric understanding of audiences, Ang (2002) pointed out that television viewing, as the activity that ratings set out to measure, was a far too complex and varied behaviour to be translated by mere numbers. Borrowing examples from both the commercial and private television domains, she argued that what used to differentiate the two sectors, namely, the conception of the audience as 'market' in one and as 'public' in the other, had gradually made way for a more unified view that presented, in both camps, the audience as a collective taxonomic term devoid of any subjective peculiarities. Seen in this light, a television audience thus becomes a generic term that is as specific as 'nation' or 'population' in terms of providing information about individual behaviour patterns. Ang (2002) delivered a very detailed argumentative journey regarding the intrinsic limitations of the kind of information that ratings deliver. Methods used at the time ranged from the classic weekly diary method or the more sophisticated but also contested Peoplemeter, or even the Scan America system, which combined viewing habits with consumption patterns. Ang saw them as manifestations of 'market feedback technology' (2002, p 7), whose primary, if not sole, role was to provide post hoc information about the size and composition of any given audience. In this pursuit, statistics achieve the ultimate prestige – or perhaps simply an undisputed faith within television circles of providing television executives with objectifying and controlling knowledge that can be converted into an economic commodity.

What we see is how the shift to digital news induced new imaginaries of publics to emerge through the new affordances of the 'digital newspaper', such as the interactive affordance of commenting. New granular representations of the audience were also made available, and audience imaginaries were increasingly intertwined with quantitative representations of the public in the form of audience dashboards. Compared to the era of the printed paper, it became hard to ignore a now ever present audience, and the technologies thus both enabled but also almost demanded that journalists and editors came to terms with this new segmented and datafied audience. This led to the reimagining of publics as productive and generative, which, as Anderson (2011) argued, is a way to legitimize this new influence of the audience in the newsroom. The same dynamics of legitimation as in the *NYT* were also present here, where certain imaginaries of the audience enabled a productive construction of the audience as consumers.

Drawing on a field theoretical framework, Jannie Møller Hartley (2011) showed how the digitalization of journalism and the technologies that came with it did not fundamentally change the field, but radicalized some values over others. Thus, she showed how the field of news production was drawn towards the economic pole as a consequence of the prevalent measurement technologies and their direct presence in the newsrooms (Møller Hartley, 2013). In turn, this made the journalist imagine the audience as more commercially oriented and not interested in, for example, foreign news, as they were confronted with the little appeal that such stories held for users. Møller Hartley (2013) also observed how this created increasing dissonance among journalists, as it became difficult to maintain an image of the audience-as-public (Ang, 2002) when constantly confronted with audience-as-market through the metrics inside the newsroom. This has led to strategies of catering to multiple audiences at the same time via content, for example, by writing a popular piece that gives clicks, but then later adding a political piece that was deemed to have societal values, thus serving a public, but which receives fewer clicks (Møller Hartley, 2013). This illustrates the continued existence of multiple audience constructions, which emerge and become intertwined with new technologies. In the current 'age of datafication', these market feedback mechanisms can even construct audiences as an abstract aggregated user: a personalized public.

The algorithmic press: publics constructed as personalized

To return to Bolin (2014), he argues that in the final phase of the digitalization of media, a *performance model* emerged, in which advertisers could pay for information about audiences, resulting in what he terms 'mass personalisation', following the rise of Big Data and algorithmic media user measurement techniques. Bolin notes though, that strangely enough, despite their finely grained measurement, the knowledge of audiences was even less social and further estranged from audiences as human beings than in the mass media era. He concludes that this development does not entail the 'death of the mass audience', as suggested in parts of the literature, but a *reconfiguring* to a mass audience 3.0: 'If the intelligence produced about the audiences in the second mass moment was an aggregated abstraction based on social characteristics, the intelligence in the era of big data is a different kind of abstraction, a commodity based in an algorithmically produced mosaic of digital information' (Bolin, 2014, p 170). Balaz Bodó (2019) picked up some of the same tenets in his work on personalization technologies, arguing that media organizations were moving into an era of 'selling news to the audience' by employing these new models of distribution.

This point is worth dwelling on. Rather than the fear of individualization, as feared by *NYT* readers, and the impossibility of the algorithm to serve collectives, the public that the *NYT* serves is still an abstract public; now just an algorithmic abstract public, presented to journalists in the form of representations of audience behaviours on screens and backend systems, available to journalists and editors.

Within the shift to the personalized press, the market representations of audiences continue to flourish, while the imaginaries of readers as preferential beings also follow, as illustrated by the case study from *NYT*. However, a new construction of the audience also emerges, namely, one in which the reader is made up of their own produced data and is predictable, creating a changing imaginary of the press as responsive to individual readers who are continuously aggregated and recomposed via data (see Table 5.1).

Conclusion

By unfolding the technological drama over the introduction of personalization technologies at the *NYT* and the historization of this case study, we have seen how measurement technologies have, to some extent, always played a role in altering and shifting the ways in which publics are constructed through imaginaries. Thus, the imaginaries of emerging technologies work as drivers of transformation in that they allow and invoke shifts in the imaginaries of publics, as we see with the introduction of the personalized recommendation algorithms. However, the imaginaries of technologies are too highly interwoven with new understandings of who the publics are, making the transformation a highly dialectic one. Particularly current or emerging ideas of the capabilities and expectation of the audience matter for this dialectic (ranging from the over- and underestimation of the printed press, to the now increasingly preferential readers). Mark Coddington (2018) has also argued that user perception plays a key role in which technologies are implemented in the first place. The technological drama also reveals how tensions arise with these shifts, as some actors, in this case the commenters, attempt to reinterpret the story by drawing on other (and more dystopian) imaginaries of technologies and their publics. This was also the case during the shift to digital news, where journalists experienced new forms of dissonance regarding the question of what public they were to serve.

In the context of media, we see how organizations, when describing emerging technologies, position themselves in the dialectics between audience-as-market and audience-as-publics and all the possible positions in between. Equally, we see how many of the users draw on the same dialectics in their reinterpretation of the emerging technology, but draw on alternative imaginaries of the technologies of social media (that is, filter bubbles) and their imagined dangerous and undemocratic publics as a way to delegitimize the shift. While these counterimaginaries exist, and have continued to flourish particularly via the concerns of, for example, 'filter bubbles' in more public discourse, we see how the discourse on news personalization initiated by the *NYT* has crystalized over the years these imaginaries of the technology and how audiences are repeated across personalization projects. This illustrates, again, why such early discourses and the connection between technological and audience imaginaries become important to understand as political constructs, because early understandings of new technologies often become 'harder' and more difficult to challenge as they mature. And as David Beer (2017) has argued, these visions and imaginaries are active in shaping and pushing back what he labels data frontiers, expanding both the reach and intensity of data-led processes in the organization, whether readers want it or not. This is further explored in the next chapter.

References

Ali, W., and Hassoun, M. (2019) 'Artificial intelligence and automated journalism: Contemporary challenges and new opportunities', *International Journal of Media, Journalism and Mass Communications*, 5(1), pp 40–49. Available at: https://doi.org/10.20431/2454-9479.0501004.

Anderson, C. (2011) 'Between creative and quantified audiences: Web metrics and changing patterns of newswork in local US newsrooms', *Journalism*, 12(5), pp 550–566. Available at: https://doi.org/10.1177/1464884911402451.

Ang, I. (2002) *Desperately Seeking the Audience*, Abingdon: Taylor & Francis.

Beer, D. (2017) 'The data analytics industry and the promises of real-time knowing: Perpetuating and deploying a rationality of speed', *Journal of Cultural Economy*, 10(1), pp 21–33.

Bilton, R. (2017) 'All the news that's fit for you: The *New York Times* is experimenting with personalization to find new ways to expose readers to stories', *Nieman Lab*. Available at: https://www.niemanlab.org/2017/09/all-the-news-thats-fit-for-you-the-new-york-times-is-experimenting-with-personalization-to-find-new-ways-to-expose-readers-to-stories/.

Bodó, B. (2019) 'Selling news to audiences: A qualitative inquiry into the emerging logics of algorithmic news personalization in European quality news media', *Digital Journalism*, 7(8), pp 1054–1075. Available at: https://doi.org/10.1080/21670811.2019.1624185.

Bolin, G. (2014) 'The death of the mass audience reconsidered: From mass communication to mass personalisation', in S. Eichner and E. Prommer (eds) *Fernsehen: Europäische Perspectiven*, Konstanz and München: UVK, pp 159–172.

Bolin, G. and Forsman, M. (2002) *Bingolotto: Produktion, Text, Reception*, Huddinge: Södertörn University.

Breed, W. (1955) 'Social control in the newsroom: A functional analysis', *Social Forces*, 33(4), 326–335.

Bruns, A. (2008) *Blogs, Wikipedia, Second Life, and Beyond: From Production to Produsage* (new edn), New York: Peter Lang.

Bucher, T. (2017) 'The algorithmic imaginary: Exploring the ordinary affects of Facebook algorithms', *Information, Communication & Society*, 20(1), pp 30–44. Available at: https://doi.org/10.1080/1369118X.2016.1154086.

Christin, A. (2020) *Metrics at Work*, Princeton: Princeton University Press. Available at: https://press.princeton.edu/books/ebook/9780691200002/metrics-at-work.

Coddington, M. (2018) 'Seeing through the user's eyes: The role of journalists' audience perceptions in their use of technology', *Electronic News*, 12(4), pp 235–250. Available at: https://doi.org/10.1177/19312 43118767730.

Coenen, A. (2019) 'How the *New York Times* is experimenting with recommendation algorithms', *Medium*, 17 October. Available at: https://open.nytimes.com/how-the-new-york-times-is-experimenting-with-rec ommendation-algorithms-562f78624d26.

Craft, S., Vos, T.P. and David Wolfgang, J. (2016) 'Reader comments as press criticism: Implications for the journalistic field', *Journalism*, 17(6), pp 677–693. Available at: https://doi.org/10.1177/1464884915579332.

Domingo, D. (2005) 'The difficult shift from utopia to realism in the Internet era: A decade of online journalism research: Theories, methodologies, results and challenges', paper presented at the First European Communication Conference, Amsterdam, 24–26 November 2005.

Flichy, P. (2007) *The Internet Imaginaire*, Cambridge, MA: MIT Press.

Gans, H.J. (1979) *Deciding What's News: A Study of CBS Evening News, NBC Nightly News, Newsweek, and Time*, Evanston: Northwestern University Press.

Garber, M. (2011a) 'The NYT adds recommendation features to its article pages', *Nieman Lab*. Available at: https://www.niemanlab.org/2011/03/the-nyt-adds-recommendation-features-to-its-article-pages/.

Garber, M. (2011b) '"You are what you read": NYT CTO Marc Frons on the paper's new article recommendation engine', *Nieman Lab*. Available at: https://www.niemanlab.org/2011/02/you-are-what-you-read-nyt-cto-marc-frons-on-the-papers-new-article-recommendation-engine/.

Gitlin, T. (1980) *The Whole World is Watching: Mass Media in the Making & Unmaking of the New Left*, San Francisco: University of California Press.

Hassan, N. (2018) 'Announcing a *New York Times* iOS feature that helps readers find stories relevant to them', *Medium*, 24 September. Available at: https://open.nytimes.com/announcing-a-new-ios-feature-that-helps-readers-find-stories-relevant-to-them-a8273f8fcca4.

Jasanoff, S. (2015) 'Future imperfect: Science, technology, and the imaginations of modernity', in S. Jasanoff and S. Kim (eds) *Dreamscapes of Modernity, Sociotechnical Imaginaries and the Fabrication of Power*, Chicago: University of Chicago Press, pp 1–33.

Kazansky, B. and Milan, S. (2021) '"Bodies not templates": Contesting dominant algorithmic imaginaries', *New Media & Society*, 23(2), pp 363–381. Available at: https://doi.org/10.1177/1461444820929316.

Mol, A. (2008) *Logic of Care: Health and the Problem of Patient Choice* (1st edn), London and New York: Athenaeum Uitgeverij.

Møller Hartley, J. (2011) *Radikalisering af kampzonen: En analyse af netjournalistisk praksis og selvforståelse i spændingsfeltet mellem idealer og publikum*, PhD thesis, Roskilde University Centre. Available at: https://forskning.ruc.dk/da/publications/radikalisering-af-kampzonen-en-analyse-af-netjo urnalistisk-praksis

Møller Hartley, J. (2013) 'The online journalist between ideals and practices: Towards a (more) audience-driven and source-detached journalism?', *Journalism Practice*, 7(5), pp 572–587. Available at: https://doi.org/10.1080/17512786.2012.755386

Møller Hartley, M. and Pedersen, L.H. (2019) 'Beyond the informed citizen? Narratives of news engagement and civic experiences among Danish news users', *MedieKultur: Journal of Media and Communication Research*, 35(66), pp 055–074. Available at: https://doi.org/10.7146/mediekultur.v35i66.112626

Møller Hartley, J., Bengtsson, M., Schjøtt Hansen, A. and Sivertsen, M.F. (2021) 'Researching publics in datafied societies: Insights from four approaches to the concept of "publics" and a (hybrid) research agenda', *New Media & Society*, 146144482110210. Available at: https://doi.org/10.1177/14614448211021045.

Nelson, J.L. (2021) *Imagined Audiences: How Journalists Perceive and Pursue the Public*, Oxford: Oxford University Press.

The New York Times Company (2011) 'NYTimes.com adds recommendations feature'. Available at: https://investors.nytco.com/news-and-events/press-releases/news-details/2011/NYTimescom-Adds-Recommendations-Feature/default.aspx?initialWidth=1108&childId=details-frame--86&parentTitle=The+New+York+Times+Company+-+News+%26+Events+-+Press+Releases&parentUrl=https%3a%2f%2fin vestors.nytco.com%2fnews-and-events%2fpress-releases%2f%23data-item%3dNYTimescom-Adds-Recommendations-Feature.

Pariser, E. (2011) *The Filter Bubble: What the Internet Is Hiding From You*, London: Penguin.

Pfaffenberger, B. (1992) 'Technological dramas', *Science, Technology, & Human Values*, 17(3), pp 282–312.

Schudson, M. (2011) *The Sociology of News* (2nd edn), New York: W.W. Norton.

Schultz, I. (2007) 'Fra Partipresse over Omnibuspresse til Segmentpresse', *Journalistica* [preprint], 5. Available at: https://doi.org/10.7146/journalistica.v2i5.1807.

Spangher, A. (2015) 'Building the next *New York Times* recommendation engine', *Open Blog*. Available at: https://archive.nytimes.com/open.blogs.nytimes.com/2015/08/11/building-the-next-new-york-times-recommendation-engine/.

Spayd, L. (2017) 'A "community" of one: The *Times* gets tailored', *The New York Times*, 18 March. Available at: https://www.nytimes.com/2017/03/18/public-editor/a-community-of-one-the-times-gets-tailored.html.

Tandoc, E.C. (2014) 'Journalism is twerking? How web analytics is changing the process of gatekeeping', *New Media & Society*, 16(4), pp 559–575.

Taylor, C. (2004) 'What is a "social imaginary"?', in D.P. Gaonkar, J. Kramer, B. Lee and M. Warner (eds) *Modern Social Imaginaries*, Durham, NC: Duke University Press, pp 23–30. Available at: https://doi.org/10.1515/9780822385806-004.

Tuchman, G. (1978) *Making News: A Study in the Construction of Reality*, Glencoe, IL: Free Press.

Turner, F. (2015) *The Democratic Surround: Multimedia and American Liberalism from World War II to the Psychedelic Sixties*, Chicago: University of Chicago Press. Available at: https://press.uchicago.edu/ucp/books/book/chicago/D/bo10509859.html.

Willig, I. (2010) 'Constructing the audience: A study of segmentation in the Danish press', *Northern Lights: Film and Media Studies Yearbook*, 8(1), pp 93–114.

6

Personalization Logics and Publics by Design

Jannie Møller Hartley, Anna Schjøtt and Jannick Kirk Sørensen

Introduction

While it might seem like personalization came like a tsunami with the arrival of Netflix, Amazon and Spotify, the first conceptualization of what personalized content distribution could look like was invented already in 1993. A group of students enrolled in the 'newspapers of the future freshman advisor seminar' at the MIT Media Lab 1993 developed the first experimental personalized online news site, 'fishWrap'.[1] Just a few years later, Nicholas Negroponte, founder of the MIT Media Lab, outlined a vision of what he labelled the 'Daily Me': 'Imagine a future in which your interface agent can read every newswire and newspaper and catch every TV and broadcast on the planet, and then construct a personalized summary. This kind of newspaper is printed in an edition of one' (Negroponte, 1995, p 153).

Negroponte's vision is often considered the moment that ignited interest in personalization in media, and it is often referenced as the first example of how this could look in practice. Since this initial project, the media landscape has increasingly digitalized the production and more and more media organizations across the globe are experimenting with personalizing their online media content distribution (Newman, 2018; Beckett, 2019). Today, Negroponte's initial vision no longer seems far from reality. As demonstrated in Chapter 5, the discursively constructed need for personalization in the news industry is intertwined with perceived changes in the audience and transformations of the technological landscape. This chapter picks up where the former left off, by moving beyond the imaginaries of personalization and into the media organizations, exploring the concrete negotiations of how to build 'good' personalization and how such processes involved changes in the constructions of publics. This shift in perspective allows us to critically examine the material and symbolic changes in news organizations and their audience constructions that occur as personalization becomes the 'natural next step' for news.

Such a critical perspective is important, because personalization has also been deeply intertwined with critical narratives of 'filter bubbles' (Pariser, 2011) and 'echo chambers' (Sunstein, 2009). Cass Sunstein (2009) – concerned with the health of the (US) publics sphere – has argued that the algorithmic personalization of news would accelerate the ongoing fragmentation of (US) society (Putnam, 2000). The concerns subsequently led to policy suggestions of regulating the exposure diversity of media (Napoli, 1999, 2011), also via algorithms (Helberger, 2012; Helberger et al, 2015), and specifically in the case of public service media (PSM) (Burri, 2015; Burri and Helberger, 2015).

In this chapter, we do not engage with what recommender systems and personalization might or might not do on a societal level; rather, our interest lies in exploring how personalization projects introduce new 'personalized logics' into the organizations and how these new logics induce subtle but significant changes in the media organizations in the way they construct publics, but also why it matters who participates in the 'constructing'.

We build this argument on two in-depth studies of personalization projects carried out by the authors of the chapter. Concretely, we draw on an almost two-year ethnographic study of a personalization project at a large regional Danish commercial media organization (Schjøtt Hansen and Møller Hartley, 2021) and on an interview study that over four years followed the personalizing of the on-demand streaming platform from a Danish PSM (Sørensen, 2020). We use quotes from interviews, transcripts from meetings we attended and fieldwork observations to exemplify our analytical points.

Both personalization projects ultimately ended with limited impact on the actual distribution of content. At the PSM only a few of the rows of content on the on-demand site were – in some periods – personalized, while the rest remained under editorial control. At the regional media organization they ultimately decided not to implement the recommender system on their online news sites and to instead use the system to produce a personalized newsletter. The fact that both projects had a minimal 'direct' impact is what makes them particularly relevant to explore the question of the evolutionary changes that occurred along with these projects. Both projects also had a strong focus on the democratic and publicist element of their personalization projects. While the PSM explicitly mentions 'the public' as a defining feature, commercial media organizations in the Nordics have always had a strong focus on the democratic role of news and through that highly democratized ideals of the public they serve, more so than in other media systems (Willig, 2010). This distinct characteristic of Danish media organizations makes these case studies well-suited for the study of the datafication of public formation by media, because the discussions of 'how to serve which publics' are highly explicit in these projects and the new ideals of the public might be more challenged than in more commercial media system contexts. We also observed that these discussions in both the commercial and PSM media organization centre around the same questions and concerns, which allowed us to draw lines across the two cases.

Personalization can technically be produced using different tools. Although the combination of the tools – for example, algorithmic models for filtering and selecting the content – play a central role for the composition of the personalized page, and thus the personalization itself, we will not discuss all the different ways such recommender systems could be comprised. Rather we will engage with how they enabled emerging 'personalized logics' to move into the media organizations and how they interact with existing media logics. In the following, we first outline what we mean with 'personalized logics' and how that relates to the construction of publics that the media seek to cultivate. We do so by drawing on existing literature on media and algorithmic logics as well as theories of audience construction. Then we empirically describe what we see as the three main logics that sum up 'personalized logics': individualism; dataism; and binarity and predeterminedness. These 'personalized logics', we argue, become drivers for how media organizations (re)construct their publics, namely as aggregated, predictable and controllable datapoints. This reconstruction of the audience allows the media organizations to engage in new form of publics cultivation – publics by design – as they now materially begin to shape and design the publics they wish to cultivate into these systems. In the last part we move onto discussing the implications of these personalization projects, where we highlight how these 'personalized logics' not only influence audience constructions but 'linger' in the organizations. Thus, even when the personalization projects fail, they are inducing an 'invisible revolution' within the organizations who undergo subtle but significant changes along with these projects.

'Personalized logics' and audience constructions

The idea of logics is in no way new to the field of media studies, rather the notion of 'media logics' was originally developed by David Altheide and Robert Snow in 1979, during the era of mass media, to describe the logics, norms, routines and formats that come to shape how mass-media content was produced. It was later defined by Altheide (2015, p 1) as a set of 'rules or codes for defining, selecting, organizing, presenting and recognizing information'. These logics do not dictate but subtly structure how media is produced and disseminated, they provide the interpretative frame for how to understand media practice. Over the years multiple iterations of the concept have been developed to describe new forms of media logics as the media landscape changed, such as social media logic (Van Dijck and Poell, 2013), new media logics (Chadwick, 2013) and network media logic (Klinger and Svensson, 2015). In his seminal work on the hybrid media system, Andrew Chadwick (2013, p 20) argues that the changes in the media landscape with new emerging logics 'calls for a reappraisal of the idea of media logic and its disaggregation into different competing yet interdependent logics'. He highlights that new emerging logics do not simply replace existing ones, rather they interact with each other and become hybridized logics. Personalization can be said to bring along yet another set of logics – personalized logic – which become hybridized with the existing hybrid media logics. However, as personalization is enabled via algorithmic techniques and machine learning, as discussed earlier, it is worth touching upon how logics have been conceptualized in relation to algorithms (see, for example, Gaw, 2022).

Robert Kowalski (1979) famously defined algorithms as 'algorithms = logics + control', where the notion of logic was used to signify the knowledge that was needed to solve the specific problem, while control signified the strategies that govern the problem solving. He connects the logic component to meaning, while control only is seen as affecting efficiency (Kowalski, 1979, pp 429–431). In the context of recommender systems, the algorithmic logics are related to the ways in which the systems produce meaning, which becomes represented via concrete predictions that guide the selection of content for the individual reader. As illustrated earlier, this meaning making is generally achieved by using different algorithmic systems that use data signals (user behaviour data, news article clicks, article similarity, predictions) to predict what content should be targeted to a specific user.

The notion of 'personalized logics' builds on this conceptualization of algorithmic logic as a meaning-making practice that is unique to the system, but also reaches beyond the system. We see them more as a type of media logic, as standardized formats are inherent in these models, which also comes with different norms and routines relating specifically to the distribution of media. Logics, that are often contraposed to existing media logics. It is this latter characteristic that makes it relevant and interesting to explore the implications of personalization for public construction and for the media organization, because as Chadwick notes: 'media logic provides a useful approach to understanding the power of media and the power relations within media' (Chadwick, 2013, p 19). Chadwick's quote here highlights how media logics can both be useful to understand power relations between media and other institutions and sites of communication, such as politics and media or legacy and social media, but also within media. In this chapter we are concerned with the latter as we engage with how the entrance of these logics and their encounter with existing media logics induce new battles of control over the cultivation of publics but also power asymmetries within the media organizations (see Chapter 3 for analysis of logics in the citizen's public formation).

In Chapter 5 the authors showed how imaginaries of audiences and their technological preferences of the 'printed paper' became a core element in the legitimizing discourse of personalization, but also how the technology the other way around enabled a reimagination of the public as these technologies come with their own ideals of publicness. In this chapter we build on those insights but explore the role of the audience construction in the development process of personalization and recommender systems. The notions of imaginaries, used in Chapter 5, and the notion of audience construction are often used interchangeably. Here we intentionally shift the vocabulary, to signal a move from discourse to practices of news making and distribution. Previous literature has highlighted that audience constructions play a crucial role in the daily routines of news making and presentation (De Werth-Pallmeyer,1997; Sumpter, 2000; Coddington, 2018) and thereby are part of the media logics that guide the selection and organization of content.

Historically, the notion of 'audience construction' has been used to describe the way journalists and editors engage with their audience and to challenge the idea that media respond to a pre-existing audience 'out there' in the world. The role of marketing data has been seen as uniquely changing the construction of the audience, and particularly the emergence of audience metrics, which granularized the knowledge available about the audience and made them highly present in the newsroom in real-time (see, for example, Willig, 2010; Anderson, 2011; Møller Hartley, 2013; Tandoc, 2014). Similarly, recommender systems used for personalization provide certain new ways to know and interact with the audience and thereby in new ways contribute to a (re)construction of the audience.

Pablo Boczkowski (2004) in his work explicated the connection between audiences and technologies using the notion of 'inscription' from Science and Technology Studies (see Woolgar, 1990; Akrich, 1992), to describe how the intended user – or in the case of media the idealized public – are built into the system. Thus, in this chapter, we engage not only with how the 'personalized logics' produce new ways of knowing and constructing the audience, but also change the way editors and journalists partake in constructing the audience. The latter becomes important to understand the evolutionary steps that these personalization projects induce and helps to underline why even failed projects or minor implementations of personalization also have implications for the media organizations. In the following we first outline the three dimensions that we argue characterize the 'personalized logics' and how they differ from existing media logics. Then we engage with how these logics become drivers in the (re)construction of the audiences, but also how they are negotiated and adapted in relation to the existing hybridized media logics and existing audience constructions.

Logics of personalization

Individualism

Since the invention of the printing press, media has been a mass-distributed product (be it on the radio, broadcasted or as a printed or online paper) and it was this distributional logic that was dominant when Altheide and Snow (1979) were first conceptualizing the notion of media logics. Over the years the 'mass' in mass media has become more segmented via the use of audience data and measurements and as a result more niche and granular audience segments have become the targets and part of the distributional logic of media. However, the current more segmented distribution logic is still considered aimed at a general 'mass' out there, which is what personalization is seen as breaking with. As emphasized by an editor at the Danish regional media organization, personalization was a way of "escaping a 200-year-old straitjacket" (interview, 2020). Personalization offers newspapers an escape from serving a 'mass' to serving the 'individual' and thereby a new distributional logic. The uniqueness of this distributional logic was highlighted by one of the data scientists involved in the personalization project in the Danish regional media organization, who explained:

> 'The editor in a city knows everything about that city. It's not that the machine is smarter than him, but it plays by different rules because it can offer individual things. If the editor were able to offer individual things to all users in that city, then it would be damn amazing if he knew what they should be. The machine knows them a little.' (Interview, 2020)

He is foregrounding how the machine can come to know the individual and via this ability can select targeted content to their interests, maybe not as well as an editor could, but on a scale that is out of reach for an editor. The scale offered by recommender systems enables a shift from a *logic of mass distribution to a logic of individualized, targeted exposure of content*. The value of serving individuals was by the media organizations seen as a way to better serve their 'publics'.

For the large regional media organization, the potential to become more locally oriented and serve the 'local democracies' better was a new and highly valued opportunity. The logic of individualism, while conflicting with the mass media logic, was not seen to conflict with the ideal of serving the (democratic) public – rather the opposite. In the context of the PSM, personalization challenges one of the core PSM characteristics, namely the special construction of 'public' as all citizens of a nation-state.

The universal reach of radio waves produced a political-economic logic of 'universalism' also when it comes to content (Van den Bulck and Moe, 2018). Personalization is thus normatively in conflict with PSM (Sørensen, 2011, 2013) but can potentially help PSM in demonstrating 'reach' – the measure for the percentage of the population using the PSM services, as well as potentially serving viewers' and listeners' special interests. Personalization exposes however also PSM's 'commercial' dilemma: at one side politically expected to be competitive and relevant, at the other side being accused of unfair competition based on state aid (Donders et al, 2020). PSM may thus have problems of political legitimacy if exploiting personalization to its maximum.

In both cases, several control strategies to contain who the individual should be and how much space they should be given were discussed and put in place in the media organizations, but the construction of audiences as individuals only referred to a small segment of the actual users, namely the users that they had data on. In both the cases discussed in this chapter, data – or the lack of it – becomes defining for the personalization. At the Danish public broadcaster, for example, only 1 per cent of clicks originate from the few personalized rows on the on-demand site and in the regional media organization the personalization was developed with mainly paying and logged-in subscribers in mind. Thus, the dimension of individualism is linked to the dimension of dataism, which we unfold in the following.

Dataism

The ways in which the system can come to know the individual brings us to the next logic, because it is in a very specific way that the system 'knows' the individual, namely via data (audience behavioural data like clicks, and so on), which become processed according to the 'logic' of the system. Personalization projects come with *a dataism logic*, as there is a strong 'belief in the objective quantification and potential tracking of all kinds of human behaviour and sociality through online media technologies' (van Dijck, 2014, p 198). In the media organizations we observed, they truly believed in the value of data and that this data could become even more valuable via the use of recommender systems. Often, a key driver for personalization is the fact the publisher already has readily available data (Bodó, 2019), as echoed by the project manager in the regional media organization when describing why they had ventured into the personalization project: "We had already built up this large data department and we had all this information about the users and their interests. At the same time, we had a bunch of articles that we found it hard to distribute" (interview, 2020). Personalization was seen to get even more value out of the data than previously. One editor explained how they had been on a year-long journey to better connect journalism and data and produce what he referred to as "data driven journalism". At the managerial level at the PSM, they also viewed the personalization project as being part of a larger organizational effort to become a data-driven organization (Sørensen, 2020). This illustrates how data had increasingly become a valorized way of knowing the audience even before personalization, but that personalization as an idea increased the value of data further. As knowledge via data becomes increasingly valorized, the existing logics of the journalistic gut feeling of knowing the audience (see, for example, Willig, 2011) becomes devalorized.

Personalization also induces a process of needing more data. On one side, producing 'good' individual recommendations requires large amounts of data. Particularly in the regional media where they wanted to provide hyper-local recommendations, it was seen as essential to have enough data about local consumption so that the system would "get enough data to make a selection for the local user", as noted by the project manager (interview, 2020). Interestingly, the need for data on audience behaviour to offer personalized recommendations, created yet another quest for data on the results of the recommendations, as the consumption and the front page is unique for each user. This resulted in a form of data puzzle of how to manage the front page: "It becomes sort of mind blowing when you think about it. How are we actually going to relate to the current news flow we have right now, if we cannot see what anyone is seeing?" (interview, 2020). This shift in distributional logic ultimately dissembles 'the news' as constituted by a 'finite arrangement of texts' (Carlson, 2018, p 5). What we can observe is that existing practices of presenting the news or media content are challenged with the logics of personalization. Previously, the importance and placement of content on the front page was prioritized in relation to the other content available coupled with user engagement metrics, but still with one overall front page. The loss of editorial prioritization practices caused by personalization led to a series of subprojects at the regional media organization. The aim of these subprojects was to ensure that new data-tracking practices were put in place, so that the editors could still assess what each individual was being presented with on the screen. Interestingly, the idea of leaving the 'public' all by themselves with no editorial oversight of the content was seen as irresponsible by project managers and editors involved in the personalization project, who struggled to maintain some form of control.

This clash between personalized and existing media logics was even more evident in the control strategies that were developed in both the regional media and PSM. Both decided to implement or discussed implementing personalization on a few selected areas on the online sites (see also van den Bulck and Moe, 2018; Schjøtt Hansen and Møller Hartley, 2021). At the PSM, a personalization specialist explained that despite the technical possibility of their new recommender system, the video on demand service

'DRTV' was only personalized to a minor degree and only for the few users using the login feature on the page. Partly this was due to the technical difficulties in scaling up the recommender system, but more importantly, it is also due to editorial hesitation to abandon the position of a mass media by no longer presenting all visitors with the same content (Sørensen, 2020). Relatively few examples of 'full personalization' can be found in the media landscape. Swedish regional media organization, MittMedia, represents one of the more extensive examples in the authors' sample of sites, where only three pieces of news at the top of the site have remained under editorial control.[2] This illustrates that while personalization might not revolutionize the actual distribution or exposure of the content, the process of personalization did intensify the already existing valorization of data (see, for example, Kristensen, 2021) and further enhances the status of data as a 'must-have' resource – the new oil of news (Rotella, 2012). The increased valorization of data systems also led to new organizational dynamics in media organizations, where employees who 'knew' and worked with data became more essential in the day-to-day practices of making and distributing news, shifting the power balance in the organizations.

Binarity and predeterminedness

The last dimension of the personalization logics we distilled from the empirical material is related to the logic of algorithmic systems and how they make sense of the world. Algorithmic systems need uniform and strictly codified data to operate, and while this might be easier for commercial products, it's not that easy for news. In the personalization project at the regional media organization, they were utilizing a recommender system they were building for a sister project, which had the goal of personalizing what deals (coupons for different experiences) to offer their users. However, as the data scientists explained, it was fairly easy to make rules for when a deal should be recommended or not; either it was active and could be purchased or it was no longer active and could no longer be purchased. With news this became more challenging as the boundaries between active and not active were no longer clear-cut. For example, some genres of news like in-depth pieces might be relevant for a longer period, while a story about a traffic jam is only relevant as long as the traffic jam is still there. This binary logic of 'either or' conflicted with the existing relational and temporal logics of media, where the relevance of media content is ongoingly determined based on the timeliness of event the content refers to (for example, the traffic jam), but also determined in relation to what new content is produced (see, for example, Møller Hartley, 2011). Such decisions of relevance and deciding what is news are made and changed consistently according to norms and routines (see, for example, Shoemaker and Reese,

1996) and values in the field. However, with the recommender system they have to be predetermined through concrete software rules that the system can handle, introducing a specific *logic of binarity and predeterminedness*. At the regional media this issue led to the development of a 'control filter' that would both ensure that journalistic values of, for example, timeliness and localness remained present even after personalizing the distribution. As the editor emphasized during a meeting discussing the future-filtering mechanism: "We need to have some filters relating to time because we cannot have ancient content there. As a news site, it must contain something relatively timely" (meeting transcript, fieldwork, 2020). Concretely, this led to the development of a new metadata 'tag' that journalists would have to assign to articles, designating their lifetime. Ultimately, timeliness as a value was reconfigured from a situational and relational value to a numeric and predetermined value. Thus, due to this rule-bound and predetermining software logic, the values went from being 'decided' to being 'designed' into the system via, for example, tags or rules (see also Schjøtt Hansen and Møller Hartley, 2021). This 'publics by design' is explored in the following – as we show how the new logics of personalization reconfigured the previous audience construction.

Publics by design

With the expression 'publics by design' we aim to signal intention rather than coincidence – also an intentional choice of the authors – because this helps to underline a shared finding across the authors' different studies, namely how personalization, via its different logics, involves a new way of reconstructing – or rather redesigning the ideal publics of media organizations. To explore this, we first return to how these systems come to know their 'individual users' and then we engage with how the editors engaged with attempting to locate the 'right' public in the data.

Users as aggregated datapoints

As noted previously, the way algorithmic systems, including recommender systems, come to understand the individual is via the input data, but the way it produces meaning of the individual is specific to the filtering model. The choice of model and thereby the core logic of how to compose and serve this new individual is left to the data scientists. In the case of the regional media it was the in-house data scientists who build the system, in the case of the PSM the in-house specialists that tried to configure and adapt a recommender system bought from an external software company, Think Analytics, that normally provides recommender systems to commercial TV. That meant that the system, until modified, was not capable of recommending the latest news as it was originally designed to recommend the first episode and first season of a TV series. The PSM was thus confronted with the logic of commercial TV.

At the regional media orgnaization, the system was 'custom built' to reflect the needs of the news organization, but that required many decisions. A data scientist explained that they had explored both content and collaborative filtering models, which are both popular models for recommendations. They had, however, decided on the collaborative model as the main component of their system. The collaborative model had gained popularity in recent years, as it requires less manual tagging of content and as many organizations already have the user data needed. While editors originally had been keen on the content-filtering model, the decision were in the end left to the 'data experts' with the backing of an external personalization expert called in to consult on the project. In a meeting he described the logic that characterizes the collaborative filtering model:

> 'The algorithm simply ordered recommendations by finding similarities between users and their reading behaviours: "Someone like you found this article good, and here, 'like you' means you have read similar articles." This, in simple terms, means that if user A reads articles A, B and C, and user B has read A and B, then that person will likely be recommended article C, but in reality, this is a calculation made with thousands of users and complicated linear algebra.' (Excerpt from observations and interview, 2020)

As the quote illustrates, the model does in fact not deal with individuals, but rather with thousands of aggregated datapoints that become continuously recombined to then produce a representation of the individual in the form of a list of recommendations – a prediction – of what a user might like to read next. This is traced back to the individual users via a user login, a cookie or some other means of identification of the individual user. As described in Chapter 5, users have throughout history been highly abstract entities, that were constructed either by the journalists themselves often based on their own high ideals of democratic citizens – either because data was not available or it was ignored (see, for example, Gans, 1979). However, with the personalized logics, the audience is abstract in a new way, as sets of nodes and vectors in a database. The data scientists noted in an interview that within the system the recommendations (and thereby the individual user) is constructed within a 50-dimensional space in which the system can find patterns (interview, 2020). This makes the construction impossible to either understand or interact with for both the data scientists and editors, who are limited to interpreting the results of the system. Hence, the audience construction is no longer tied to ideals of the editors or journalists but to the logics of the system.

The personalized logic introduced with personalization also produces a very different construction of the individual, compared to when, for example, an editor constructs an idea of who they are serving, such as thinking of the reader as '43-year-old Lisa from the city of Kolding – a middle sized city in Denmark'. While it is an imagined person, it is still a person. Even with audience metrics, journalists would make sense of who the audience was based on the data (see, for example, Anderson, 2011). With the personalized logics the user is constructed via aggregated datapoints, similar to what Deleuze (1992) has called 'dividuals', an unstable cybernetic subject that is continuously constructed out of datapoints, codes and passwords (see also Zwick and Denegri Knott, 2009). The system is continuously recomposing the individual, based not only on what they click, but also on what other users click, which means the user becomes a modular and dynamic entity assembled in and by accumulated data. Contrary to the use of explicit personalization, where the user creates their own profile – a stable representation of them as individuals – implicit personalization, which is what was used in both projects, dissolves the individual, making the user as fragmentable and combinable as aggregated datapoints (see also Vedder [1999] on de-individualization). As audiences are becoming 'dividualized', the power to design publics is transferred into the hands of data science and data analysis departments. Compared to past audience formats that were part of the more segmented media logics of targeting segments based on data (for example, focus groups or later audience metrics), the difference is that here the construction is moved out of the newsroom. Where audience data and reader profiles were interpreted by editors and journalists, here the interpretative work takes place within the system, and it is the data scientists that ultimately decide the logic of interpretation. However, as we shall see in the following section, the editors and project managers feared a loss of 'the audience-as-publics' and embarked on developing control strategies.

Finding publics in data

The personalization allowed the media organizations to reinterpret the news value of relevance. As the digital editor stated: "It is a different relevance than the one you get taught when studying journalism, where relevance means the societally important events" (interview, 2020). 'Relevant' in the context of personalized news distribution meant content which could engage the audiences, constructing them as consumers, as exemplified by the following quote:

'It is important that this system will reward the right kind of content, because in our data we can see that the content that really engages our users is something as simple as a news piece regarding a new store opening because it matters in their daily life as they now have new possibilities to shop in their local area.' (Interview during fieldwork, 2020)

What this quote helps to highlight is that 'publics' are being reconstructed via the data hypothesis of what matters to the audiences. This should be seen in relation to the dataism dimension discussed earlier, and the fact that the traditional journalistic 'gut feeling' over the years has become more and more datafied. In turn, this changes what content is deemed important, namely more service or useful content.

With personalization the editors saw the potential to 'seek out' new publics via the scalability, namely hyper-local public, as the data editor explained during a meeting:

'Right now, we do not have a lot of hyper-local content out there because we are collecting, for example, house sales and prizes in joined articles, as they would otherwise be too many small fragments to present for people, but the goal is that these small pieces should have a life of their own. The problem is that right now we do not know who is in the market to read such hyper local news from your local village.' (Excerpt from meeting during fieldwork, 2020)

While they were unsure of the market for this content, the availability of data and the idea that local content was valuable to the user (based on data) made personalization an ideal way to cultivate this local public, as both could be seen as economically beneficial, and both could deliver on their editorial mission of supporting local democracies. This illustrates how the strengthened logic of dataism both drives ideas of value in terms of utilizing content and data available, but also produced a change in how the audience was constructed. Now the audience, due to the scalable abilities of personalization, could be targeted even beyond segments and in hyper-local communities – one that the digital editor referred to as a 'street level relevance' (fieldwork observations, 2020). As he described: "If a house is sold down the street, then that story has value on my street, but probably not three streets away" (interview, 2020). This not only affected how the audience was constructed but shifted what could be considered 'relevant' or newsworthy content. Interestingly, this exact type of hyper-local relevancy was what originally provoked Eli Pariser in his popular book (2011) on filter bubbles. In the introduction chapter, Pariser quotes Mark Zuckerberg: 'A squirrel dying in front of your house may be more relevant to your interests right now than people dying in Africa' (2011, p 1). With this, Pariser highlights the inherent tension between personal and societal relevance, where the latter has historically been seen as the core task of journalism. The logics of personalization, therefore, in some ways challenged the notion of societal relevance as the editors, through personalization, could move beyond local segments to individual users (represented in data), making previous non-newsworthy content newsworthy. However, as we will see in the next section, the personalized logics of audiences-as-data were also challenged when confronted with ideals of the audiences-as-publics.

During the personalization projects, the editors involved would, together with the data scientists, also have to assess whether the recommendations by the recommender systems could be deemed 'good'. At the regional media organization this involved looking at spreadsheets that contained the headlines of the articles that a user had read in the past and comparing that to the suggested articles that the system had recommended. For the data scientists this was a way to do 'reality checks' on the machine, in terms of seeing whether the recommendations seemed completely off. However, they did not solely rely on this in testing the machine, but also on multiple accuracy measurements that would help assess the workings of the system. The editors, on the other hand, had to rely solely on these sheets to assess the quality and accuracy of the recommendations, which sometimes became enigmatic for the editors, when reader habits did not fit with their understanding of the audience. During one of these assessment moments, an editor noted in relation to a reader who had read much sports news and as a result was getting several sports recommendations, "[t]here, we might need the manual filter to ensure that there is also a fair amount of local content and not just – what can you say? – sports news" (fieldwork observations, 2020). This tension also emerged in relation to the ideal to cultivate a local public, because in validating the results, the editors were confronted with new data in the form of Excel sheets that showed what any given reader had read in the past (the input data to the personalization system) and the recommendations that the system had produced. While most users were seen as having 'suitable' reading patterns, this user had what was considered a 'wrong' consumption and as a result the 'individual' produced by the system as a result of his sports-heavy input data was deemed problematic. The editor, as a result, found it necessary to push content that could cultivate a form of local public, which the editor considered most important for their audience and the mission of the newsroom.

Concretely, such concerns led to control strategies of ensuring that the individuals produced by the recommender system would also fit the editorial mission. This meant, for example, experimenting with having a filtering mechanism that, similarly to the timeliness, would filter the recommendations so that 50 per cent of what would be recommended would be local content. It also led to discussions of how much to personalize the site and at both the PSM and regional news, the fear of 'losing' the collective public led to decisions to only personalize certain locations on the sites to ensure the most important content was still presented to 'everyone' (a fictive construction). This unwillingness to transfer control to the algorithm was also evident during the implementation of personalization at the PSM, where the project leader stressed that the algorithm would not be allowed to dominate publication or exposure for 'the foreseeable future', highlighting that: 'We are a house of editors. We will not for the foreseeable future let the algorithm drive the exposure. We would lose our identity. What would be our livelihood?' (Sørensen, 2020, p 101). As the quote highlights, it is not only the construction of a certain public, but also the role of media in relation to that public that comes to be at stake. The control of the editorial product is central to the identity of the media. The control strategies should prevent one looking stupid, as the editor at the regional media organization brought up during a meeting: "[T]here are so many ways to make something that will be really stupid because the situation and placement matters" (meeting excerpt, fieldwork observations, 2020). It has been proved difficult to make 'rules' to govern the algorithm that could account for all potential situations, relating back to the highly situational logic of the presentation of news (see Willig, 2011; Møller Hartley, 2013).

What these examples illustrate is that while the existing media logics remained dominant in how the content ultimately becomes distributed or was planned to be distributed, the personalized logics provided the editors with completely new ways of algorithmically designing the public they wanted to cultivate based on their interpretation of the data with which they were presented. While reader profiles or audience metrics equally have served to guide the routines of production and presentation of content with the aim of cultivating publics, here the logics of personalization enabled a further shift by enabling the editors to make numeric and predetermined 'settings' of cultivation, such as the case with always ensuring 50 per cent local content. This is a temporal shift in the cultivation of publics. Audience metrics allows the editors to make changes post hoc based on clicks, but with personalization they could ex ante decide how to compose their ideal public. Rather than make decisions based on the data of the public, they could now actively pursue the publics they wanted to cultivate – making publics much more of a question of design, namely an entity whose shape and size could be predetermined and made into operationalized rules.

Merging logics and new 'publics'

The analysis illustrates how a hybridization of existing media logics and personalized logics, on one side, led to transformations in existing understandings of who the public is and how it can be cultivated. On the other side, the strong ideas of serving a collective public and the value remaining for a publisher in presentation of such content, remained at the core of the discussion and ultimately became the dominant factor in the limited role played by personalization. In many ways these projects revived the classic conflict between the audience-as-publics and audience-as-markets (Ang, 2002; Willig, 2010), while also adding a new twist to the conflict by producing new contexts for audience construction, which as discussed became machinic and where audiences became aggregated datapoints in an unimaginable 50-dimensional space. This is a rather different audience construction process than previously, because the audience is essentially also pushed to the background. They exist purely in data processes, or what Christin (2020) called algorithmic publics, namely as metrified representations of a public. This shift in audience construction on one hand afforded editors new agency in designing publics ex ante, rather than having to respond and cultivate the public based on the data post hoc. On the other hand, it also limited the editor's agency, as they were forced to engage with the constructions via simple representations in spreadsheets due to the system's lack of interpretability. This lack of access was not unique to the editors because even the data scientists were forced to attempt to make meaning of what the system produced, as one data scientist from the regional media organization noted during an interview: "It can be difficult to say why you get something recommended. That is just what the machine thinks" (interview, 2020). However, the data scientists remained more in control of the systems, by being the ones who would make decisions on input data, model selection and also continuously tweaking the model, thereby directly contributing to the construction of the audience, while the editors were mainly left to add layers of control on top of the machine – such as filtering rules.

This layering practice becomes a clear example of how logics become hybridized even highly materially. However, as we mentioned in the beginning, both these projects ended up with minimal effects on the actual distribution and therefore also in the ways in which the editors began to algorithmically cultivate publics. In many ways this dispels the fear of filter bubbles, because these systems do not revolutionize media practices as expected, which has remained one of the strong negative discourses relating to these projects. With regards to the tale of journalism's crisis in the cultivation of publics, we here see that while the projects are often a response to this discourse and fear of losing the audience (often supported via data), there is more nuance that must be attended to, which comes to the foreground when exploring the hybridization of new and old media logics.

Conclusion

Although the personalized newspaper was originally presented by Negroponte (1995) as a revolution that would bring full consumer freedom to the user, the actual trajectory of personalized news has rather been a silent and careful evolution (see also Winston, 1996, 1998). Many of the expectations set up by Negroponte came at odds with the inherent logics in the newsrooms, as shown in this chapter. Given the possibility of creating a personalized newspaper or video on demand service, editors and media organizations envisioned radical changes, but their approach to the development was characterized by caution, as they kept a constant eye on how the algorithms behaved. The fear of losing control and potentially losing identity as a news organization, or PSM, resulted in relatively limited personalization that emulated the existing non-personalized news offer, only with few incremental changes.

However, even if personalization of news does not materialize as a revolution visible to the audience or the public, we argue in this chapter that personalization − more than processing news through algorithms − has introduced or reinforced three new personalized logics in the media organizations. These logics, contrarily to personalization itself, contribute to a transformation in the media organizations, as they via these projects become normalized and affect both how news is perceived and how publics can be constructed. First, we see how news or video content is increasingly becoming constructed via its datafied properties − as just another digital product − as it is produced, distributed and measured via data and digital tools. If a personalized revolution is to be discussed, it is more pertinent to highlight how personalization has silently and gradually contributed to transforming the news story into a news product, and towards finally becoming mere 'content' (just as the commercial products that personalization originally was used to sell). This transformation is not without resistance, which was expressed in the tensions between data scientists − representing the normalization of the news as a 'product' − and the editors insisting on the uniqueness of news and the wider purpose of media, when attempting to control the algorithms.

The second way to discuss a revolution is to highlight how these logics induced a relocation of power. In the regional media organization, personalization changed the ways in which editors could know and interact with the audience, because editors increasingly rely on data people to produce intelligible ways of understanding how this algorithmic public is produced. The efforts to give more agency to editors to personalize content distribution and cultivate the desired publics also induced a new dependency on, and thus shift in power to, the data scientists.

This essentially moved much decision-making power out of the hands of the editors and into the hands of the data scientists, who through their access to (organizational ownership) and control over the data, as well as model choices, gained a new power through materials (see Latour, 1987). This power through materials (the data, the algorithms) shifted the long-discussed boundary between the newsroom and the marketing department (which is where the data scientists were based) (see Gans, 1979; Willig, 2010; Schjøtt Hansen and Møller Hartley, 2021). The revolution may thus not be that visible to the outside, to the public. A public who – if we follow Negroponte (1995) – only waited in vain to dissolve itself into individual personalized news consumers. Despite the fact that personalization is not implemented 1:1, the audiences are nevertheless becoming datafied and subject to the optimization of audiences and attention. The promised revolution of personalized news has in the end perhaps more become an invisible process of business optimization and organizational transformation, which is continuing to change the ways in which decisions of what becomes news and questions of which publics to serve are approached and answered in media organizations.

Notes

[1] http://www.mit.edu/afs.new/athena/astaff/reference/olc-stock/stock_answers.real/other/fishwrap

[2] https://medium.com/@katarinaellemark/why-we-choose-to-simplify-our-newsfeed-7aa2d2268dd0

References

Akrich, M. (1992) 'The de-scription of technical objects', in W.E. Bijker and J. Law (eds) *Shaping Technology/Building Society: Studies in Sociotechnical Change*, Cambridge, MA: MIT Press, pp 205–224.

Altheide, D.L. (2015) 'Media logic', in G. Mazzolini (ed) *The International Encyclopedia of Political Communication*, New York: John Wiley & Sons, pp 1–6.

Altheide, D.L. and Snow, R.P. (1979) *Media Logic*, Beverly Hills: SAGE.

Anderson, C. (2011) 'Between creative and quantified audiences: Web metrics and changing patterns of newswork in local US newsrooms', *Journalism*, 12(5), pp 550–566.

Ang, I. (2002) *Desperately Seeking the Audience*, Abingdon: Taylor & Francis.

Beckett, C. (2019) 'New powers, new responsibilities: A global survey of journalism and artificial intelligence', *Polis*, London School of Economics and Political Science. Available at: https://blogs. lse. ac. uk/polis/2019/11/18/new-powers-new-responsibilities.

Boczkowski, P.J. (2004) *Digitizing the News: Innovation in Online Newspapers*, Cambridge, MA: MIT Press.

Bodó, B. (2019) 'Selling news to audiences: A qualitative inquiry into the emerging logics of algorithmic news personalization in European quality news media', *Digital Journalism*, 7(8), pp 1054–1075.

Burri, M. (2015) 'Contemplating a "public service navigator": In search of new (and better) functioning public service media', *International Journal of Communication*, 9, pp 1341–1359.

Burri, M. and Helberger, N. (2015) 'Public service media and exposure diversity: Introduction', *International Journal of Communication*, 9, pp 1319–1323.

Carlson, M. (2018) 'Automating judgment? Algorithmic judgment, news knowledge, and journalistic professionalism', *New Media & Society*, 20(5), pp 1755–1772. Available at: https://doi.org/10.1177/1461444817706684.

Chadwick, A. (2013) *The Hybrid Media System: Politics and Power*, Oxford: Oxford University Press.

Christin, A. (2020) *Metrics at Work: Journalism and the Contested Meaning of Algorithms*, Princeton: Princeton University Press.

Coddington, M. (2018) 'Seeing through the user's eyes: The role of journalists' audience perceptions in their use of technology', *Electronic News*, 12(4), pp 235–250.

Deleuze, G. (1992) 'Postscript on the societies of control', *October*, 59, pp 3–7.

Donders, K., Raats, T. and Tintel, S. (2020) '(Re)defining public service media from an economic perspective: Damned if they do, damned if they don't', in M.B. von Rimscha (ed) *Management and Economics of Communication*, Berlin, Munich and Boston: De Gruyter Mouton, pp 203–222.

DeWerth-Pallmeyer, D. (1997) *The Audience in the News*, New York: Routledge.

Gans, H.J. (1979) *Deciding What's News: A Study of CBS Evening News, NBC Nightly News, Newsweek, and Time*, Michigan: Northwestern University Press.

Gaw, F. (2022) 'Algorithmic logics and the construction of cultural taste of the Netflix Recommender System', *Media, Culture & Society*, 44(4), pp 706–725.

Helberger, N. (2012) 'Exposure diversity as a policy goal', *Journal of Media Law*, 4(1), pp 65–92.

Helberger, N., Kleinen-von Königslöw, K. and van der Noll, R. (2015) 'Regulating the new information intermediaries as gatekeepers of information diversity', *Info*, 17(6), pp 50–71.

Klinger, U. and Svensson, J. (2015) 'The emergence of network media logic in political communication: A theoretical approach', *New Media & Society*, 17(8), pp 1241–1257.

Kowalski, R. (1979) 'Algorithm = logic + control', *Communications of the ACM*, 22(7), pp 424–436.

Kristensen, L.M. (2021) 'Audience metrics: Operationalizing news value for the digital newsroom', *Journalism Practice*, DOI: 10.1080/17512786.2021.1954058.

Latour, B. (1987) *Science in Action: How to Follow Scientists and Engineers through Society*, Cambridge, MA: Harvard University Press.

Møller Hartley, J. (2011) *Radikalisering af Kampzonen – en analyse af netjournalistik praksis og selvforståelse*, PhD thesis, Roskilde University.

Møller Hartley, J. (2013) 'The online journalist between ideals and audiences: Towards a (more) audience-driven and source-detached journalism?', *Journalism Practice*, 7(5), pp 572–587. Available at: https://doi.org/10.1080/17512786.2012.755386.

Napoli, P. (1999) 'Deconstructing the diversity principle', *Journal of Communication*, 49(4), pp 7–34.

Napoli, P. (2011) 'Exposure diversity reconsidered', *Journal of Information Policy*, 1, pp 246–259.

Negroponte, N. (1995) *Being Digital*, New York: Vintage Books.

Newman, N. (2018) *Journalism, Media, and Technology Trends and Predictions 2018*, report, Reuters Institute. Available at: https://reutersinstitute.politics.ox.ac.uk/our-research/journalism-media-and-technology-trends-and-predictions-2018.

Pariser, E. (2011) *The Filter Bubble: How the New Personalized Web is Changing What We Read and How We Think*, London: Penguin.

Putnam, R.D. (2000) *Bowling Alone: The Collapse and Revival of American Community*, New York: Simon & Schuster. Available at: http://bowlingalone.com/.

Rotella, P. (2012) 'Is data the new oil?', *Forbes*, 2 April. Available at: https://www.forbes.com/sites/perryrotella/2012/04/02/is-data-the-new-oil/.

Schjøtt Hansen, A. and Møller Hartley, J. (2021) 'Designing what's news: An ethnography of a personalization algorithm and the data-driven (re) assembling of the news', *Digital Journalism*, [Preprint]. Available at: https://doi.org/10.1080/21670811.2021.1988861.

Shoemaker, P. and Reese, S. (1996) *Mediating the Message: Theories of Influences on Mass Media Content*, White Plains: Longman.

Sørensen, J.K. (2011) *The Paradox of Personalisation: Public Service Broadcasters' Approaches to Media Personalisation Technologies*, PhD thesis, University of Southern Denmark.

Sørensen, J.K. (2013) 'Public service broadcasting goes personal: The failure of personalised PSB web pages', *MedieKultur: Journal of Media and Communication Research*, 29(55), pp 43–71.

Sørensen, J.K. (2020) 'The datafication of public service media dreams, dilemmas and practical problems: A case study of the implementation of personalized recommendations at the Danish public service media "DR"', *MedieKultur: Journal of Media and Communication Research*, 69, pp 90–115.

Sunstein, C.R. (2009) *Going to Extremes: How Like Minds Unite and Divide*, Oxford: Oxford University Press.

Sumpter, R.S. (2000) 'Daily newspaper editors' audience construction routines: A case study', *Critical Studies in Media Communication*, 17, pp 334–346.

Tandoc, E.C. (2014) 'Journalism is twerking? How web analytics is changing the process of gatekeeping', *New Media & Society*, 16(4), pp 559–575.

Van den Bulck, H. and Moe, H. (2018) 'Public service media, universality and personalisation through algorithms: Mapping strategies and exploring dilemmas', *Media, Culture & Society*, 40(6), pp 875–892.

Van Dijck, J. (2014) 'Datafication, dataism and dataveillance: Big data between scientific paradigm and ideology', *Surveillance & Society*, 12(2), pp 197–208.

van Dijck, J. and Poell, T. (2013) 'Understanding social media logic', *Media and Communication*, 1(1), pp 2–14.

Vedder, A. (1999) 'KDD: The challenge to individualism', *Ethics and Information Technology*, 1(4), pp 275–281.

Willig, I. (2010) 'Constructing the audience: A study of segmentation in the Danish press', *Northern Lights: Film & Media Studies Yearbook*, 8(1), pp 93–114.

Willig, I. (2011) 'The journalistic gut feeling: Journalistic doxa, news habitus and orthodox news values', in D.A. Berkowitz (ed) *Cultural Meanings of News*, Thousand Oaks: SAGE, pp 83–98.

Winston, B. (1996) *Technologies of Seeing: Photography, Cinematography and Television*, London: British Film Institute.

Winston, B. (1998) *Media Technology and Society: A History From the Telegraph to the Internet*, Abingdon: Routledge.

Woolgar, S. (1990) 'Configuring the user: The case of usability trials', *The Sociological Review*, 38(1_suppl), pp 58–99.

Zwick, D. and Denegri Knott, J. (2009) 'Manufacturing customers: The database as new means of production', *Journal of Consumer Culture*, 9(2), pp 221–247.

PART III

Infrastructured Publics

Classifying the News: Metadata as Structures of Visibility and Compliance with Tech Standards

Lisa Merete Kristensen and Jannick Kirk Sørensen

Introduction

In pre-digital times, the visibility of a news story was determined by the newspaper layout, the size of its headline and placement on the page, reflecting the editors' assessment of the relevance of the story. Visual means of attention management applied by typographs signalled hierarchy of stories and the genre, topic and author, which were placed accordingly. With news on the web, new tools for managing attention have emerged. What was previously called 'news articles' or 'news stories' are now 'content' in a database (Caswell, 2019). Most importantly, with today's news audiences increasingly encountering news on third-party platforms (Newman et al, 2022), being visible to audiences requires being visible to the external platforms for news.

Metadata are often explained as 'data about data', underlining that they are a secondary layer of knowledge describing a primary entity. For example, for a photo, its timestamp is a piece of 'metadata'. In the field of information science, 'metadata' are defined a little more precisely to demonstrate how data in this respect are not just any information. As such, '[m]etadata is a statement about a potentially informative object' (Pomerantz, 2015, p 26). Metadata are essential for storing and retrieving information in most databases; if the information is not organized, it would be nearly impossible to find specific pieces of information again. Thus, all data must be filed using the same rules, following existing standardizations, and this is where metadata schemes come in: 'A metadata schema is a set of rules about what sorts of subject-predicate-object statements (called triples) one is allowed to make and how one is allowed to make them' (Pomerantz, 2015, p 28).

The logic of databases, as argued by Manovich (2002), changes how narratives are constructed. Narratives are composed of discreet elements that are selected by an algorithm based on their formal metadata descriptions; think of the autogenerated feeds of social media, for example the 'for you page' (fyp) on TikTok or the Spotify playlist called 'Girl's Night' which has 2.8 million followers. As such, metadata become key to exposure for content online while simultaneously telling a story about, for example, what a girls' night 'sounds' like. The nature of a database is to 'know' its content; it demands metadata to match content with, for example, data on user preferences, in essence, what is something that is 'for you' when opening your TikTok app. Hence, databases set requirements for the creation of news; that is, new news content can only be added to the database if the obligatory metadata is provided. In this way, the visibility of the content now depends on its metadata, indexing and other means of making news narrative readable for an algorithm. This chapter, thus, has the concepts of visibility and legitimacy at its core. This also applies to the publics that media ideally serve. As Bengtsson and Schøtt observed in Chapter 3 in this volume, hashtags added to media content help structure conversations and create publics. However, contrary to the metadata discussed in this chapter, hashtags do not follow a specific ontology; in the so-called 'folksonomy' of hashtagging, every user is free to invent a new concept, as Chapter 3 also observed in practice (Marlow et al, 2006).

To understand the dynamics of the data-driven creation of the public, we must deconstruct the notions of tagging, of metadata and indexing. We must also understand how old pre-digital news professionalism is inherited in the new formal description of news content, along with the conflicting interests associated with news indexing. A description is more than a condensation of information; rather, it is an interpretation – a new layer of meaning. Anyone who attempted to describe something (for example, a photo or a music number) knows this: the description must be socially recognizable, it must draw on the shared knowledge of humans, one might even consider whether descriptions are socially acceptable. Hence, the chosen description may also reveal something about the person providing the description, for example, the person's opinion or worldview. The nature and implications of categorization are famously discussed by Star (1998) and Leigh Star (2010), who argue that what is not included in descriptions remains invisible; hence, categorization results in a rectification and standardization that, in line with this argument, may reduce diversity and inhibit innovation. Thus, we can ask the following question: Can the metadata indexing of news and other media rectify their interaction with the reader, thus inscribing specific interpretations into the news? Furthermore, what is the power balance between the description and the meaning of the text? Does the news story lose its agency when becoming 'content' and description? In that process of metadata description, news is treated as a scientific object and inscribed in the traditions of classification – from linguistics, informatics and even natural sciences. In this way, the news story becomes a specimen for scientific inspection, description and analysis. This classification and standardization relate to what Bowker and Star (1999) called 'information structures'.

Following the logic of databases and algorithms, metadata may have a greater influence on the visibility of a news story than the actual message it wants to convey to the public. The metadata description wraps a news story in an interpretation. However, a data scientist may see this differently: the metadata description is just a formal reduction of information – a condensed summary. Arguably, all metadata descriptions are not a matter of interpretation to the same degree (for example, a timestamp for uploading or releasing the content, the author's name, the URL and copyright information). However, we argue that these firm entities are also social constructions participating in the game of interpretation. An example could be a news story not performing as expected: by rewording and resubmitting a news article to the database, the story gets a second chance, as it looks 'new' to the algorithm, and it once again has a chance at being placed at the top of search results.

The process of categorization raises the following questions: Who defines the categories? What counts as metadata? How do these descriptions become acknowledged as a standard? Once established and acknowledged, a standard appears as an authority to which one must align. A standardization is introduced to streamline differences in the name of the common good: a commonly known metadata structure for library search is the 'Dublin Core',[1] which has existed since 1999. An even more ambitious metadata standardization project, which was intended for multimedia, was the MPEG-7 standard (Martínez, 2002; Martínez et al, 2002). The latter may serve as an example of an 'over-engineered' standard, capable of describing everything but is too complex for practical use. Similar things can be said about the various suggestions for a 'semantic web' that gives webpages machine-readable tags that allow for automatic categorization (Berners-Lee et al, 2001; Shadbolt et al, 2006). However, not many approaches have been successful (Hogan et al, 2020). Instead of an official standard, Big Tech companies ended up defining their own indexing system, that is, the Schema.org, which is a structured data vocabulary founded in 2011 by search engine providers Microsoft, Yahoo!, Google and Yandex.[2] A year after its foundation, the standardization organization for the World Wide Web, the World Wide Web Consortium (W3C) and representatives from academia joined the Schema.org project, signifying its ongoing expansion, both in terms of use and the numbers of classes and relations (Guha et al, 2015).

The question discussed in this chapter concerns the importance of metadata for the public: How do metadata as datafication of news items influence or shape publics? To narrow the scope of the larger question, in this chapter, we look at how media and news websites apply metadata in their presentations of content on the web. This is achieved via interviews with media practitioners and analyses of webpages from 260 primarily European news media sites for the presence of metadata tags. Specifically, we look after tags that comply with Schema.org and Google's guidelines for tagging. The use of Google's catalogue of how to structure data has implications for the visibility/exposure of news stories in Google's services and, arguably, for the shaping of publics.

The remainder of the chapter is structured as follows. First, we decipher the use of descriptive and structured metadata in media organizations, as we argue that the datafication of news is an understudied, but much needed, avenue to uncover its effects on the classic role of journalism in the *construction of reality* (Tuchman, 1978). Following this, we explore the extent of conformity to Schema.org structured data of news organizations' news sites, then we move on to examine the presence of those tags that are recommended by Google to signal the authoritativeness, relevance and freshness of news content. Finally, the chapter illustrates how media organizations reflect on this by presenting findings from semi-structured qualitative interviews with developers from a Danish broadcasting company (TV 2[3]), UK news outlet (*The Guardian*[4]) and Norwegian media group (Amedia[5]). This leads to a discussion of the role of Google and Schema.org tagging in the dissemination of media content and the wider consequences of the news media's ability to cultivate publics. In essence, the presence of certain metadata structures demonstrates the perceived importance of news media connecting news articles to the web and its potential many publics.

Categorizing news through metadata

In her seminal 1978 collection, *Making News: A Study in the Construction of Reality*, Gaye Tuchman found that journalists tended to intuitively classify news into the categories of 'soft' or 'hard', 'developing' or 'continuing', and 'spot news' (Tuchman, 1978, p 47). These categories have been reproduced and shown to overlap with various news criteria and values in both the professional and academic literature (Parks, 2019; Kristensen, 2021). To the *newsmen* in Tuchman's fieldwork, soft news were typically feel-good stories that did not need urgent publication, while hard news consisted of the 'real' and factually driven stories that were, almost by definition, prone to expiration. As this example demonstrates, categorization inherently signifies relevance as it is: 'the classification of objects according to one or more relevant characteristics' (Tuchman, 1978, p 50). In practice, this categorization of news connects the time and typification of news (Tuchman,

1978), and this resonates in the metatags used on news article pages and in the recommendations given by search engines to allow for the relatively seamless crawling and classification of news. The point is that a process of standardization happens according to several variables when labelling and, in essence, datafying news.

One process is to describe the basics of a news story. Another is to assess whether such a story lives up to professional journalistic qualities. For example, a staple of journalism is to work rigorously to provide accurate accounts and evidence and carefully select sources. When a search engine or social media service 'looks' for content to show in search results or in a user's feed, it uses the metadata attached in the code of the article to understand it. However, how can a search engine determine whether a fact, author or a media organization is trustworthy? Along with other Big Tech companies, Google encourages news media to use specific metadata tags in the HTML code of their news webpages. This metadata signals to the search engine that, for example, the webpage content – the news story – stems from a reliable source, is relevant and is not outdated. Metadata makes it more likely that news articles and their links show up in search results, social media feeds and aggregation applications, because it helps crawlers understand how to make sense of the text in the news article. One can say that, while the journalist of a news item writes and reads the same language as the reader, the search engines' web crawlers need a different kind of language to understand what a news article is about. For example, the metadata tags containing the time and date of publication signal to the search engine the timeliness of the news article. An article presenting the latest news on the war in Ukraine has likely been updated multiple times, and maybe the news organization has multiple article pages covering the war but in the context of international politics, local politics, energy resources, and so on.

Schema.org and Google structured data

Most importantly, implementing Schema.org markup in the page HTML is a way to make it more likely that search engine crawlers find and adequately understand what the page is about and who is behind it. Some applications, such as Apple News, use schema markup for aggregation; otherwise, it would be more difficult for algorithms to understand the unstructured data representing news article text. A coveted place to be featured, especially for media companies, is in Google Rich Results, which is highlighted information in search results (think of the Wikipedia box that appears alongside most search results). Schema.org has specific properties pertaining to creative work, and under this umbrella, we find tags specifically relevant to journalism. The Schema.org vocabulary specifies that news content falls under the term 'NewsArticle', which again has several terms that describe the news content (Schema.org, ndb). According to the vocabulary, 'A "NewsArticle" is an article whose content reports news or provides background context and supporting materials for understanding the news' (Schema.org, ndb). However, this tag can be used even if the article is not entirely factual or opinionated, and Google has specific recommendations for implementing Schema.org metadata to news media websites so that Google Search can 'elevate original reporting' (Gingras, 2019, para 11). In the following section, we focus on these tags.

Google pays special attention to news content that fall in the 'Your Money or Your Life (YMYL)' category, as described in Google's 'Search Rater Guidelines' (Google, 2021). This means that news must adhere to higher standards than other content found on the web (Google, 2021). According to the Google News Initiative blog (ndb), the factors authoritativeness, relevance and freshness are essential factors for a news story to be selected and ranked.[6] Media organizations may implement certain structured data in page HTML to make sure that web crawlers recognize the presence of these factors (Google Search Central, nd). Both generic tags (employed universally on websites, such as publishing dates and times) and news markups (tags specifically relevant to news media websites) are recommended for publishers.

Google offers four categories of tags that news media can add to news pages to respectively signal authoritativeness, relevance, freshness and compliance with Google's systems. These tags will, according to Google, boost the visibility of the news story in Google's services, such as in search results and in the highlighted search results ('rich results'). Furthermore, the Google News app and the Fact Check Tools function on the basis of these metatags (Google, nd). In the following, we briefly lay out the categorizations we have found and how they matter to the visibility of the content connecting news content with the wider internet.

Authoritativeness

The Google News Initiative blog states: 'Our algorithms are designed to elevate news from authoritative sources, and we require publishers to be transparent and accountable in order to be represented in news results.'[7] As touched upon briefly in the preceding section, the 'NewsArticle' tag does not necessarily signal journalistic integrity as it can be used by anyone, including company blogs. Instead, the @type-class makes it possible for publishers to indicate whether an article is produced in adherence to journalistic quality criteria, as demonstrated by an example from the Spanish daily elpais.com:

'@type':['NewsArticle','ReportageNewsArticle'].

Furthermore, publishers can include 'award' and 'publishingprinciples' in their HTML to communicate that they are trustworthy, as shown by an example from Belfast.co.uk:

> itemtype='https://schema.org/NewsMediaOrganization'><meta itemprop='publishingPrinciples' content=https://www.belfastlive. co.uk/about-us/. (Black, 2022)

Relevance

While relevance in journalism studies refers to news, which will likely have impact on the future and has impact for a large number of people (Caple and Bednarek, 2016, p 439), for Google, '[a] news article is relevant if it has the information you are looking for' (Google News Initiative, ndb). The algorithms determine this, according to the Google News Initiative, by matching keywords from an article to the search terms of the searcher – 'but our algorithms also have more advanced ways to determine relevance' (Google News Initiative, ndb). While we cannot know how algorithms determine relevancy, the preferred (that is, clicked) news article by users searching for the same keywords, along with the geographical position of the user searching, are part of the calculation. To get an idea of rigorous use of metadata keywords, we can observe keywords implemented in the HTML of an article on Spanish daily elpais.com:[8]

> 'keywords':['España', 'Política', 'Congresos PP', 'Alberto Núñez Feijóo', 'Pablo Casado Blanco', 'PP', 'Sevilla', 'Andalucía', 'Cuca Gamarra', 'Nombramientos', 'Congresos políticos', 'Políticos', 'Partidos políticos', 'Mariano Rajoy', 'Soraya Sáenz de Santamaría']

Freshness

Freshness can be likened to the news value of 'timeliness' in journalism studies: 'The relevance of an event or issue in terms of time: recent, ongoing, about to happen, or seasonal' (Caple and Bednarek, 2016, p 447). Also, we see a parallel to the journalists in Tuchman's (1978) newsroom study, who articulated and classified news in relation to time. In Google Search and Google News products 'freshness' is operationalized similar to this: 'Freshness refers to how recently the article is published and how important to this story having the freshest content is. When news is happening, our algorithms may determine that an article with up-to-date information is likely more useful than an older one' (Google News Initiative, ndb). Tags such as 'DateTime' and 'DateModified' are used across the web for all types of content (they are what we call 'generic' tags), but they are likely given extra weight in the context of news stories. An example of the metadata tag appearing in the HTML of a news article page on BBC.co.uk:

'datePublished':'2022-04-01T17:26:00.000Z', 'dateModified': '2022-04-01T17:26:00.000Z'.

Compliance tags

Two metadata tags explored in this study, namely, 'SchemaFound' and 'googleSiteVerification', are universally employed on webpages across the web. They are, however, unique to Schema.org (the former) and Google (the latter) and can therefore bring into view how compliant the news media in our sample are to these entities. 'SchemaFound' simply signals to the algorithm that the news page can be understood through the vocabulary of Schema.org (Pomerantz, 2015). 'googleSiteVerification' signals that the news site has gone through a series of steps to become verified, which allows for access to data sensitive to the site on Google Search Console (Search Console Help, nd, para 5).

Metadata use in news organizations

As we have seen with the semantic web, the availability of a technical standard or solution does not guarantee its uptake. Google offers a system, but how do media organizations understand and perceive the role of metadata? Based on our interviews with media practitioners from four media companies, we find very different approaches, but all are structured around the argument of usefulness: Do the metadata tags help the media organization obtain its goals? Specifically, usefulness is expressed in the prioritization of resources. We find that resources in general and resources allocated to the technical department vary greatly, and this notion seems to play a key role in these cases, especially in terms of compliance.

The Danish daily newspaper *Information*[9] has few resources in the technical department. Between working on subscription flows, troubleshooting login solutions and the like, the developers do not have much time to worry about metadata:

'It is useful to do a reality check on your schema markup, maybe a couple of times a year or so. Once a year, in our case. In my previous jobs (as a communications consultant), I hired specialists to go over the markup and spit out a report. It is fast and easy for the developers to correct the mistakes, but it is a drag to inspect the site to look for inconsistencies or missing stuff, or to replace old tags with newer versions.' (Digital director, *Information*, 2021)

The opposite can be observed at the Danish media group, TV 2,[10] a broadcaster of national and regional news, operator of a streaming service and one of the most visited news sites in the country. The publisher is adamant about using data models, most importantly to allow content to be independent from its presentation in the future. In their case, several different vocabularies are used as inspirations, and Schema.org is only one of them: "Schema.org is well known and used in other companies and organizations. It is not the only standard we have our eye on, but we have to look towards those who are furthest along in some of this" (journalist and developer at TV 2, 2021). Furthermore, TV 2 is moving towards using the Google Knowledge Graph, thereby moving from thesaurus to ontology: "When we build our model, we try to look at how the open models on the internet, like Google's, work. We try to apply those standards instead of our own to match models and connect content more easily" (journalist and developer at TV 2, 2021).

Meanwhile, *The Guardian*[11] has worked with its own content Application Programming Interface for a decade. However, this does not mean that the news organization avoids integrating with off-platforms[12] or implementing tech company solutions into their architecture:

> 'I think a lot of tech companies, though, depend on those tech giants. So, the question for the future of society is, is it the right model or not? It's difficult to say, right. I think we are conscious that if the entire world depends on individuals, that's probably not sustainable. Right. But at the same time, right now, I think those companies are offering incredible value for money, and being an independent newspaper organization, being cost efficient, is incredibly important for us.' (Head of engineering at *The Guardian*, 2021)

In the Danish public service media organization, DR,[13] the lack of suitable metadata created major challenges when a personalization algorithm was introduced for the video on demand service 'DRTV'. Like other public service broadcasters, DR has a long tradition of applying categories to TV and radio programmes for the purpose of public service auditing. However, these categories (for example, 'Enlightenment and Culture' or 'Current Affairs and Debate') are too broad to make sense of by the personalization algorithm. Thus, the entire DRTV catalogue was tagged with categories intended for the algorithm (Sørensen, 2020; Lassen and Sørensen, 2023).

The practitioners' experiences with and opinions about metadata tagging for publishing are mixed and express some degree of hesitation. This could be rooted in strategic considerations about the relationships between the news organization and the much bigger tech companies and in the practical prioritization of work: How do the media organization get the most out of the programmers they have hired? The interviews also illustrate a gap between media management's technology-deterministic visions of increased efficiency, competitiveness and growth, which can be achieved via semantic metadata (for example, Pellegrini, 2017) and the practical programming work necessary before Google can get what it wants.

Patterns in the use of Google-specific metatags

The interviews could indicate that media companies may be less interested in increasing the visibility of their content via metadata to search engines and other content aggregators, but in the introduction of this chapter, we suggested that metadata is the only 'layout' that databases and search engines understand. Assuming that news sites will do everything in their power to be seen by Google's algorithms, we can thus examine how many media websites are using specific Google tags. The addition of tags to a webpage does not require Google's approval, and it is free of charge. The benefits of tagging for news organizations should be convincing: platforms such as Google are key mediators of news for an overwhelming share of the audience worldwide (Nielsen and Ganter, 2018). About 73 per cent of respondents in the 2021 Reuters Digital News Report said that they obtained news mainly through social media, searches, mobile alerts and emails, in that order (Newman et al, 2021, p 25). Thus, we are curious to see how many of 32 metadata tags we can find on 260 news sites.[14] We chose the top news story page[15] for each of the 260 websites. Then, we visited the websites three times over a period of one month (spring 2022) and counted the presence of 32 different tags.[16]

Surprisingly, only six tags were used frequently and not at all news sites. These six tags are not particularly intended for news sites but for all types of webpages. One tag, 'schemaFound', indicates that the site is compliant with the vocabulary of Schema.org, while another, 'dateModified', indicates the page's attention to timeliness. For news webpages, using the 'dateModified' tag is a way to signal actuality to the search engine, thus avoiding 'old news' being recommended. Continuously updated articles are often more relevant when it comes to breaking or ongoing news. Diving a bit deeper into the findings, we see considerable variations among countries and different categories of news media. We also see a clear difference between non-EU European countries and EU/EEA countries. In particular, four tags ('Google Site Verification', '@type', 'about' and 'Article Section') appear more often at news sites from EU/EEA (and sites from outside Europe). The reasons for this require further research, but earlier research has shown that sites from non-EU countries in general have a lower number of third-party sites involved, possibly indicating a less complex technological web infrastructure compared to others (Sørensen and Kosta, 2019).

Although large legacy news media are more likely to implement Google tags, we do not see strong coherence. Conversely, in some cases, we see media outlets that do not have any particular credibility using tags that indicate such. This points to a central property of the tags: news media, as well as any other publisher of websites, can, as mentioned, freely – without any restrictions – add tags of any kind to the webpage HTML. However, it is unknown to what extent Google and other news aggregator services consider the tags when recommending content to users; thus, the effects of tagging remain unknown.

As already mentioned, the Schema.org ontology contains both generic tags and those related to creative work, such as news journalism. As mentioned previously, the Google News Initiative presents tags in three groups: authoritativeness, relevance and freshness (Google News Initiative, ndb). In Table 7.1, we see very large variations in the appearance of the tags. While two tags are present in a large proportion of the sites, other tags are barely used, if at all.

We observe that the group of 18 news sites that use the 'Award' tag is highly heterogeneous and that well-established legacy news brands of quality news are accompanied by search portals or popular press sites.[17] Only a few media sites actually use tags that signal 'news' and 'journalism' to Google's algorithm. We do not find any clear patterns in the use of tags in relation to, for example, the type of news publication, the country of origin or whether the media outfit is private or for public service. Rather, we see a very scattered image looking beyond the tags recommended by the Google News Initiative, namely, at the full range of Schema.org tags we have found at the news sites. The sparsity of the tags could indicate that news publishers are either unaware of the more detailed and redundant tags or expect the outcomes gained by using the more specific tags to be too little to justify a systematic implementation of the relevant tags. Tentatively, we can conclude that the news sites examined only to a very limited degree follow the tag recommendations from the Google News Initiative. In any case, except for a few frequently used tags, the appearance of Google tags looks more or less random.

The heterogeneity of the appearance of tags also points to the tags as self-declared statements: any webpage can publish as many tags as it wants. There is a parallel to this in the history of the World Wide Web: in the early days of HTML, web developers believed that adding even irrelevant keywords in the <meta> section of their webpage would generate more traffic; hence, words, such as 'porn', were often used. Then, two Stanford PhD students invented an alternative to the <meta> keyword tags to indexing webpages, namely, a search-based analysis of the actual content of the page and its links (Brin and Page, 1998). As their research project gained popularity, they founded a company they eventually called Google. In this way, attracting attention via 'popular' keywords gradually lost its relevancy, giving room for a new industry: that of search engine optimization. Thus, one can participate

Table 7.1: Characteristics and prevalence of metadata tags

Tag category	Tag	Description (Schema.org)	Percentage of sites	Characteristics
Authoritativeness	'@type'	'NewsmediaOrganization' indicates that the article is published by a news outlet, while 'NewsarticleReportage' indicates that the news article adheres to journalistic principles	69% of all sites	Appears more often at private media sites (73%) than on public service media sites (43%); appears more often at sites from the EU (69%) than non-EU sites (47%)
	'award'	'An award won by or for this item'	18 sites or 6% of all sites	A mixed group: well-established legacy news brands of quality news, search portals and popular press sites
	'publishing Principles'	Contains a description or URL that points to 'the editorial principles of an organization (or individual, such as person writing a blog) that relate to their activities as a publisher (for example, ethics or diversity policies)'	Six sites or 2.3% of all sites	Appears only at the following: elmundo.es, 20minutos.es, elpais.com (Spain), belfastlive.co.uk, bbc.com (UK) and scmp.com (Hong Kong)
Relevance	'keywords'	'Keywords or tags used to describe some item'	60% of all sites	In 32 of the 44 countries, more than half of the media sites use 'keywords'
Freshness	'Expires'	'Date at which the content expires and is no longer useful or available, for example, a VideoObject or NewsArticle whose availability or relevance is time-limited, or a ClaimReview fact check whose publisher wants to indicate that it may no longer be relevant (or helpful to highlight) after some date'	Eight sites or 2.7% of all sites	A very diverse group of sites: cdm.me, dagbladet.no, derstandard.at, edition.cnn.com, laprovincia.es, mail.ru, politiken.dk and tilestwra.com
	'DateModified'	'The date at which the CreativeWork was most recently modified'	One site	suomenkuvalehti.fi
	'SchemaFound'	Indicates that the page adheres to the Schema.org structured data vocabulary	42% of all sites	No clear pattern found, slightly higher appearance in sites found in countries outside Europe (25%)
Compliance tags	'google-site-verification'	Indicates that a website owner has been verified by Google	18% of all sites	

Sources: Gingras (2019); Google (2021); Google Search Central (nd); Schema.org (nda)

in the game for attention and publicity by trying to guess which tags will generate attention, but as long as one does not know the rules of the game, tagging remains a blind business.

Google News Initiative informs publishers that freshness, authoritativeness and relevance can be signalled to crawlers using 'technology to organize the news, and then surface the most relevant and useful results based on the content and the source, as well as data like your location and, in some cases, interests' (Google News Initiative, nda, para 'approach'). Authoritativeness is signalled by being transparent about publishing principles and making it known through metadata that the content on the page is produced by a media organization ('@type'). In our empirical data, we observe that very few media organizations use news media-specific tags (for example, 'publishingprinciples'). Google also reports that it highlights original reporting from trusted sources. As observed in our empirical data, there seems to be a connection between the use of journalism-specific metadata tags and the prominence of the news organization. One might fear that this can lead to a situation wherein smaller news outlets that cannot or will not prioritize the engineering and strategic design effort that goes into tagging consciously to gain editorial privileges on Google Search will be ranked below large players, such as *El Pais* and the *New York Times*. While Google is resolute about its societal aim of supporting quality journalism, there remains the question of what it means to news and publics that Google and the three other search engines involved in building the Schema.org vocabulary are involved in making sense of the news. In essence publics are being constructed by the newspapers' tagging and the platforms' automated selection of news based on that tagging. While the monopoly is worrying to, for example, *The Guardian's* head of engineering, it is also helpful to publishers aiming to make their content available now and in the future across various platforms and interfaces (TV 2, for example). However, further research is required to fully understand this phenomenon, along with the consequences to publics and their world-building in this set of semantic logics.

Discussion

Using the analogy of learning how to 'dress to impress', we conclude that most of the news sites do not make much effort to appear as *news* sites in the algorithmic 'eyes' of information-hungry search engines. In fact, most news sites do very little to get noticed, and only a few use tags that specifically signal (quality) 'news'. In comparison, more sites use basic tags, indicating that the (news-)content is fresh or that the site is a reliable source. We do not know the reasons for all of the websites examined, but the interview quotes presented in this chapter do not express a sense of urgency to be noticed by the algorithms. However, there could be good reasons for not 'dressing up for Google's party' as we phrase it. Since the introduction of Google News (Ojala, 2002) and the appearance of news summaries in Google's search engine, we have seen repeated conflicts between news publishers and Google on the topic of intellectual property rights (Van Asbroeck and Cock, 2007; Marcos Recio et al, 2015; Saiz García, 2022). Furthermore, newspapers have followed different and often changing strategies in distributing news outside their own platforms. This is driven partly by the fear of losing readers by not being present on the external sites and partly by concerns regarding losing traffic on their own sites, with the implications of the declining sales of advertisements and sparse, data-driven consumer insights. The lack of legitimacy in using the tags could be another reason for the reluctant uptake. When everybody can claim that they have, for example, won an award, the value of mentioning this is diminished. Currently, to our knowledge, there is no verification of a news media's use of tags, but Google reports that it internally evaluates the quality of the web sources (Google, 2021).

As a surprising finding, we see that 'Big Tech' apparently favours 'Big Media', meaning major news media outlets that are already established. In the Google News Initiative blog, Richard Gingras, Google VP of News, explains how Google has made changes to its algorithms to favour original reporting (Gingras, 2019).[18] In addition, the Google-employed human search raters are, in their guidelines, instructed to look for reputation of websites: 'you might find that a newspaper (with an associated website) has won journalistic awards. Prestigious awards or a history of high-quality original reporting are strong evidence of positive reputation for news websites' (Google, 2021, p 22). As we have observed in our interviews and in the metadata, large, established legacy media organizations are more likely to have their metadata optimized. When authoritativeness is operationalized through accumulated trust, awards and exclusive reporting, there are arguably advantages to being part of the 'old' media. In comparison, newer media outlets may struggle to be seen, falling behind in terms of accumulated integrity in the eyes of Google and possessing the resources to conduct investigative reporting. Furthermore, implementing the proper metadata tags takes developer resources, as we observed in our interviews. In combatting disinformation and providing the most relevant answers to user queries, this might be a step forward as opposed to the approach applied by Facebook: 'everything is news' and source does not matter. However, it might come with its own risk of encouraging some media organizations, overlooking other journalistic forces working to get accreditation and utilizing the same journalistic principles and ideals as major players. The Google News Initiative does work with smaller publishers and local news and gives them tools and resources to report and do better financially; however, there seem to be diverging strategies between these two actions.

As discussed, metadata is a prerequisite for storing, retrieving and making information useful (Pomerantz, 2015). As such, metadata organizes the world so we can document it and subsequently remember it, make it available and, perhaps, act upon it. When we consider journalism and its aims to serve the public, metadata serves the functions of making news reach the public and linking information about the world as it is covered by the media. For example, linking articles to one another to make a collection of coverage on a given US presidential period requires an agreement on how we might describe the content of an article in relation to our understanding of a period in history, its actors and its relevance to adjacent topics, among others. In addition, it requires an agreement as to what constitutes journalism, who can deliver on the normative principles of journalism and how we might operationalize these principles in metadata markup.

One could also argue that metadata tagging, particularly in the form of hashtags, rectifies and homogenizes multifaceted life-world experiences into simple arguments and predictable opinions. Related to this, a question arises as to who is to blame: the providers of the technology or those who use it. That classic news media hesitate to apply Google's metadata tags to their content could thus be seen not only as a lack of business interest in making the content even more accessible to Google, but also as a sign of keeping the power of interpretation – in terms of metadata indexing – 'in-house': If media organizations via internal metadata systems are capable of presenting the public and the readers with a good product, why would they delegate the power of describing and organizing the news to Google? By insisting on controlling the metadata indexing, the media may insist that they see themselves as the creators of the datafied publics and not mere tech platforms; that is, metadata indexing is not a technical activity, but an editorial one.

Conclusion

As previously discussed at the beginning of this chapter, external platforms are increasingly used by audiences worldwide to access news (Newman et al, 2021, 2022). While there are many ways to seek or consume news, there is no avoiding the fact that search engines are important in getting the news delivered to the public. Furthermore, according to Google's News Initiative, the search engines' understanding of relations among events, topics and issues of the world influences what, how and when users are shown which news in search results (Google News Initiative, nda). This could influence not only individual media organizations' ability to reach an audience but also the representation of the news story being covered. From our data, we have reason to conclude that most news organizations do not prioritize, are against or possibly unaware of the opportunities in using the metadata tags introduced by Google and Schema.org. The publics created via search engines, based on metadata, could thus be skewed by giving more visibility to news articles that are the most compliant with the metadata recommendations of Schema.org and Google for publishers. However, we will reserve this question for future research. Another limitation of our research is the lack of a full picture of how media companies internally use metadata. In particular, we do not know the metadata architecture of the news organizations, such as whether they have metadata vocabularies other than those implemented by Schema.org (most do, according to samples). Finally, Google's methods for selecting and ranking news remain one of the most under-researched areas in the media industry.

In this work, we have examined the idea that metadata is the key to search engine attention, and thus for the datafied construction of the public. First, we examined a technology-deterministic argument that metadata is to search engines and news aggregators what newspaper/webpage layout is to humans: a way to get attention. As no constraints or restrictions exist to which or how many tags a news website can add to its webpages, one should – following a simple logic of exposure – assume to find a multitude of tags. Instead, we found that the 260 websites we examined use a few very generic tags. We do not know whether news organizations are not considering tags as a way to make news stories more visible, or whether applying the strategic intention of not prioritizing readers from search engines play a role in this phenomenon. With respect to tagging, the power of search engines and content aggregators seems to be limited, and many news media outlets do not do much to help search engines find relevant content faster. However, for the public, there might be a bias, as not all news media do equally much (or equally little) to be discovered by search engines. Furthermore, tags may add dubious credibility to low-quality 'news sites' (for example, certain web portals in our sample) that, in reality, do not meet journalistic principles. Thus, tagging is not a sign of quality, as its reliability for the public is little.

Notes

[1] https://www.dublincore.org.
[2] https://schema.org/docs/datamodel.html.
[3] tv2.dk.
[4] www.theguardian.com.
[5] https://www.amedia.no.
[6] https://newsinitiative.withgoogle.com/hownewsworks/mission/help-you-make-sense-of-the-news/.
[7] https://newsinitiative.withgoogle.com/hownewsworks/mission/help-you-make-sense-of-the-news/.
[8] https://elpais.com/espana/2022-04-01/el-pp-recupera-el-legado-de-rajoy-para-volver-al-pp-mas-clasico.html.
[9] At Information.dk, we found five tags: @type, dateModified, about, articleSection and genre.

[10] At tv2.dk we found two tags: @type and audience. This does not mean there are not other tags, this only reflects the tags inspected for this chapter.

[11] At theguardian.com we found five tags: schemaFound, @type, dateModified, associatedMedia and audience.

[12] Off-platform refers to a platform on which news can be featured or distributed. For example, Google News.

[13] www.dr.dk.

[14] The 260 news websites were selected to represent 43 countries in Europe (EU, EEA, non-EU) and a few countries from outside Europe. For private media, we chose the top five most popular news sites (a total of 117 websites) for countries featured in the Reuters Institute Digital News Report 2017. For other countries, we used Alexa's list of top news sites (78 websites) and manual search via Google (7 sites). For public media, membership in the European Broadcasting Union was used as a criterion. For links redirecting to the same website (for example, the case for many German public service websites), only one page was analysed. We visited each news site three times with an interval of 14 days (24 February 2022, 10 March 2022 and 24 March 2022, respectively), selecting a new page for every visit. We see a high stability of the appearance of the tags (except the 'about' tag), which means that we are confident in drawing conclusions based on the three samples.

[15] The top news story was defined as the biggest picture at the top-left side of the page that was not an advertisement or an internal link. At pages where no pictures were shown, we selected the text link found on the top left.

[16] https://schema.org, 'google-site-verification', '@type', 'dateModified', 'about', 'articleSection', 'Backstory', 'Speakable', 'Abstract', 'alternativeHeadline', 'Archived', 'associatedMedia', 'audience', 'Award', 'character ', 'citation', 'contentLocation', 'correctionCorrection', 'creativeWorkStatus', 'Date Created', 'datePublished', 'Expires', 'Genre', 'Keywords', 'interactionStatistic', 'Mentions', 'publishingPrinciples', 'schemaVersion', 'sdDatePublished', 'sdPublisher', 'alternateName' and 'disambiguatingDescription'.

[17] heute.at (Austria), mail.ru (Belarus), vrt.be (Belgium), sigmalive.com (Cyprus), yahoo.com (Greece), independent.ie (Ireland), tvm.com.mt (Malta), stirileprotv.ro (Romania), eldiario.es, elconfidencial.com (Spain), expressen.se (Sweden), dailymail. co.uk, belfasttelegraph.co.uk, buzzfeed.com, belfastlive.co.uk (UK), nytimes.com, washingtonpost.com, newyorker.com (US).

[18] https://blog.google/products/search/original-reporting/.

References

Berners-Lee, T., Hendler, J. and Lassila, O. (2001) 'The semantic web', *Scientific American*, 284(5), pp 34–43. Available at: https://www.jstor.org/stable/10.2307/26059207.

Black, R. (2022) 'Roy Reynolds suffered "barbaric injuries", court told', *Belfast Live*, 1 April. Available at: https://www.belfastlive.co.uk/news/belfast-news/roy-reynolds-suffered-barbaric-injuries-23563257.

Bowker, G.C. and Star, S.L. (1999) *Sorting Things Out: Classification and Its Consequences*, Cambridge, MA: MIT Press.

Brin, S. and Page, L. (1998) 'The anatomy of a large-scale hypertextual Web search engine', in *Proceedings of the Seventh International Conference on World Wide Web 7*, Elsevier Science, pp 107–117.

Caple, H. and Bednarek, M. (2016) 'Rethinking news values: What a discursive approach can tell us about the construction of news discourse and news photography', *Journalism*, 17(4), pp 435–455.

Caswell, D. (2019) 'Structured journalism and the semantic units of news', *Digital Journalism*, 7(8), pp 1134–1156. Available at: https://doi.org/10.1080/21670811.2019.1651665.

Gingras, R. (2019) 'Elevating original reporting in Search', *Google*. Available at: https://blog.google/products/search/original-reporting.

Google (nd) 'Fact check markup tool', *Google*. Available at: https://toolbox.google.com/factcheck/about#fcmt.

Google (2021) 'Search quality evaluator guidelines', *Google*. Available at: https://static.googleusercontent.com/media/guidelines.raterhub.com/da//searchqualityevaluatorguidelines.pdf.

Google News Initiative (nda) *How News Works*. Available at: https://newsinitiative.withgoogle.com/hownewsworks/mission.

Google News Initiative (ndb) *Surfacing Useful and Relevant Content*. Available at: https://newsinitiative.withgoogle.com/hownewsworks/approach/surfacing-useful-and-relevant-content/.

Google Search Central (nd) *Documentation: Understand How Structured Data Works*. Available at: https://developers.google.com/search/docs/advanced/structured-data/intro-structured-data.

Guha, R.V., Brickley, D. and MacBeth, D. (2015) 'Schema.org: Evolution of structured data on the web: Big data makes common schemas even more necessary', *Queue*, 13(9), pp 10–37. Available at: https://doi.org/10.1145/2857274.2857276.

Hogan, A., Hitzler, P. and Janowicz, K. (2020) 'The semantic web: Two decades on', *Semantic Web*, 11(1), pp 169–185.

Kleis Nielsen, R. and Ganter, S.A. (2018) 'Dealing with digital intermediaries: A case study of the relations between publishers and platforms', *New Media & Society*, 20(4), pp 1600–1617. Available at: https://doi.org/10.1177/1461444817701318.

Kristensen, L.M. (2021) 'Audience metrics: Operationalizing news value for the digital newsroom', *Journalism Practice*, pp 1–18.

Lassen, J.M. and Sørensen, J.K. (2023) 'From broadcast volume to on-demand value: DR's 2019 strategic response to changes in Danish media policy', in M. Puppis and C. Ali (eds) *RIPE@2021 'Public Service Media's Contribution to Society'*, Göteborg: Nordicom.

Leigh Star, S. (2010) 'This is not a boundary object: Reflections on the origin of a concept', *Science, Technology, & Human Values*, 35(5), pp 601–617.

Manovich, L. (2002) *The Language of New Media*, Cambridge, MA: MIT Press.

Marcos Recio, J.C., Sánchez Vigil, J.M. and Olivera Zaldua, M. (2015) 'Google News y el impacto de la Ley de Propiedad Intelectual en la prensa: un nuevo amanecer para la información', *Documentación de Las Ciencias de La Información*, 38, pp 67–81.

Marlow, C., Naaman, M., Boyd, D. and Davis, M. (2006) 'HT06, tagging paper, taxonomy, Flickr, academic article, to read', in *Proceedings of the Seventeenth Conference on Hypertext and Hypermedia 2013 HYPERTEXT '06*, Odense: ACM Press, pp 31–40.

Martinez, J.M. (2002) 'Standards: MPEG-7 overview of MPEG-7 description tools, part 2', *IEEE Multimedia*, 9(3), pp 83–93.

Martínez, J.M., Koenen, R. and Pereira, F. (2002) 'MPEG-7: The generic multimedia content description standard, part 1', *IEEE Multimedia*, 9(2), pp 78–87.

Newman, N., Fletcher, R., Schulz, A., Andi, S., Robertson, C. and Nielsen, R.K. (2021) *Reuters Institute Digital News Report 2021*, Reuters Institute for the Study of Journalism. Available at: https://reutersinstitute.politics. ox.ac.uk/digital-news-report/2021.

Newman, N., Fletcher, R., Schulz, A., Andi, S., Robertson, C. and Nielsen, R.K. (2022) *Reuters Institute Digital News Report 2022*, Reuters Institute for the Study of Journalism. Available at: https://reutersinstitute.politics. ox.ac.uk/digital-news-report/2022.

Ojala, M. (2002) 'Google expands Google News', *Information Today*, 19(10)

Parks, P. (2019) 'Textbook news values: Stable concepts, changing choices', *Journalism & Mass Communication Quarterly*, 96(3), pp 784–810. Available at: https://doi.org/10.1177/1077699018805212.

Pellegrini, T. (2017) 'Semantic metadata in the publishing industry: Technological achievements and economic implications', *Electronic Markets*, 27(1), pp 9–20.

Pomerantz, J. (2015) *Metadata*, Cambridge, MA: MIT Press.

Saiz García, C. (2022) 'Spain: The return of Google News', *GRUR International*, 71(2), pp 99–100.

Schema.org (nda) *ReportageNewsArticle*. Available at: https://schema.org/ ReportageNewsArticle.

Schema.org (ndb) *Markup for News*. Available at: https://schema.org/docs/ news.html#acks.

Search Console Help (nd) *Verify Your Site Ownership*. Available at: https:// support.google.com/webmasters/answer/9008080.

Shadbolt, N., Berners-Lee, T. and Hall, W. (2006) 'The semantic web revisited', *IEEE Intelligent Systems*, 21(3), pp 96–101.

Sørensen, J.K. (2020) 'The datafication of public service media dreams, dilemmas and practical problems: A case study of the implementation of personalized recommendations at the Danish public service media "DR"', *MedieKultur: Journal of Media and Communication Research*, 69, pp 90–115.

Sørensen, J.K. and Kosta, S. (2019) 'Before and after GDPR: The changes in third party presence at public and private European websites', *WWW '19: The World Wide Web Conference*. Presented at the WWW '19 Companion Proceedings of the Web Conference 2019.

Star, S.L. (1998) 'Grounded classification: Grounded theory and faceted classification', *Library Trends*, 47(2), pp 218–232.

Tuchman, G. (1978) *Making News: A Study in the Construction of Reality*, New York and London: Free Press.

Van Asbroeck, B. and Cock, M. (2007) 'Belgian newspapers v Google News: 2–0', *Journal of Intellectual Property Law & Practice*, 2(7), pp 463–466.

Appendix

Tags monitored

SchemaFound, googleSiteVerification, @type, dateModified, about, articleSection, Backstory, Speakable, Abstract, alternativeHeadline, Archived, associatedMedia, audience, Award, character, citation, contentLocation, correctionCorrection, creativeWorkStatus, Date Created, datePublished, Expires, Genre, Keywords, interactionStatistic, Mentions, publishingPrinciples, schemaVersion, sdDatePublished, sdPublisher, alternateName and disambiguatingDescription.

Countries covered

Albania, Austria, Belarus, Belgium, Bosnia-Herzegovina, Bulgaria, Canada, Croatia, Cyprus, Czech Republic, Denmark, Estonia, Finland, France, Germany, Greece, Hong Kong, Hungary, Iceland, Ireland, Italy, Latvia, Lithuania, Luxembourg, Malta, Moldova, Montenegro, Netherlands, North Macedonia, Norway, Poland, Portugal, Romania, Russia, Serbia, Slovakia, Slovenia, Spain, Sweden, Switzerland, the UK, Ukraine and the US.

8

Infrastructuring Publics: Datafied Infrastructures of the News Media

Lisa Merete Kristensen and Jannick Kirk Sørensen

Introduction

Digital platforms are increasingly intertwined with everyday lives of citizens and are even argued to take on infrastructure status, being fundamental to the functioning of society at large (Helmond, 2015; Plantin et al, 2018; van Dijck et al, 2018). Our goal here is to empirically investigate how platformization is making its way into the sector of journalism through being part of the technological foundation of media websites, thereby potentially becoming an infrastructure of not only the media, but also of the societal function of media as a cultivator of publics. By combining a platformization perspective and an infrastructures perspective, this chapter sets out to dissect the vast number of intertwining actors and interactions sustaining public formation. From the perspective of journalistic media organizations, we examine the reciprocal influence of digital infrastructures on the media's ability to maintain the journalistic ideals of facilitating public access to and deliberation of information as participants in a democratic society. In practice, our analysis examines the systems consciously built into the web architectures of media organizations' websites, such as content management practices and audience measurement techniques, as well as the structures, or off-platform integrations, connecting the organizations' content and services to the audience – that is, potential publics. We rely on a predominantly material approach to the concept of infrastructure proposed by, among others, Flensburg (2020), which entails looking at the composition and design of systems to uncover the ways in which they are used, the capabilities they afford, and subsequently how they might affect the social world (Flensburg, 2020, pp 81–82).

We argue that this empirical perspective allows for a more comprehensive look at the influence of Big Tech, which we argue to be important. In narratives on technology, Big Tech is regularly cast as both a vessel for progress and objectivity in decision-making and a threat to fundamental areas of public and private life (see also Chapter 1 in this volume). Here we argue that the (otherwise very justified, as this chapter will also reveal) significance placed on companies like Google, Amazon, Facebook and Microsoft can hinder exploration of the full scope of the dynamics involved, encompassing large, medium and many small technological players. This, to borrow from photography terminology, wide-angle lens is reflected throughout the individual parts of this chapter:

We begin by introducing the theoretical backdrop and conceptual argument for this chapter, stressing the need to address technological players of all levels and sizes to understand their significance for the digital infrastructures upholding the media and, thus, to understand the role media plays for the infrastructuring of publics. In the second section, we focus on the individual components of the technological infrastructures surrounding the media, operationalized as systems and technologies that ensure the media's ability to make information available to the public and make deliberation and discussions on issues possible in a democracy. By outlining the most widely used systems in the media, while paying specific attention to the providers of these systems, we developed an overview of the many actors involved in sustaining the production and distribution of news. We argue that they are by default also involved in the cultivation of publics by means of providing infrastructures for the distribution of news. In the third part we dig deeper into the extent to which Big Tech is involved in sustaining media websites and present the results of a mapping of external third-party web services on 361 European media websites over a period of 20 months. Finally, the chapter discusses the implications of this interdependency between news media and its underlying technologies for the ability of media to serve the public.

Media and the public

In an ideal world, media organizations serve more than advertisers and audiences (Picard, 2005): they provide a service to the public, who rely on the media for 'information gathering, deliberation and action' (Fenton, 2010). According to Caple (2018), journalists honour these needs of the public by scrutinizing powerful actors from society and by enabling publics and potential publics through 'stories that are important for people to know in order to participate in democratic governance and to function effectively and knowledgeably in society' (Caple, 2018, p 2). Ahva and Heikkilä found that people do in fact use media coverage as a starting point for private and offline discussions (2016, p 320) and argue that the act of sharing news online not only makes more people in the network aware of public issues but encourage sharing news and opinions altogether (2016, p 321). Strömbäck highlighted how upholding the social contract between journalism and society requires 'a system for the flow of information, for public discussion and for a watchdog function independent of the state' (2005, p 332). Of course, as Strömbäck noted, these statements are broad, and they are bound to both normative standards of democracy and normative expectations of the public (2005, p 337). Nevertheless, we find these three requirements, or functions, of the democratic press to be of analytical guidance, as it connects the 'old' world of journalism to 'the new' in which a new set of potentially powerful actors are present. Thus, this is a key point in our empirical interest in interdependencies between the media and the technologies sustaining journalism.

Media infrastructures

Those who want to communicate a message need an infrastructure to support that communication. Strömbäck's earlier-mentioned 'system for the flow of information' (2005) is just that. Infrastructure, in crude terms, refers to an 'underlying foundation or basic framework' (Merriam-Webster, nd). For example, outside the range of a broadcast transmitter, a radio programme cannot be heard, and a television programme cannot be seen. The placement of radio transmitter pylons on hillsides and mountains and the strong emitting power they often possess, thus, have been prerequisite to the fulfilment of the national broadcasting projects (Lewis, 1991) and, accordingly, the cultural-political institution of public service broadcasting. In the digital world, the infrastructure is no longer comprised of a series of discrete entities, such as 'transmission tower' and 'radio receiver', but, instead, contains several layers in each entity. Smartphones, for example, hold apps, as well as an operating system, and they depend on a WiFi connection provided by an Internet service provider or on the base station of a mobile operator (see Flensburg and Lai, 2020). When a webpage or an app is accessed through a smartphone, the phone employs various protocols to establish and maintain the communication with a web server. These protocols themselves use more basic protocols to keep the connection alive. Finally, the user's antenna and location, including country, define how well the user receives the signal. Communicating a message (or a news article in this context), in today's datafied news media similarly depends on several subsystems, variables, parameters, operating systems, browsers and more.

Infrastructure as a concept is not easy to grasp as it takes on many meanings and functions in research contexts (Flensburg, 2020; Hesmondhalgh, 2021). Here, we rely on the material approach used by Sofie Flensburg which entails looking at the underlying foundations that sustain communication

(Flensburg, 2020, pp 78–81). Individual systems mentioned by other scholars taking this approach to examining digital infrastructures include 'software, data, and technologies from outside newsrooms' (Ananny and Finn, 2020), 'search engines and related systems' (Nardi and O'Day, 1999) and 'protocols (human and computer), standards, and memory' (Bowker et al, 2009, p 97). The approach here is a micro perspective on the relation between the media tech stack as an infrastructure of a given media outlet which we use as a foundation for discussing the internet and its platforms as an infrastructure of media and publics. Here we draw analytically on the reflections of Elizabeth Shove; 'something becomes an "infrastructure" when it stands in an infrastructural role in relation to one or more practices' (Baringhorst et al, 2019, p 77). There are of course characteristics of infrastructures that we can employ to determine what possesses the 'status' of an infrastructure. To illustrate, the internet fits the overall characteristics of any infrastructure, as it is:

> [R]eliable, transparent, widely shared, and visible to users mainly when it breaks down. Its many uses are learned as part of membership in contemporary society. It provides essential services, so much a part of commerce, government, work, and everyday life that whole societies would be crippled if some catastrophe caused it to collapse. (Plantin et al, 2018, p 301)

Focusing on the tech stacks of the news media might at first glance seem insufficient in the grand scheme of digital communication infrastructures, but in working our way from inside the media and out, we can reveal both dependencies and interdependencies at play between the media and the technologies supporting the media's service to the public and ability to cultivate those publics. Thus, if we are to make sense of the positions and narratives put forth in the literature and in public discourse, we must consider where we in practice can observe the actual interactions and exchanges between media and media infrastructures that are potentially infrastructuring the formation and cultivation of publics.

Mapping the infrastructural components of media websites

As mentioned earlier, we take our point of departure from tech stacks – the combination of technologies that a news site is composed of or 'runs on'. Then we examine how this local architecture both reaches out to the wider infrastructure of the internet and how platforms, themselves considered infrastructural players (Plantin and Punathambekar, 2019), are entrenched in tech stacks. The mapping is based on qualitative interviews with developers in legacy news media, fieldwork, attendance at industry conferences, a systematic reading of media profiles on the stackshare.io website, Reuters Institute reports, a mapping of third-party cookies on media websites for this chapter and by searching for systems marketed for the media industry that publish media customer testimonials. In our mapping we identify three categories of technologies in the media tech stacks:

1. production and publishing technologies;
2. distribution technologies; and
3. technologies that enable the commercial viability of media.

The technologies are to different degrees the foundations of the news media. We summarize this effort in Table 8.1, where we organize these widely used systems in the tech stacks of Western media according to their function in practice while also noting the corporate ownership of systems. Not all media organizations make use of each individual technology, and if so, not necessarily to the same extent. In addition, as is the nature of infrastructures, there are many overlaps between versions and functions of systems.

Technologies enabling commercial viability of news media

We start by observing a group of technologies that are perhaps relatively unappreciated in the newsroom, but nonetheless make up a significant part of the average media tech stack: technologies that enable the news media to manage user profiles, online subscriptions, market analysis and advertising. Although the media historically has aimed to keep advertising and editorial interests separate, the commercial viability of a media organization serves as a prerequisite for contributing to the flow of quality news.

Media companies traditionally generate revenue through advertising and subscription sales, along with possible subsidies or donations. Online advertising can be sold the 'old-fashioned way' practised during the days of the printed paper, selling ads and banners for the website directly by communicating with potential advertisers. Alternatively, advertising can be sold programmatically through ad exchanges via the process of real-time bidding. Particularly in the latter case, extensive knowledge about the target group and group members' behaviours and preferences is the basis of the interaction, as the sales price for the ad depends on the level of detail in the profiling for the specific user visiting a specific webpage. Therefore, both media and ad brokers have a strong financial interest in user profiling. Technologies that facilitate this programmatic ad-exchange process include, for example, customer data platforms, ad server plug-ins and audience measurement systems tailored for commercial analytics. Depending on the business model of the media organization, technologies that register, recognize and categorize audience members also indirectly contribute to the flow of information. For example, a premium business model may focus on recruiting subscribers and reaching new potential subscribers, thus directing selected pieces of content in the direction of possibly interested users by promoting it on Facebook. However, the advertising industry has been forced to find new methods to sell ads to audiences because the General Data Protection Regulation (GDPR) and many browsers have made the well-known cookie technology obsolete (Acar et al, 2014; Urban et al, 2020; IAB Europe, 2021). The public, in the advertising context, equals the optimization of exposure, ideally the audience segment of 'one' person (cf Peppers and Rogers, 1993). To summarize, media firms are dual-demand companies, serving both advertisers and audiences (Picard, 2005), and audiences are rather considered segments than potential publics in the development of these systems.

Production and publishing technologies

This category includes technologies that assist journalists in producing the news, traditionally involving the steps: access and observation, selection/filtering, processing/editing, distribution and interpretation (Domingo et al, 2008, p 328). For example, content management systems (CMS) allow journalists to write stories directly into a template without worrying about HTML coding. Visualization tools embedded in a CMS can be used to create interactive maps if needed. The journalist can then press 'publish' to distribute the news article, and the editor can prioritize its placement on the front page. All without worrying too much about technical functionality.

Most systems allow journalists to add relevant in-text hyperlinks ('read more'), but some media organizations use recommender algorithms to calculate the relevant hyperlinks according to user preferences, content characteristics and other factors deemed relevant (Just and Latzer, 2017). By monitoring web metrics – powered by web analytics tags automatically placed in the HTML of each news page – an editor may assess whether the article needs a new headline, a follow-up or any other change. Audience measurement systems are usually used by managers and journalists to evaluate and make decisions about news selection and the prioritization of resources for existing and new editorial projects.

Distribution technologies

The distribution technologies category contains infrastructurally critical technologies that connect news items to the internet. News audiences in the 21st century are more prone to being 'discovered' by the news than to 'discovering' it themselves. Therefore, most news organizations place high priority on establishing visibility outside their news website. This can be done by meta-tagging news articles to be indexed by search engines, by posting or accepting posts on social media platforms, by allowing others to feature news content on other web pages (public APIs, RSS), allowing content to be featured on news aggregators, signing up for Google AMP and so on. These technologies share a common feature in that they require the signing over part of the autonomy by the media organization, editorially and economically. For example, being visible on news aggregators or being featured on voice assistants may result in fewer ad views on the news site, while being visible on social media and in search results means adhering to community standards and norms and their regulations. This can influence the type of content that is produced, as selection decisions may be made to avoid having content banned or to try to 'game' the algorithms to be more visible (Napoli, 2014, p 343). This can also add to the menu of news genres already existing as content produced for TikTok or Facebook is bound to differ from content published on the news site.

Table 8.1 sums up our mapping of technologies and their different functions in sustaining media. Once again, we note that many of the systems cross over categories.

The table is not intended to represent all systems and corporate owners. For instance, Development Operations and productivity tools such as Google Workspace are not included. Moreover, we do not include journalistic tools for monitoring news, like Crowdtangle; only systems within the web architecture of the news media are considered. Again, we note that technologies should not be perceived as the determinants of how news and publics are infrastructured, nor should ownership of technologies. For example, some media companies develop their own solutions and are aware that they can switch providers when existing options are not suitable, as we will touch upon later in the chapter.

A journey into the forest and underwood of third-party services

Thus far we have mapped multiple web services, both popular and less known. We discovered that a few services, those provided by the Big Tech companies, get ample attention in the literature and public discourse, but we lack knowledge about the full picture of systems. To elaborate on van Dijck's metaphor of infrastructural layers as a tree (2020): what is the significance of the underwood in comparison to the redwoods of Big Tech in the deep forest of web services?

Indeed, publishing news in the digital age is a highly complex matter. In 2016, Kasper Lindskow published an analysis of the complex and large ecosystems of technology providers on which media organizations depend

Table 8.1: Technologies sustaining journalistic news media

Categories of infrastructural technologies in the media	Facilitation in practice	Technologies	Commonly used service providers
Technologies enabling commercial viability of media	Advertising	Ad exchange server	Google ads, Oracle responses
	Handling of subscriptions, log-in, customer profiles, customer engagement	Customer data platform	Twilio
		Audience measurement (for marketing purposes), customer relationship management, data warehouse	Tealium, Adform
	Audience insights, business intelligence		Google Analytics
	Strategy/resource allocation		BigQuery (Google), ElasticSearch
Production and publishing technologies	Content storage, content delivery	Server/database, content delivery network	Amazon DynamoDB, Fastly, AWS, CloudFront (Amazon), Cloudflare, Akamai, Microsoft Azure, Firebase
	Producing and publishing news to the news site and/or news app	CMS/publishing platform	Stibo CUE, Wordpress VIP, Sitecore, Drupal
	Adding storytelling elements and data to news articles	Storytelling and visualization tools	Infogram.com, Google Fusion Tables, Tableau Public
	Testing different versions of headlines on news articles	A/B testing	Chartbeat, Optimizely, Google Analytics
	News selection and prioritization of day-to-day editorial resources	Audience measurement system real time and aggregated over time (for editorial purposes)	Google Analytics 360 (Realtime Content Insights), Chartbeat, Parse.ly, ComScore, Gemius, Moat, Facebook Insights

Table 8.1: Technologies sustaining journalistic news media (continued)

Categories of infrastructural technologies in the media	Facilitation in practice	Technologies	Commonly used service providers
	Content organizing, analysis for automation and tagging	Transformer models (NLP) Topic/language modelling	Think Analytics, Cxense, Contentwise, GDP 1, 2, 3 (OpenAi/Microsoft), Google (BERT), Facebook (XLM Roberta), Huggingface (Huggingface), Google Tag Manager
	Automatic curation of news on the website	Recommender systems	Think Analytics, Cxense, Contentwise
Distribution technologies	News links shared to external platforms (by users and journalists)	Social media/debate fora, message apps	Facebook, Twitter, SnapChat, WeChat, Instagram, TikTok, Reddit
	Newsletters	Email newsletter services	MailChimp, HubSpot, SubStack
	Making news articles available on external platforms	Aggregation services (including podcast apps), voice assistants, pre-load article solutions	Apple News, Google News, Nachtrichten.de Apple Podcasts Alexa, Google Assistant Google AMP, Facebook Instant Articles News APIs
	Search	Search engines	Google Search (Alphabet), Bing (Microsoft), Yahoo

Sources: Interviews, provider websites, stackshare.io, fieldwork, Reuters Digital News Reports 2021/2022

when delivering news to the public (Lindskow, 2016). Using the US media as an example, Lindskow examined the extent to which external technology partners were involved when a media organization delivered a webpage to a user. He uncovered and mapped an impressive complexity of small tech and Big Tech companies, such as advertising, audience measurement, news content delivery, editorial tools and so on, participating in varying components of news production operations. Some three years later Sørensen and Kosta (2019) examined the equivalent ecology for 361 European media sites in a longitudinal study spanning 20 months between February 2018 and October 2019. Sørensen and Kosta (2019) and Sørensen et al (2020) applied a web privacy measurement perspective (Acar et al, 2014; Englehardt and Narayanan, 2016; Lerner et al, 2016) to observe possible changes in the ecosystem before and after commencement of a new European privacy regulation (GDPR), but the nature of the dataset allowed for an analysis inspired by the one presented by Lindskow (2016).

Our analysis draws on the longitudinal dataset collected by Sørensen and Kosta (2019) and it uncovers a picture that adds perspective to the narrative of the hegemony of Big Tech. Following Sørensen and Kosta (2019), we observed which so-called 'third-party' web services are loaded into users' browsers when they visit a news website. In the current study our focus was on how they help deliver the news product, sell advertisements or measure user behaviour. We found 3,669 distinct URLs. As was to be expected, Google accounted for 22 per cent of all third-party web service appearances, with a slow trajectory of expansion for other companies, including Facebook, with nine URLs[1] or 5 per cent of all appearances, and Twitter, with four URLs[2] or 2 per cent. Moreover, the top ten third-party companies, with their 76 URLs, accounted for 39.8 per cent of all appearances, whereas the 3,593 other URLs accounted for 60.1 per cent (see Figure 8.1 and Table 8.2). Table 8.2 sums up the number of third-party services found by provider and the prevalence of services pertaining to that provider.

Thus, the underwood of third-party services plays a perhaps too long overlooked role when news travels the web. As Scott Brinker showed in his yearly mapping of the marketing technology landscape, this underwood is big; for 2022 he finds 9,932 solutions for all types of publishing and advertising needs.[3] However, the omnipresence of the big web services provide these with a considerable advantage in terms of overview and data aggregation, for example, for trend prediction. Google's advertising service 'DoubleClick' is present at 85.87 per cent of the 361 news websites, Google Analytics is present at 84.21 per cent of the sites. In Figure 8.2 we show the distribution of the presence of URLs at the 361 news websites; a few URLs can be found at almost every news site. These are Google, Facebook, Twitter, Amazon, Chartbeat and Criteo. For other larger companies also present at many sites, see Box 8.1. A few companies

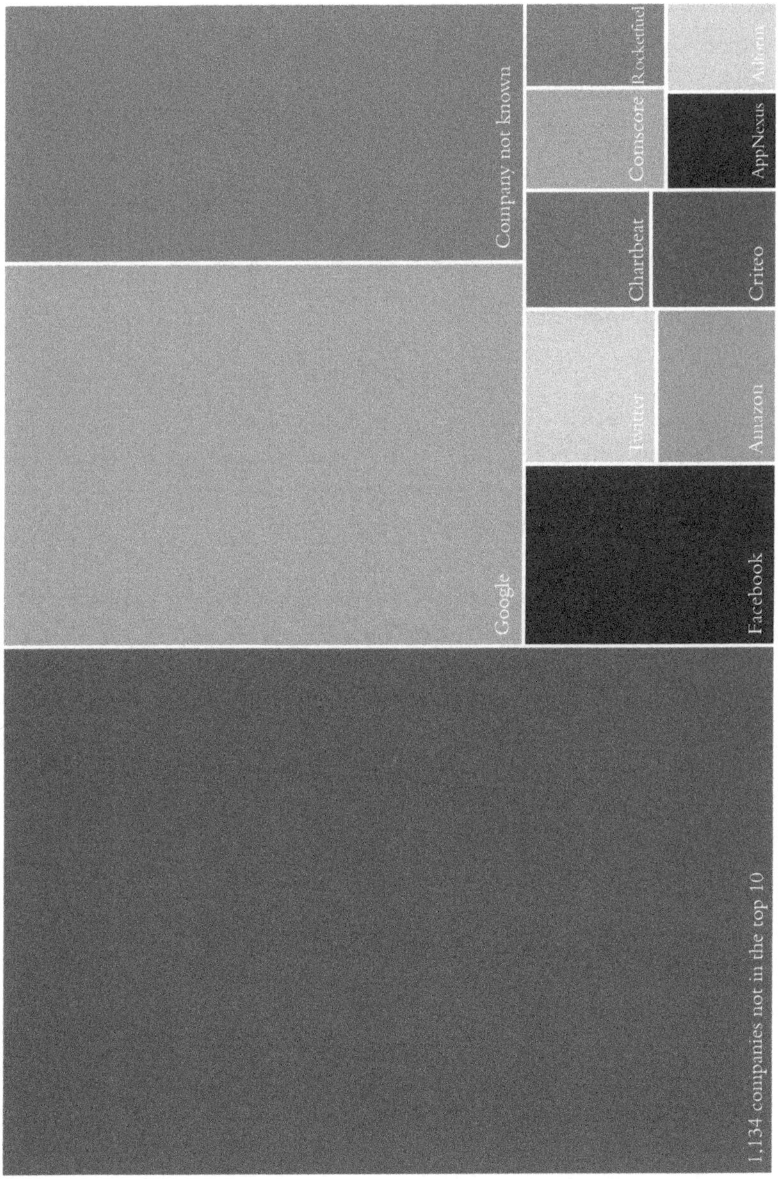

Figure 8.1: Prevalence of companies in the 'underwood' of third-party URLs

Table 8.2: Number of URLs and prevalence of third-party URLs

Third-party service	No of appearances	No of URLs
Companies not in the top 10 (1,134)	203,970	1,510
Google	99,456	33
Company not known	67,236	2,083
Facebook	22,781	9
Twitter	10,134	4
Amazon	9,243	12
Chartbeat	7,454	2
Criteo	7,423	2
Comscore	7,182	5
RocketFuel	5,958	3
AppNexus	5,414	2
Adform	4,931	4

Box 8.1: Other top ten third-party companies

Amazon: 12 URLs (cloudfront.net, amazonaws.com, amazon-adsystem.com, wp.com, amazon.fr, assoc-amazon.com, assoc-amazon.fr, prgmt.com, wpdigital.net, adtechjp.com, media-amazon.com, ssl-images-amazon.com); *Criteo*: two URLs (criteo.com, criteo.net); *Comscore*: five URLs (scorecardresearch.com, voicefive.com, sitestat.com, zqtk. net, adxpose.com); *RocketFuel*: three URLs (2mdn.net, rfihub.com, rfihub.net); *AppNexus*: two URLs (adnxs.com, prebid.org); *AdForm*: four URLs (adform.net, seadform.net, adformdsp.net, adform.com).

thus play a leading role in the ecology of news production, while a large underwood of URLs is performing specialized tasks for each individual news site. However, the underwood has declined over time, while the number of Google appearances have grown slightly. We cannot make any conclusions as to why this is the case.

Figure 8.3 visualizes a classification of the third-party web services according to their purpose. It illustrates that advertising constitutes the biggest share, followed by web analytics, which was an outcome we expected.

Five categories accounted for fewer than 1 per cent of all appearances: 'plug-in' (0.8 per cent), 'retail' (0.77 per cent), 'malicious' (0.595 per cent), 'privacy' (0.4 per cent) and 'cybersecurity' (0.04 per cent). For a detailed definition of categories, see Sørensen and Kosta (2019). Overall, we see that the category of

Figure 8.2: The long-tail of third-party presence at 361 news sites

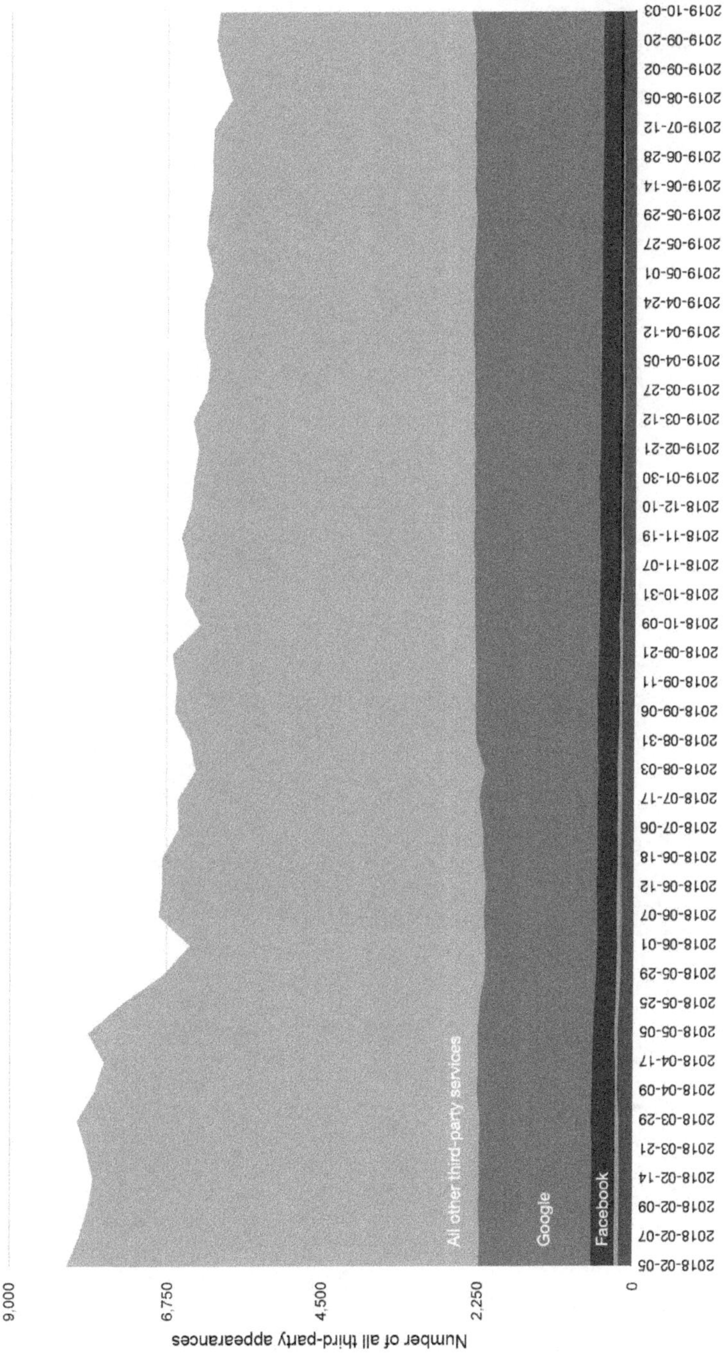

177

Figure 8.3: The total number of third-party appearances at the media sites arranged by category

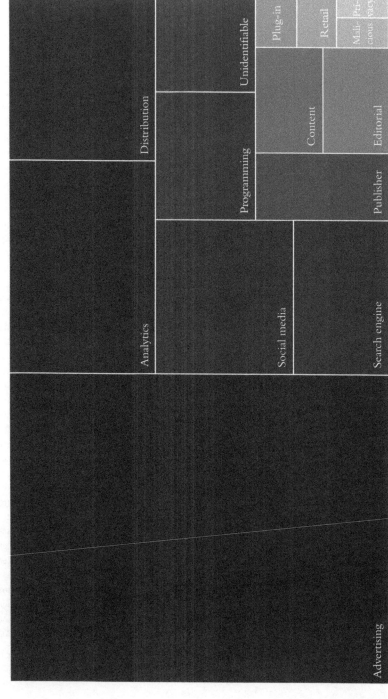

Note: Cybersecurity is the least occuring third-party and represents 170 of the total number of appearances (431.440). See the box in the bottom right-hand corner.

technologies enabling the commercial viability of media holds the biggest share when we take a functional view of the third-parties sustaining the media online.

Discussion

In the following, we discuss the significance of the interdependencies between media and the infrastructures sustaining it. We structure our discussion of this chapter's findings according to the following themes:

- public access to information;
- legitimization of issues and publics; and
- audience imaginaries and journalistic production.

Public access to information

It is evident from our empirical data that a multitude of systems inside the tech stack of media websites function to further chances of being visible on the internet, in essence providing potential publics with information. A clear observation was the extent to which the 'Big Tech' companies were present in all categories of our tech stack mapping. Alphabet's (Google's parent company) products are used to keep track of subscribers and visitors to the website, they are used to create visualizations for news stories, they are used to sell advertisements programmatically, they are used to structure the unstructured data that is news, they are setting standards for how to classify news and users, and they are used to distribute news via for example voice assistants and search (see Table 8.1). By the sheer prevalence of Google products in our empirical data we can see that the company holds significant power in deciding which classifications are appropriate for users, for news content, and which variables are best suited to evaluate the needs of users in terms of receiving the information relevant to them. To incorporate systems built by companies that are taking on an infrastructural status (Plantin et al, 2018) means standardizing data variables so data and content can move smoothly between platforms (Star and Ruhleder, 1996; Helmond, 2015). For the individual and potential member of multiple publics this means that you are defined using the same characteristics as others, while other immeasurable characteristics or overlooked characteristics are not accounted for. Worries are that the standardization would further the commercialization of news and segmentation of audiences and would negatively affect the diversity of information being presented on third-party platforms. This means that the access to information might be based on an anticipation of the public one could potentially belong to or already belongs to (Ananny and Finn, 2020).

An overlooked aspect is the disparity of legitimacy, visibility and ability to keep data within the news organization between news media outlets such as the *New York Times*, a local newspaper and a digital native news startup. One immense difference is resources – larger news organizations are able to make choices in regard to building their own systems or tailoring the existing systems. For example, *The Guardian* developed Ophan to circumvent the role of external companies dictating which metrics were appropriate. Ophan still runs on the ElasticSearch data platform, however. Smaller media outlets seem less likely to take control over elements in their tech stack as it would be difficult to maintain and troubleshoot the systems. Being affiliated with systems out of Big Tech is more reliable and cheaper, which is key in a trying media market. We did see the medium-sized news outlet *Information* dropping the services of MailChimp and instead choosing an external system provider with an accessible developer team to sustain its distribution of news via email. Still, legacy media companies are more likely to hold the resources to explore new technical possibilities. An example of this is the use of Natural Language Processing (NLP) transformer models to tag content which among other things allows for a smoother analytics flow and structure news texts to make it recognizable to search engines and 'ready' for other platforms, now and in the future. We argue that this is a gap in the literature where there is a need for examining the influence of legacy media players and what it means for smaller media outlets that are not in advance marked 'authoritative' or 'trusted' by, for example, the Google Search crawlers. This could mean that perspectives are lost, insights from sources not usually used by legacy media are lost, and this would greatly affect the ability of publics to be aware of issues and form around them.

Public cultivation and formation

In normative accounts of the media's role as an infrastructure of public cultivation and formation, the media should be active in connecting all types of citizens to 'foster public discussions characterized by rationality, impartiality, intellectual honesty and equality' (Strömbäck, 2005, p 341). In the digital age, news sites can provide the public with a forum for engaging in debate and calling for debate on matters of public interest on news sites by allowing comments to be posted under articles, by hosting discussion forums, by incorporating participatory live feeds in the coverage and by posting letters to the editor or to the authors of news stories. This requires a website integration of these functionalities, which can be provided by companies such as Facebook, Scribble, Disquss or Wordpress. Much debate among and interaction with the public happens on social media; however, the media organization can post on its own pages on sites like Facebook and Twitter. The audience can share or post news stories and, therefore, interact with others based on the news article. As we argued previously, having important functionalities taking place 'off-platform' potentially requires giving up autonomy for the sake of distribution and, in this case, also for the sake of nature of debate and what can be debated, for example, who can participate, who will be highlighted by algorithms, what can be uttered, and so on. We note that we do not know of the extent to which the enabling technologies are present from our particular empirical data. When problematizing the loss of autonomy of the media as an infrastructure of publics, one runs the risk of casting the media as the protagonist fighting against the villain of Big Tech and other technology providers. If debate is moved from the opinion sections in newspapers, we have the potential that people who debate on the news platforms such as Twitter and Facebook will have an easier time connecting instantly and perhaps mobilizing. The use of automatic tagging helps further the chances of news content appearing in algorithmically ordered feeds, and one might argue that when media utilize this technology to connect their own news site to the higher layer and wider infrastructure of communication that is the internet, it makes it easier for potential publics to discover and share news and perhaps agree and assemble around a cause that is inspired by the news article. Opinion pieces are very much shared (Ahva and Heikkilä, 2016) and this might be a signal to us that there is a specific appeal to the debate content. One of the authors of this chapter previously worked with the opinion section of a major legacy newspaper in Denmark, and the opinion pages were slow, to say the least, in sparking debate. Each day around seven debate articles were chosen for the print paper, and the following day we had responses to it that had to be sorted through before publishing the following day, if any. The work felt meaningful, but we often received letters from the same people: politicians and the same few representatives of grassroot causes. When media utilize the possibilities of adding structured data to the opinion pieces published online, they are more likely to be viewed by more people through third-party platforms, also including search results. Furthermore, the ease and speed with which people can discuss issues is much different than in the printed papers – for better or for worse, of course. The point being, however, that potential members of publics no longer have to subscribe to a print paper to view or participate in discussions. Again, the arena and curation of debate is then in the hands of third-party platforms, and the downside to this is that the selection criteria are opaque, although this might have been the case in the example of print media. By looking at the interface of Facebook, we do know that politicians and other actors considered 'elite' are promoted in the discussion section on Facebook. For the formation and cultivation of publics this could mean that the reliance of media on third-party platform infrastructure for debate risks that issues and points of view in the debate around them are suppressed and essentially being delegitimized by algorithmic selection.

In the previous paragraph we discussed the imperative to classify content to make it understandable to algorithms for distribution and the decision to choose web measuring services that measure the 'right things' about the audience. For both news content (including the media sharing articles, questions and opinion pieces on social media) and individual users, legitimacy is the core question of the cultivation of discussion and potential gatherings around an issue. According to Warner, publics must be recognized and recognize themselves to be a public (2002) and this requires being visible to algorithms and journalists alike. Following Ang, audiences and publics are 'produced and invented, made and made up, by the institution itself' (1991, p 26). While the media has the power to legitimize causes and publics, they, based on our findings, outsource and share this function with third-parties large and small, sharing this power and responsibility.

Audience construction and journalistic production

In the first category structuring the discussion we noted how the classification of users, content and the underlying values built into platforms might affect the way users are presented with news. Here we get into how these classifications, due to them being built into media websites' tech stacks, might create a 'trickle-down' effect that influence the journalists in creating an image of the audience and perhaps unknowingly tailoring content to certain segments and platforms for news consumption (Welbers et al, 2016; Coddington et al, 2021). In this chapter we found that advertising and analytics systems make up a large share of systems comprising the tech stack. Especially audience measurements in the newsroom have been described extensively in the literature and have been found to affect news selection (Welbers et al, 2016) and imaginaries of the audience (Nelson, 2021). All production and publishing processes can incorporate audience measurement systems (Kristensen, 2021). Companies such as Parse.ly and, especially, Chartbeat, managed to take over a significant market share with their editorially mindful metrics, placing weight on such factors as 'time spent' reading an article (Petre, 2021). In March 2019, Google launched its own newsroom analytics dashboard, Realtime Content Insights (RCI). After dominating the market for commercial web analytics, with RCI, the company was shifting its focus to the same consumers that Parse.ly and Chartbeat targeted: journalistic news media. Google was already a competitor for attracting advertisers and organizing and distributing information; with the launch of RCI, the company also delivered audience measurement insights for long-term planning, for marketing and for digital newsroom journalists. Lee et al (2014) and Welbers et al (2016) conducted natural experiments to evaluate how audience click rates affected their news judgement. Both experiments revealed positive effects in regard to the influence of audience metrics, although journalists did not report this in subsequent interviews. This highlights a classical tension in the media between 'giving the people what they want' and 'giving the people what they need'. This also touches upon the issues of platform influence on the format of news content and the censorship of certain issues and visuals on platforms. For journalists to be investing much time in gaining market share on displaying news on TikTok, for example, the autonomy of journalists could be challenged.

Based on our findings, the media seem to overall invest heavily in the category of technologies ensuring the viability of media. In the case of being independent from the state, advertising and subscription revenue could be seen as key factors of removing oneself from government subsidies, for example. In our scraping of third-party cookies we found that advertising and analytics technologies account for a large amount systems, suggesting that efforts to make profit are present. The systems are often provided by Big Tech companies (for example, BigQuery from Google), which are often scorned for having overtaken advertising revenue once made by the media. Again, we find ourselves in a twilight zone where taking charge of one's own infrastructure can end up making the media more intertwined with external providers of technology, for good and bad. This makes visible the complexity of these interdependencies, where both media and technology providers are each other's customers.

The findings from this chapter convincingly showed that Big Tech is enthralled in the tech stacks of European media to a very large degree and that the trend over time is that the prevalence of Google products in particular are on the rise (see Figure 8.3). As this section of the book is exploring the narratives surrounding the power of Big Tech, an important finding is that there is as much reason to explore what we call 'small tech' – the underwood of systems sustaining the media. By combining a material and relational perspective on infrastructuring, we can investigate empirically how these systems function, how they are designed, and how they are employed and reworked in practice in the news media. Only this will allow for a full picture of how publics are enabled through the media and to which degree they are infrastructured by the systems sustaining both the media and society.

Conclusion

In this chapter we inspected the platforms and technologies currently supporting digital journalism. Drawing on the fields of platform studies and infrastructure studies, we argue that media can be both an infrastructure of society and democracy while simultaneously being supported by a much larger infrastructure of the internet and the platforms supporting fundamental media functions. Taking our departure from the relation between these infrastructures we set out to investigate extent to which media organizations rely on external systems for the production and distribution of journalistic content via the internet and discuss the significance of this for the service for the public in terms of access to information in the form of news, public discussion, and the ability of news media in keeping up its previously idealized role in the infrastructure of democracy. In our discussion, we pointed to several implications of our findings for maintaining the journalistic ideals of facilitating public access to and deliberation of information as participants in a democratic society. Overall, we argue that the potential involvement of Big Tech on every level of the web architecture of media outlets, along with the sheer prevalence of services from especially Google, Amazon, Facebook and Microsoft, on the 361 media company websites, is indeed an indicator that we should encourage continued watchfulness of interdependencies and dependencies. Classifications of news content, users (that is, potential publics) and the algorithmic variables linking content to content, users to users and content to users on third-party platforms and, via audience measurement systems perhaps also on media websites themselves, create imaginaries of users and publics that create uncertainty about the diversity of and access to information for the public. This uncertainty also applies to the possibilities of publics to form, as issues, sources and publics are legitimized through prioritization and recognition in classification by media and platforms. To be datafied is to be a public, one might say.

There are nuances to this, as is illustrated throughout this volume. For one we note that legacy news ('Big News', we might call them) are to some extent favoured by Big Tech and are also able to distance themselves from third-party systems by reworking them and even developing new systems on top of them. This calls for more empirical research on the meaning and workings of this relation. Based on our mapping of the web services used by media organizations, we observed that, while the 'Big Five' technology companies are, by far, the largest providers of services, combined they still do not have more of a market share than the collective underwood of smaller providers. If we continue the tree metaphor of van Dijck (2020), our findings suggest that there is an underwood of technologies that should not be overlooked. A large conglomeration of smaller third-party services that have a significant importance to a specific country, market or publisher remain unexplored in the context of information provision and in relation to the role of news media in public formation. First, by understanding the ecosystem of third-parties and, second, continuously evaluating their importance in facilitating the public's engagement, in combination with that of other actors and actants, in the building, use, maintenance and reworking of the infrastructure, as prompted by Parks and Starosielski (2015), Korn et al (2019) and Hesmondhalgh (2021). Although the highest trees are more easily seen, Big Tech is not the only vegetation in the forest participating in the co-creation of publics.

Notes

[1] facebook.com, facebook.net, instagram.com, tapad.com, atdmt.com, fbcdn.net, cdninstagram.com, sundaysky.com, fbsbx.com.
[2] twitter.com, twimg.com, t.co, ads-twitter.com.
[3] https://chiefmartec.com/wp-content/uploads/2022/05/martech-map-may-2022.jpg.

References

Acar, G., Eubank, C., Englehardt, S., Juarez, M., Narayanan, A. and Diaz, C. (2014) 'The web never forgets: Persistent tracking mechanisms in the wild', in *Proceedings of the 2014 ACM SIGSAC Conference on Computer and Communications Security*, Scottsdale: ACM, pp 674–689. Available at: https://doi.org/10.1145/2660267.2660347.

Ahva, L. and Heikkilä, H. (2016) 'Mass, audience and the public', in T. Witschge, C.W. Anderson, D. Domingo and A. Hermida (eds) *The SAGE Handbook of Digital Journalism*, London: SAGE, pp 315–325. Available at: https://doi.org/10.4135/9781473957909.

Ananny, M. and Finn, M. (2020) 'Anticipatory news infrastructures: Seeing journalism's expectations of future publics in its sociotechnical systems', *New Media & Society*, 22(9), pp 1600–1618. Available at: https://doi.org/10.1177/1461444820914873.

Ang, I. (1991) *Desperately Seeking the Audience*, London: Taylor & Francis.

Baringhorst, S., Marres, N., Shove, E. and Wulf, E. (2019) 'How are infrastructures and publics related and why should we care? An email conversation', in M. Korn, W. Reißmann, T. Röhl and D. Sittler (eds) *Infrastructuring Publics*, Wiesbaden: Springer Fachmedien Wiesbaden (Medien der Kooperation), pp 69–86. Available at: https://doi.org/10.1007/978-3-658-20725-0_4.

Bowker, G.C., Baker, K., Millerand, F. and Ribes, D. (2009) 'Toward information infrastructure studies: Ways of knowing in a networked environment', in J. Hunsinger, L. Klastrup and M. Allen (eds) *International Handbook of Internet Research*, Dordrecht: Springer Netherlands, pp 97–117. Available at: https://doi.org/10.1007/978-1-4020-9789-8_5.

Caple, H. (2018) 'News values and newsworthiness', in H. Caple, *Oxford Research Encyclopedia of Communication*, Oxford: Oxford University Press. Available at: https://doi.org/10.1093/acrefore/9780190228613.013.850.

Coddington, M., Lewis, S.C. and Belair-Gagnon, V. (2021) 'The imagined audience for news: Where does a journalist's perception of the audience come from?', *Journalism Studies*, 22(8), pp 1028–1046. Available at: https://doi.org/10.1080/1461670X.2021.1914709.

Domingo, D., Quandt, T., Heinonen, A., Paulussen, S., Singer, J.B. and Vujnovic, M. (2008) 'Participatory journalism practices in the media and beyond', *Journalism Practice*, 2(3), pp 326–342. Available at: https://doi.org/10.1080/17512780802281065.

Englehardt, S. and Narayanan, A. (2016) 'Online tracking: A 1-million-site measurement and analysis', in *Proceedings of the 2016 ACM SIGSAC Conference on Computer and Communications Security*, New York: Association for Computing Machinery (CCS '16), pp 1388–1401. Available at: https://doi.org/10.1145/2976749.2978313.

Fenton, N. (2010) 'Drowning or waving? New media, journalism and democracy', in N. Fenton, *New Media, Old News: Journalism & Democracy in the Digital Age*, London: SAGE, pp 3–16. Available at: https://doi.org/10.4135/9781446280010.n1.

Flensburg, S. (2020) *Det Digitale Systemskifte: En historisk analyse af digitaliseringen af det danske kommunikationssystem*, PhD thesis, Det Humanistiske Fakultet, Københavns Universitet.

Flensburg, S. and Lai, S.S. (2020) 'Mapping digital communication systems: Infrastructures, markets, and policies as regulatory forces', *Media, Culture & Society*, 42(5), pp 692–710. Available at: https://doi.org/10.1177/0163443719876533.

Helmond, A. (2015) 'The platformization of the web: Making web data platform ready', *Social Media + Society*, 1(2), 205630511560308. Available at: https://doi.org/10.1177/2056305115603080.

Hesmondhalgh, D. (2021) 'The infrastructural turn in media and Internet research', in P. McDonald (ed) *The Routledge Companion to Media Industries*, Abingdon: Routledge, pp 132–142.

IAB Europe (2021) *A Guide to the Post Third-Party Cookie Era*. Available at: https://iabeurope.eu/wp-content/uploads/2021/02/IAB-Europes-Guide-to-The-Post-Third-Party-Cookie-Era-Feb-2021-Update.pdf.

Just, N. and Latzer, M. (2017) 'Governance by algorithms: Reality construction by algorithmic selection on the Internet', *Media, Culture & Society*, 39(2), pp 238–258.

Korn, M., Reißmann, W., Röhl, T. and Sittler, D. (2019) 'Infrastructuring publics: A research perspective', in M. Korn, W. Reismann, T. Rohl and D. Sittler (eds) *Infrastructuring Publics*, Wiesbaden: Springer Fachmedien Wiesbaden (Medien der Kooperation), pp 11–47. Available at: https://doi.org/10.1007/978-3-658-20725-0_2.

Kristensen, L.M. (2021) 'Audience metrics: Operationalizing news value for the digital newsroom', *Journalism Practice*, 0(0), pp 1–18. Available at: https://doi.org/10.1080/17512786.2021.1954058.

Lee, A.M., Lewis, S.C. and Powers, M. (2014) 'Audience clicks and news placement: A study of time-lagged influence in online journalism', *Communication Research*, 41(4), pp 505–530. Available at: https://doi.org/10.1177/0093650212467031.

Lerner, A., Simpson, A.K., Kohno, T. and Roesner, F. (2016) 'Internet jones and the raiders of the lost trackers: An archaeological study of web tracking from 1996 to 2016', in *Proceedings of the 25th USENIX Conference on Security Symposium*, Austin: USENIX Association (SEC'16), pp 997–1013.

Lewis, T. (1991) *Empire of Air: The Men who Made Radio*, New York: Edward Burlingame Books.

Lindskow, K. (2016) *Exploring Digital News Publishing Business Models: A Production Network Approach*, PhD thesis, Copenhagen Business School. Available at: https://research.cbs.dk/en/publications/exploring-digital-news-publishing-business-models-a-production-ne.

Merriam-Webster (nd) 'Infrastructure', in Merriam-Webster.com dictionary. Available at: https://www.merriam-webster.com/dictionary/infrastructure.

Napoli, P.M. (2014) 'Automated media: An institutional theory perspective on algorithmic media production and consumption', *Communication Theory*, 24(3), pp 340–360. Available at: https://doi.org/10.1111/comt.12039.

Nardi, B.A. and O'Day, V. (1999) *Information Ecologies: Using Technology with Heart*, Cambridge, MA: MIT Press. Available at: https://doi.org/10.7551/mitpress/3767.001.0001.

Nelson, J.L. (2021) *Imagined Audiences: How Journalists Perceive and Pursue the Public*, Oxford: Oxford University Press.

Parks, L. and Starosielski, N. (2015) *Signal Traffic: Critical Studies of Media Infrastructures*, Urbana: University of Illinois Press.

Petre, C. (2021) *All the News That's Fit to Click: How Metrics are Transforming the Work of Journalists*, Princeton: Princeton University Press.

Peppers, D. and Rogers, M. (1993) *The One to One Future: Building Relationships One Customer at a Time*, New York: Currency Doubleday.

Picard, R.G. (2005) 'Unique characteristics and business dynamics of media products', *Journal of Media Business Studies*, 2(2), pp 61–69. Available at: https://doi.org/10.1080/16522354.2005.11073433.

Plantin, J.-C. and Punathambekar, A. (2019) 'Digital media infrastructures: Pipes, platforms, and politics', *Media, Culture & Society*, 41(2), pp 163–174. Available at: https://doi.org/10.1177/0163443718818376.

Plantin, J.-C., Lagoze, C., Edwards, P. N. and Sandvig, C. (2018) 'Infrastructure studies meet platform studies in the age of Google and Facebook', *New Media & Society*, 20(1), pp 293–310. Available at: https://doi.org/10.1177/1461444816661553.

Sørensen, J. and Kosta, S. (2019) 'Before and after GDPR: The changes in third party presence at public and private European websites', in *The World Wide Web Conference*, San Francisco: ACM Press, pp 1590–1600. Available at: https://doi.org/10.1145/3308558.3313524.

Sørensen, J.K., Van den Bulck, H. and Kosta, S. (2020) 'Stop spreading the data: PSM, trust, and third-party services', *Journal of Information Policy*, 10, pp 474–513. Available at: https://doi.org/10.5325/jinfopoli.10.2020.0474.

Star, S.L. and Ruhleder, K. (1996) 'Steps toward an ecology of infrastructure: Design and access for large information spaces', *Information Systems Research*, 7(1), pp 111–134.

Strömbäck, J. (2005) 'In search of a standard: Four models of democracy and their normative implications for journalism', *Journalism Studies*, 6(3), pp 331–345. Available at: https://doi.org/10.1080/14616700500131950.

Urban, T., Tatang, D., Degeling, M., Holz, T. and Pohlmann, N. (2020) 'Measuring the impact of the GDPR on data sharing in ad networks', in *Proceedings of the 15th ACM Asia Conference on Computer and Communications Security. ASIA CCS '20: The 15th ACM Asia Conference on Computer and Communications Security*, Taipei: ACM, pp 222–235. Available at: https://doi.org/10.1145/3320269.3372194.

van Dijck, J. (2020) 'Seeing the forest for the trees: Visualizing platformization and its governance', *New Media & Society*, 23(9), pp 2801–2819. Available at: https://doi.org/10.1177/1461444820940293.

van Dijck, J., Poell, T. and de Waal, M. (2018) *The Platform Society: Public Values in a Connective World*, Oxford and New York: Oxford University Press.

Warner, M. (2002) 'Publics and counterpublics', *Public Culture*, 14(1), pp 49–90. Available at: https://doi.org/10.1215/08992363-14-1-49.

Welbers, K., Van Atteveldt, W., Kleinnijenhuis, J., Ruigrok, N. and Schaper, J. (2016) 'News selection criteria in the digital age: Professional norms versus online audience metrics', *Journalism*, 17(8), pp 1037–1053. Available at: https://doi.org/10.1177/1464884915595474.

9

Conclusion: Datapublics as a Site of Struggles

David Mathieu and Jannie Møller Hartley

Introduction

In 2009, David Beer noted that the time was ripe for an academic discussion of the power of algorithms, following a decade of research focused on user participation, empowerment and democratization that new and social media had made possible on a global scale. If the research of the first decade of the new millennium can be described as utopian, the following decade has arguably traced a darker portrait of new and social media as dystopian, focusing on misinformation, massive surveillance, prejudices and exploitation. In emphasizing a sociocultural perspective to be placed alongside a political economy perspective on media production, this volume welcomes a coming decade (and hopefully more) of 'topian' research.

In this volume, we have suggested and developed the concept of datapublics to understand the transformations – even the turmoil – taking place in the broad field of journalism and media. In this field, technology is typically either decried or celebrated for its role in forming and transforming publics. As argued in the Introduction (Chapter 1) and explored in several chapters of this book, we can observe a tendency in the literature to emphasize or overstate the role of technology in the formation of publics, giving the impression that the latter is the outcome of the former. In the two decades of utopian and dystopian research, media users have been mostly conceived as the effects of media (both social and legacy), either lifted by the new potential of media or sent down to darker corners by that same very power. In the same vein, journalistic media have been described as victims of processes of datafication led by Big Tech surging over them. This volume has focused on avoiding such determinism and instead foregrounds the interplay between emerging technologies, both their materialities and imaginaries, in relation to other objects, subjects, processes and practices.

By recognizing consumption and civic engagement practices as moments of agency, this volume has recognized the sociocultural perspective of actors and their agency as playing a mediating role on par with technology and the datafied realities afforded by those technologies. In focusing on actors and agency, we do not want to return the pendulum to an understanding of citizens as all-powerful. In short, we are not trying to introduce cultural determinism as a response to the overemphasis on technological determinism. Rather, the volume has made a point of assessing the negotiation between technological and sociocultural processes and representations.

By insisting on publics as (socially) constructed, we have emphasized an approach that is neither technologically deterministic nor media-centric. Rather, we have examined the dialectics between different forces and dynamics, which included analysing media production and reception, imagined and actual audiences, structure and agency, online and offline contexts of civic engagement, social and technological processes, legacy and new media, as well as private and public spheres of activities. Therefore, we argue, datapublics are indeed hybrid publics, not connected to any specific media space or enabled by any specific technology. The same platform can both function as a training ground for civic practices and as a contested space where civic practices are shut down or delegitimized.

The importance of sensitizing one's approach to hybridity, Chadwick argues, is that 'hybridity offers a powerful mode of thinking about media and politics because it foregrounds complexity, interdependence and transition' (2013, p 4). Accordingly, this volume has contributed many empirical examples and discussions of how new forms of civic practices emerge and transform in the intersections between infrastructures of data, the workings and affordances of platforms and interfaces, the civic practices of users and the discursive imaginings of publics by journalists and media organizations as they entangle themselves in data flows. Thus, a central line of inquiry in the book was to investigate the ways in which power, agency and structure are being (re)negotiated in the new datafied context.

Complexifying datapublics

The first section of this volume, which takes its point of departure in a sociocultural approach, paints a more nuanced and complex picture of the role of data in the formation of publics than the drama presented in the Introduction (see Chapter 1). A focus on actors and their agency allows us to view the contradictory logics or tensions at play in the formation of publics or in the work of data. Datafication is not some large-scale and inevitable top-down process but something that is constantly negotiated in the practices of actors in relation to their cultural environment, which other actors contribute to shaping. Publics are far from passive, but they have remained largely invisible as actants in both public discourse and research on datafication.

The first section of the book provides some useful pointers that help reveal less visible or recognized sites of agency for everyday citizens. Chapter 2 stressed that media users are active (as if the claim needed to be made again). It sought to detail the gaps between, on the one hand, the practices of users and, on the other hand, their capture through data as behavioural traces of their media use. The gaps between media use and practice provide spaces of reflexive agency for users to inspect the datafication of their uses and inscribe their practices in the data loop (Mathieu and Pruulmann Vengerfeldt, 2020). This does not entail that media users are suddenly in control or fully empowered by their reflexive capability, because the looping of data goes beyond their reach and involves other actors, structures, processes and contexts that also matter for how data travel in the loop. Yet, Chapter 2 is a good example of the need to look elsewhere if we do not wish research to be confined to regard citizens as victims of datafication.

On that count, this volume has contributed to illuminating a wider range of dynamics than those heard recently. In Chapter 3, we saw attempts by citizens to gather as counterpublics, but struggling for visibility and legitimacy against different ways in which they are imagined by other actors or articulated by technology. For example, representations of these counterpublics as sceptics, or even as 'tin foil hats', in traditional media played against the self-understanding of these publics and hindered their formation. Whether or not one sides with their cause is indeed a normative question, which highlights that public formation is also a question of legitimacy. The chapter insists on the hybrid character of publics in today's landscape, which does not simply depend on the affordances of a given digital platform, but results from a set of complex processes, discourses and values that at times clash and at times align to provide possibilities for publics to emerge.

The need to look elsewhere and to detail less visible spaces or practices of public formation is also demonstrated in Chapter 4. This chapter deconstructs how our conception of the public is hierarchized by revealing that less legitimate strata of the population engage as publics via the sphere of the private, to which social media have largely contributed. The mundane and the everyday become sources of engagement for a neglected part of the population that does not identify with the more elitist form of engagement associated with those with more cultural capital. Correspondingly, social media have contributed to enlarging the space by which citizens can form publics, although we show how this space is contested and in constant negotiation. Publics should therefore not be conceived in opposition to the private domain, or as linked to formal politics alone.

Further, we have shown that the dynamics of datafication are more than a single and encompassing process that imposes itself on other fields, such as journalism. In fact, we have seen how datafication co-constitutes and is co-constituted not only by other social processes or actors but also through means other than the processual. In Chapter 6, we depicted how, as personalization processes are set in motion, both conceptions of journalism and publics are being reconfigured. The role and reach of journalism are currently being renegotiated, while the field must learn to live with other actors, who are taking part in the cultivation of publics. However, even when public formation takes place in spaces outside the realm of news journalism, it is unreasonable to claim that journalism has been made irrelevant. As Chapter 3 previously demonstrated, public formation occurs in conjunction between new and old media platforms, between online and physical spaces.

As revealed in Chapter 5, emergent technologies have always altered and shifted the ways in which publics have been constructed. Journalism has overlived its past technological and cultural transformations. What we can observe is that journalism is adapting and adjusting to the pace and logics of datafication but has not been made irrelevant. While it is true that, like many other legacy media, the news media undergo a period of economic uncertainty and that, for the moment, advertising revenues are streaming towards platforms, this economic uncertainty cannot be directly translated into a cultural crisis concerning the role that journalism can play in forming publics. As Chapter 3 showed, journalism plays a significant role for public formation, cultivating publics though processes of legitimatization and visibility.

The activity of implementing these technologies such as personalization or artificial intelligence in a field such as journalism becomes an activity of designing publics, as we argue in Chapter 6. We see how these technologies have no meaning in themselves but are meaningfully deployed in relation to existing sociocultural realities. Chapter 6 illustrates that processes of datafication do set in motion certain organizational changes in 'power' and 'logics' inside the media organizations. These shifts in power matter for the role that journalistic media play in the construction of publics, for example shifting the balance in how they construct the audience-as-markets and struggle to make processes of datafication fit the construction of audiences-as-publics.

Thus, it should come as no surprise that datafication is so tightly intertwined with the commercial rentability of media organizations. However, we see that datafication is also being developed as a discourse relevant to the formation of publics by news editors and reacted to as such by the public. If we believe the readers of the *New York Times*, the public does not always agree with the positive implications of data for its self-understanding as audiences of the *New York Times* or users of its website. The datafied system of valorization, constructing publics as aggregated datapoints, is at odds with those normative professional ideals of journalism as foundational for democracies and the autonomy those media organizations have towards the economic market. Nevertheless, it is likely that the economic crisis in which they find themselves because of losses in advertising revenue will drive journalistic media towards increasing processes of datafication, making citizens lose sight of how the journalistic media differ from all the other offers available in the media's repertoires.

Lastly, how are publics infrastructured and what is the role of Big Tech? While the likes of Facebook and Google allegedly play an important role, they are only a part of the larger picture. Not only do these platforms participate directly in the construction of publics, but they also support the work of journalistic media by providing these with a large infrastructure on which they become dependent for the production and distribution of content. However, the emphasis on Big Tech overshadows the role of small tech in this infrastructure and the efforts of journalistic media to steer or affirm their public interest against a system developed for commercial purposes or mould the system for their own (and often less commercial) purposes.

The analyses presented in many of the chapters warn against technological (and platform) determinism, as processes of datafication are negotiated at all levels in all practices. In Chapter 7, we also discern how these negotiations are reflected in categorizations of media content. For media content to be distributed to the internet, it needs to be recognized by systems and databases. While the argument in the literature has emphasized dependencies on, for example, search engines, Chapter 7 illustrates how this dependency cannot be taken for granted but is negotiated and unevenly distributed across media organizations. The interviews with media organizations illustrate how the relationships with different tech companies are at best ambivalent and at worst constrained, pushing media organizations that can afford to do so in their own processes of datafication and platformatization. Thus, we can argue that the concept of 'media' and 'tech' is becoming even more blurred. A great number of actors are involved in the infrastructuring of publics, with different resources available and different normative ideals of what public formation entails and how they are best served and cultivated.

In Chapter 8, we showed that tech companies both small and large, and the infrastructural tech systems they provide, are pivotal to media organizations for almost every process, from production and publishing to marketing and measurement; there would be no digital media without these tech companies and their services. But the heterogeneity of services used by media organizations points rather to the importance of 'small tech' and a multiplicity of actors involved in tandem with 'Big Tech'. Also, the lack of compliance towards the technical requirements of Big Tech indicates a more complex relationship between Big Tech, media and publics in all their forms.

Datapublics as normative sites of struggle

The notion of public often comes with normative connotations – a yardstick against which we measure the shape of our democracies. For example, if publics become filtered by algorithms, a crisis of democracy is assumed and feared. This normative division into good and bad publics is not foreign to the technological drama formulated in the introduction of this volume (see Chapter 1). Passive publics, ripped out of their agency by technology, who are led by forces outside journalism into dark participation (Quandt, 2018) are but a manifestation of the normativity involved in public formation. Thus, the drama and its portraying of the main characters provide a rather negative judgement on the state of public formation in datafied societies.

As we have argued, the chapters of this volume trace a picture that is more complex, varied and nuanced. However, we observe that normative conceptions of the public are changing and diversifying in the wake of datafication. Public formation is therefore not just a process, an empirical reality, but an idea, even a stake – or, as Charles Taylor formulated it, 'a social imaginary': 'The social imaginary is that common understanding that makes possible common practices and a widely shared sense of legitimacy' (Taylor, 2005, p 23).

As such, the normative conceptions associated with public formation become a site of struggle in the new and data-infused landscape, testifying to the diversity and heterogeneity of spaces, technological means and social processes now available for citizens to make themselves heard and be recognized (or misrecognized). This is because the construction of publics is a constant struggle, an ongoing negotiation between actors or between ways of imagining or affecting technology. Thus, the technological dramas addressed by this volume are in fact echoes from the spaces in which the normativity of public formation manifests itself. They are dynamic and ongoing sites of struggle brought by technological transformations, not the result or effect of these.

Datapublics appear constantly contested and always negotiated rather than something that emerges as a matter of fact or by manipulating the right brakes and levers. Not all algorithmic attempts aimed at public construction, for example, personalization, filtering or hashtagging, result in the formation of publics; conversely, not all agentic uses of media lead to public formation. Hence, it is no surprise that this volume documents a broad range of heterogeneous dynamics by which publics are not only imagined but also actualized, always in struggle – both with and against processes of datafication.

Interactions in Facebook groups, as shown in the analyses of Chapters 3 and 4, illustrate how politics is everywhere and how these groups function as sites of struggles for legitimacy and training grounds for publicness.

Thus, we cannot say that public formation is first and foremost made up by mediated connections to a public world of matters beyond 'purely private concerns' (Couldry et al, 2010, p 65) defined as classical politics. Publics cut across mediated spaces, occur and are maintained in numerous spaces both private and public, where citizens struggle to define and legitimize what those shared issues should be and what politics is.

Chapters 5 and 6 have laid out some of these valorizations and negotiations following the clash of values in journalism at odds with the logics of personalization. In this ongoing struggle to define what shared issues should be, the perceptions and imaginaries of audiences by journalistic media play a lead role. The way they imagine audiences as publics legitimizes certain civic practices and certain issues as important. However, new actors have come onto the stage, demanding a different role to play in the cultivation of publics, and finding their way into news media by means of essential datafied infrastructure and tech services.

Subsequently, Chapters 7 and 8 have illustrated just how the valorizations of tech providers (small and large) are built into systems of news distribution and how the categorizations of content through data also routinize the distribution of the flow in specific directions. Hence, we see a quantification of previously qualitative gatekeeping logics in journalistic practice. In addition, we observe how this is contested (and to some degree rejected) by media organizations, as they refuse to 'dress up for Google' or abandon personalization because making the algorithm the gatekeeper based on previous user history conflicts with their self-understanding of their normative role in (democratic) public formation.

Given these stakes, it comes as no surprise that news media institutions seek to rely on a complex data infrastructure to capture citizens' attention and construct the audience-as-publics. On the other hand, publics are increasingly constructed and legitimized as social constructs through many media formats and platforms other than legacy media. In the process, the visibility and legitimacy of different media institutions are constantly negotiated and do, to varying degrees, guarantee access to a wider public. As such the infrastructural tech solutions matter for visibility of information and journalistic content, and for the media's ability to provide access to information. Thus, these tech solutions and emerging technologies can be said to be infrastructuring publics, legitimizing certain formations of public, and standardizing flows of information around these publics.

The normative ideals associated with publics seem to be overlooked or taken for granted in the debate of the journalistic media versus Big Tech. With this volume, we are arguing against the Manichean narrative of seeing Big Tech as purely commercial and journalistic media as a purely public good. Instead, we have examined their struggle to legitimize themselves as the dominant cultivator of publics through providing information, debates and civic engagement. Further, they position themselves as the proper infrastructure supporting information flows and deliberative spaces, while trying to black box, to some extent, those ideals and valorizations inherent in how they themselves design the infrastructures of content distribution.

Technology is but one driver in challenging and constructing the normative publics, creating instability and heterogeneity. Yet, it is not a deterministic driver, for we have seen that actors resist technological and algorithmic logics and processes as much as they are investing in these technologies with their discourses and interests, interfacing with public formation in various ways. The imaginaries invested in emerging technologies work as drivers of transformation in that they allow and invoke shifts in the construction of publics, as we saw with the case of personalized recommendation algorithms in Chapters 5 and 6.

Some public formation struggles become more prominent in political and popular discourses than others, often because they clash with normative ideals of the public sphere, ideals that have always been far from the everyday practices of citizens and media. Misinformed and conspiratorial forms of publicness have received a great deal of attention because these conceptions are part of established ideas about the healthy functioning of the democratic public formation. Not that this attention is undeserved, but it might distract us from investigating other dynamics of public formation that are less sensational or controversial.

Some of these dynamics are not, as sometimes rendered, anti-democratic per se. We must be wary of judging some public formations as anti-democratic on the grounds that we disagree with their message. Instead, we encourage analysis of how different actors gain recognition, visibility and attention. As we saw in the Introduction (Chapter 1) and in Chapter 4, counter-publics such as the COVID-19 protesters that position themselves against the mainstream are simply pursuing the goals of visibility and legitimacy that we see characterize all publics. While we might disagree with the message of these counterpublics, we must also recognize that their engagement is not necessarily anti-democratic, although it is aimed against the establishment and an established common ground of legitimacy.

We suggest seeing the construction of publics as a struggle between different normative ideals and to conceptualize public construction as a process involving different modalities of publicness, as seen in Figure 9.1. We argue, based on the empirical analyses across sites in this book, that publics are spaces (physical, virtual and imagined) in which struggles for attention, visibility, legitimacy, hierarchization (or stratification) and valorization take place, not only for publics themselves, but also for all actors involved in the formation of publics.

Figure 9.1: The (social) construction of datapublics

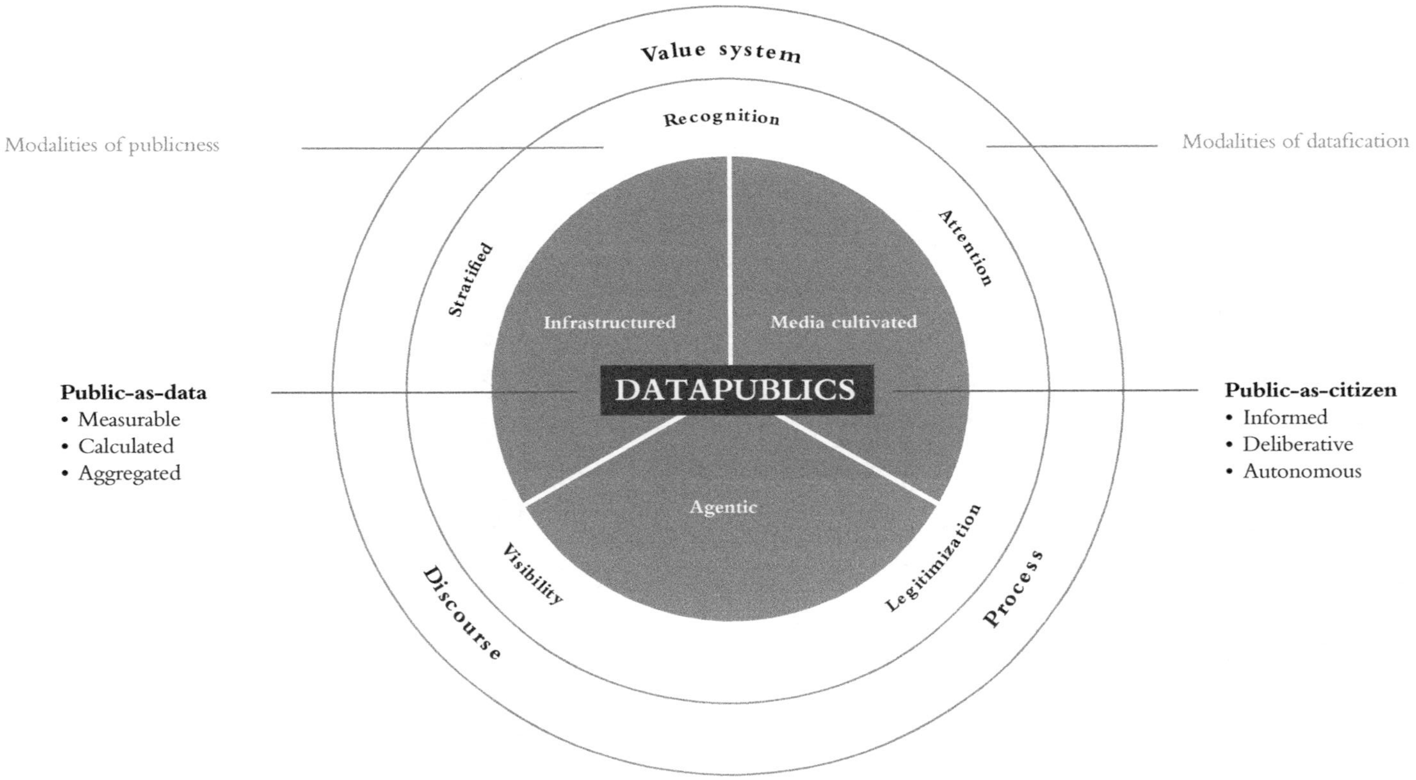

Figure 9.1 also highlights what we label 'different modalities of datafication'. The book has emphasized the processual modality of datafication, as we see how datafication is acted upon differently by actors with different resources, and also unfolds differently in different contexts. As datafication is being negotiated by news media, different discourses of datafication are drawn upon, constructing positive or negative imaginaries of publics. Additionally, many of the chapters show that datafication is not a one-way tsunami, but a value system, which affords and quantifies some of the modalities of publicness. For example, by bringing about logics of personalization into the newsroom, logics which emphasize individualism, dataism and binarism.

As such, Figure 9.1 synthesizes the findings of this volume by suggesting that publicness and datafication involves a complex of modalities that, in combination or in opposition, construct datapublics. This new normative conception of publics as *datapublics* expresses the tensions and resolutions between understanding publics-as-citizens and publics-as-data. We do not suggest the concept of datapublics has been fixated; rather it is in constant negotiation through the work of citizen agency, media organizations as cultivators of publics and technological infrastructures. Citizens do play a role in their agentic practices of public formation, but of course always in relation to how they are cultivated by media and infrastructured by technology.

The formation of publics takes place at the intersections of distinct processes, sites, means, norms and discourses, which do not harmoniously contribute to the formation of a given public, but must be constantly negotiated. Hence, we see the importance of recognizing the valuation inscribed in diverse practices, technologies or discourses. In that respect, datafication is not simply a process but also an idea and ultimately a value system, whose power is also discursive and social. Datapublics are not simply an empirical reality with clear borders or the result of an overarching force or impulse but are always co-constituted through hybrid dynamics.

Final remarks

We encourage future research on datafication to continue the sociotechnical turn developed in this book and already initiated elsewhere (see Kitchin, 2017; Bucher, 2018; Seaver, 2019). Future scholars should examine not only the processual effects of the algorithmic black box but also how the algorithm is used to value certain practices and devalue others, hence influencing or co-constructing transformations in the social order. In particular, we must consider, for example, what it means to be an audience, a journalist, an editor, and so on, in the midst of these transformations.

Furthermore, we suggest considering datafication not only as a (top-down) process, but also as a discourse and a value system. This entails that, in searching for the consequences of datafication, we must look beyond single instances and anecdotical evidence of filter bubbles or dark participation to look holistically at the whole (hybrid) picture. It is then that we can hope to understand the consequences of datafication for public formation or for societies at large. We believe that the approach embraced both implicitly and explicitly in this volume can provide inspiration when searching for answers to questions that combine both technological assumptions and cultural realities.

The fact that data are always embedded in other practices might be good news compared to claims that data (and algorithms that process the data) are impenetrable black boxes. As we have shown elsewhere (Mathieu and Møller Hartley, 2021), users rely on heuristics to assess data. As data are embedded in practices of control, commodification, news distribution or discussions on news values, and so on, the work of data and its meaning not only become more visible but also understandable for citizens. The embeddedness of data in public formation might ultimately allow citizens and civil society actors to discuss data in terms that are intelligible and meaningful to them and their practices, rather than in computational or engineering language, as the notion of the black box suggests. In fact, we hope that this volume will contribute to the intelligibility of data in matters of publicness.

There is no simple answer to what defines or constructs datapublics. Therefore, we should be wary of suggestions that perceive technology as playing, if not the only role, then the lead role in these stories of rise and fall that we wish to leave behind. This is perhaps the beauty and usefulness of the concept of datapublics: neither one nor the other, but endless combinations and fixations of its meaning and impact on today's democratic societies.

References

Beer, D. (2009) 'Power through the algorithm? Participatory web cultures and the technological unconscious', *New Media & Society*, 11(6), pp 985–1002. Available at: https://doi.org/10.1177/1461444809336551.

Bucher, T. (2018) *If… Then: Algorithmic Power and Politics*, New York: Oxford University Press.

Chadwick, A. (2013) *The Hybrid Media System: Politics and Power*, Oxford: Oxford University Press.

Couldry, N., Livingstone, S. and Markham, T. (2010) *Media Consumption and Public Engagement: Beyond the Presumption of Attention*, New York: Springer.

Kitchin, R. (2017) 'Thinking critically about and researching algorithms', *Information, Communication & Society*, 20(1), pp 14–29. Available at: https://doi.org/10.1080/1369118X.2016.1154087.

Mathieu, D. and Pruulmann Vengerfeldt, P. (2020) 'The data loop of media and audience', *MedieKultur: Journal of Media and Communication Research*, 36(69), pp 116–138. Available at: https://doi.org/10.7146/mediekultur. v36i69.121178.

Mathieu, D. and Møller Hartley, J. (2021) 'Low on trust, high on use: Datafied media, trust and everyday life', *Big Data & Society*, 8(2), 205395172110594. Available at: https://doi.org/10.1177/20539517211059480.

Quandt, T. (2018) 'Dark participation', *Media and Communication*, 6(4), pp 36–48. Available at: https://doi.org/10.17645/mac.v6i4.1519.

Seaver, N. (2019) 'Knowing algorithms', in J. Vertesi and D. Ribes (eds) *digitalSTS: A Field Guide for Science & Technology Studies*, Princeton: Princeton University Press, pp 412–422. Available at: https://doi.org/10.1515/9780691190600.

Taylor C. (2005) *Modern Social Imaginaries*, Durham, NC: Duke University Press.

Index

References to figures appear in *italic* type; those in **bold** type refer to tables. References to endnotes show both the page number and the note number (68n2).

A

Actor-Network Theory 30
AdForm 176
advertising 169–170, 176
  and analytics systems 182, 183
  Google 'DoubleClick' 174
  online 169
  revenue 192, 193
agency 7, 30, 66, 67
  communicative 39–41
  consumption and civic engagement
    practices as 190
  for everyday citizens 191
  human agency 30
  inscriptive 41
  inspective 40
  user 28, 41
Ahva, L. 166
AI (artificial intelligence) 2, 3
algorithmic control 16, 27–48
  as discursive control 34, 42
  as an extension of audience measurement 33–34
  problems with the notion of 28–33
algorithmic drama 4
algorithmic logics 56, 123, 124, 196
algorithmic press **113**, 115–116
algorithmic publics 8, 12, 29, 31, 136, 137
algorithmic resistance 7, 53, 65
algorithms 6, 27, 53, 99, 124, 129, 130
  definition of 124
  recommender algorithms 170
  users influencing outcomes of 33
Alphabet (Google's parent company) 9, 179
Altheide, D.L. 56–57, 123, 126
Amazon 9, 166, 174, 176, 184
Anderson, C. 4, 114
Ang, I. 28, 33, 34, 102, 106, 114, 182
Apple Inc. 9
Apple News 149
Application Programming Interface 2, 153

AppNexus 176
Arab Spring 12
Arendt, H. 73
argumentation 5
Aristotle 5
artificial intelligence (AI) 2, 3
audience constructions 101, 110–116, 122,
    123, 131, 136
  and journalistic production 182–183
  personalized logics and 123–126
  role in personalization and recommender
    systems 125
audiences
  algorithmic control and measurement of 33–34
  audience-as-citizen 112
  audience-as-consumer 112
  audience-based business model 113
  data loop of media and 39–41
  imaginaries of 13, 31, 33, 101, 111, 113,
    114, 117
  institutional and sociocultural perspectives
    on 28
  as markets 116, 136
  measurement systems 125, 170, 182
  as publics 136
automatic tagging 181

B

Bakardjieva, M. 77, 89
Bartlett, Jamie 6
Beer, David 30, 117, 189
behavioural data 38
behavioural research 38
Bell, G. 15
Bengtsson, Mette 146
Beyond Measure (Vincent) 15
Big Data 6, 38, 115
'Big Five' technology companies 9, 184
Big Tech 8, 9–10, 18, 166, 174, 183, 184,
    185, 189
  versus journalistic media 195

and major news media outlets 158
role of 193
Birkbak, A. 31
Boczkowski, Pablo 125
Bodó, Balaz 115
Bolin, Göran 14, 113, 115
Bourdieu, Pierre 73, 78, 91
Bowker, G.C. 147
boyd, d. 12
Breed, Warren 111
Brinker, Scott 174
Bruns, A. 12
Bulgaria, mundane (digital) citizenship in 89
Burgess, J. 12
Butsch, R. 78

C

calculated publics 12, 29, 31
Caple, H. 166
Carlsen, H.B. 31
Carrigan, Mark 38
categorization 146, 147
Chadwick, Andrew 53, 57, 124, 190
Chartbeat 174, **176**, 182
ChatGPT 2
Christin, A. 12, 136
citizens, as counterpublics 191
class 78
clicking, on news items 35, 36–37
climate change and environmental issues 87
Coddington, Mark 116
Coenen, Anna 104, 106
collaborative filtering models 131
Comscore 176
content management systems (CMS) 170
cookies 131, 169, 170, 183
Couldry, Nick 7, 35, 36, 50, 73, 83, 91
counter-tactics 57–58, **59–60**, 62–65
counterimaginaries (alternative) 102, 107–108,
    109, 110, 116–117
counterpublics/counterpublicness 11, 50, 56,
    57, 58, 65–66, 68, 196
  citizens as 191
  subaltern 54
COVID-19 67
  civic engagement during the pandemic 50
  emoji 63
  misinformation 2
  protesters 1, 196
  sceptics 1, 16, 49, 50, 55–56, 68n2
Crawford, K. 33
Criteo 174, 176
Cukier, Kenneth 13

D

Dahlgren, P. 89
Danish Facebook groups 55–56, 84, *85*
  active engagement 84, 92n3

mapping of 76
political conversations in 87–88
space and civic engagement in *86*
see also Denmark; Facebook groups
Das, R. 40
data 13
  behavioural 38
  categorization of content through 195
  collection by media 15
  data loop of media and audience 39–41
  ontology of 38–39
  in public formation 199
  publics in 132–135
  subjects 30, 38
datafication 6–7, 18, 40, 53–54, 67,
    190–191, 192
  future research on 198
  modalities of 198
  of news 148
  and public formation processes 13, 14,
    16, 51
datapublics
  definition of 10–13
  as hybrid publics 190
  introduction to 1–3
  as normative sites of struggle 194–198
  social construction of *197*
de Certeau, M. 57
Deleuze, G. 132
demonstrations 66
Denmark 3, 64, 82, 181
  Federation of Danish Media 9
  negotiations of media support in 9
  public lifestyle patterns in 75
  public sphere in 83, 91
  Socialist People's Party 89
  see also Danish Facebook groups
designing publics 136, 192
Dewey, J. 10, 11, 73
Dewey–Lippmann debate 10, 52
digital media 35, 36, 43n8, 76, 79
digital (mundane) citizenship 77, 89
digital news 114, 116
  Reuters Digital News Report 2021 154
digital press 113–115
digitalization 15, 61, 115
Distinction (Bourdieu) 78
distribution technologies 170–171
Dourish, P. 15
DR (Danish public service media
    organization) 58, 153
DRTV 129, 153

E

echo chambers 9, 122
editors 102, 137
ElasticSearch data platform 180
elite/digital public 81–82, 88
  engagement in Facebook groups 86–87

elite/traditional public 80–81
emerging technologies 99–120, 192

F

Facebook 9, 29, 158, 166, 171, 174, **176,**
181, 184, 193
algorithm 1, 6, 27
backup/alternative profiles 64
newsfeed 36
Facebook groups 49, 55, 62, 75–76,
78–79, 88
citizen-led 73
for Covid-19 sceptics 58, 67
as small-scale digital publics 83–87
see also Danish Facebook groups
Fact Check Tools 150
fake news 8
filter bubbles 5, 9, 109, 122, 133, 136
filtering mechanism 134
Fisher, E. 33
Flensburg, Sofie 165, 167
Flichy, Patrice 102
Fraser, Nancy 11, 54
Frederiksen, Mette 66
Freedom Movements Council 49
Frons, Marc 105

G

Gans, H.J. 111
General Data Protection Regulation
(GDPR) 170, 174
Giddens, A. 38
Gillespie, Tarleton 12, 29, 38
Gingras, Richard 158
Gitlin, Todd 111–112
Google 6, 18, 166, 174, **176**, 184, 193
AdWords 32
Alphabet Inc. (Google's parent
company) 9, 179
'DoubleClick' advertising service 174
Google Analytics 174
Google News 150, 151, 158
Google News Initiative 150, 151, 155, 157,
158, 159
Google Search 150, 151, 157, 180
Google Search Console 152
'googleSiteVerification' 152
Knowledge Graph 153
metatags 154–157
News Initiative blog 150
Realtime Content Insights (RCI) 182
Rich Results 149
Schema.org and Google structured
data 149–150
'Search Rater Guidelines' 150
tags for news media 150
GPT-3 2
Graham, T. 77
The Guardian 66, 157

content Application Programming
Interface 153
Ophan 180

H

Habermas, J. 11, 52, 54, 73
Hall, Stuart 28, 31
hard news 148
Harju, A. 77
Hartley, J. 76
hashtags 4, 12, 52, 146, 159
Hassan, Norel 105
Heikkilä, H. 166
Hesmondhalgh, D. 185
Heunicke, Magnus 67
Hovden, Jan Fredrik 73, 75, 77, 78
HTML 149, 150, 151, 152, 155, 170
hybrid ethnography 55
hybrid media 3, 16, 17, 53, 124
hybrid quantification logic 51, 68
formation tactics and 57–67
hybridity 190
of public formation processes 52–53

I

imaginaries 102–104, 125
of audiences 13, 101, 102, 110, 111, 112,
125, 182, 195
of personalized news system 106–107
of technologies 17, 101, 102, 103, 110,
116, 125, 196
see also recommender systems
information, public access to 179–180
Information (Danish daily
newspaper) 152, 180
infrastructures 193
of media websites 168–171
public cultivation and formation 180–182
internet 4, 55, 153, 168, 170, 179, 181, 183,
184, 193
issue publics 88

J

Jasanoff, Sheila 102
journalism 7–9, 159, 192
journalistic news media 195
technologies sustaining 169, 171, **172–173**
journalists 102

K

Kaplan, Bruce 109
Karakayali, N. 33
Kennedy, Helen 7, 13–14
Kluge, Alexander 54
Kormelink, Groot 36
Korn, M. 184
Kosta, S. 174, 176
Kowalski, Robert 124
Kozinets, R. 76

L

Lee, A.M. 182
legacy news 184
Leigh Star, S. 146
Lindskow, Kasper 171, 174
LinkedIn 64
Lippmann–Dewey debate 10, 52
Lippmann, Walter 10
Livingstone, Sonia 35, 50
local public 133, 134

M

MCA (multiple correspondence analysis), of
   Facebook groups 17, 74, 75, 76, 79, 88
*Making News: A Study in the Construction of
   Reality* (Tuchman) 148
Manovich, L. 146
marginalized groups 51, 54
Markham, Tim 50
mass media 56, 66, 115, 123, 129
   logics 57, 65
Mayer-Schönberger, Viktor 13
media
   data collection by 15
   data loop of media and audience 39–41
   dependency of audience on 31
   infrastructures 167–168
   journalistic 169, 171, **172–173**, 195
   as a prerequisite for political acts and
      orientations 15
   production of 28, 31
   and the public 166–167
   usage of 75, 92n1
   use and practice 191
media consumption 16, 28, 30, 31, 39,
   42, 105
media content 34, 193
media logics 56–57, 123–124, 126
   merging personalized logics and 135–136
media tech stacks 18, 169
media websites 18, 168–171
mediated public 12, 77
Mehozay, Y. 33
Meijer, Costera 36
Men in Black group 49, 56, 61, 62
Messenger 64
Meta 1, 2, 9
   see also Facebook
metadata 18, 145–164
   categorization of news through 148
   definition of 145
   description 147
   use by media companies 160
   use in news organizations 152–154
metadata tags 18, 149, 159
   @type-class 150
   authoritativeness **156**, 157
   characteristics and prevalence of **156**
   compliance 152, **156**

'dateModified' 154
freshness 151–152, **156**, 157
'googleSiteVerification' 152
patterns in the use of Google-specific
   metatags 154–157
relevance **156**, 157
'SchemaFound' 152, 154
Microsoft 2, 9, 166, 184
Min, S.J. 33
misinformation 8, 55
MIT Media Lab 121
MittMedia 129
Moe, H. 77
Mol, Anne Marie 105
Møller Hartley, Jannie 12, 115
MPEG-7 standard 147
multiple correspondence analysis (MCA), of
   Facebook groups 17, 74, 75, 76, 79, 88
mundane citizenship 77, 89
mundane/digital public 82, 87, 88
mundane/traditional public 82
music listening 30, 33

N

Natural Language Processing (NLP)
   transformer models 180
Negroponte, Nicholas 121, 136, 137, 138
Negt, Oskar 54
netnography 17, 74, 76, 84, 87, 89
networked publics 12
Neumayer, Christina 68
New York Times Media Group 99
New York Times (NYT) 17, 99–101,
   103–108, 180, 192
news
   audience click rates and news
      judgement 182–183
   authoritativeness 150–151
   classification of the 145–164
   clicking on news and interest in 36
   compliance tags 152
   consumption of 38
   datafication of 148
   digital 114, 116, 154
   distribution 106, 132, 195
   metadata categorization 148
   personalized 99, 100, 106, 132, 137, 138, 194
   relevance of 133, 151
news journalism 77
news media 18, 31, 192, 195
   audiences for 102
   datafied infrastructures of the 165–188
   tags 150
   tech stacks 168
   technologies enabling commercial viability
      of 169–170
news organizations 8, 10, 17, 18, 122, 137,
   148, 159, 160, 179–180
   metadata tags and prominence of 157

metadata use in 152–154
use of AI by 2
visibility of 170–171
news reading 33, 35–36
news websites
Award tag 155
tags 148, 149, 157, 160
third-party services present at 177
newspapers, personalized 136–137
newsrooms
ethnographies 111
social control in the 111
work of metrics in 12
Norway, people's public lifestyles in 78
NYTimes.com 99

O

omnibus printed press 112, **113**
O'Neil, Cathy 6
online news 4
personalized 121
OpenAI 2

P

Papacharissi, Zizi 12, 92
Pariser, Eli 109, 133
Parks, L. 184
Parse.ly 182
participation
dark 8, 55, 194, 199
political 76, 81
uncivil 55
passive publics 194
People vs. Tech (Bartlett) 6
personalization 99–100, 101, 192
data and 127–129
dismissal of by users 107
implicit 132
recommender systems used for 125
tools for 123
user control and 105
personalization logics 17, 121–141
and audience constructions 123–126
binarity and predeterminedness 129–130
dataism 127–129
individualism 126–127
in media organizations 137
merging logics and new publics 135–136
personalized content distribution 17
personalized news 99, 100, 106, 132, 137, 138
Pfaffenberger, Bryan 101, 102–103, 106, 109
Phillips, L. 31
Picone, I. 76
Poell, Thomas 14
political groups 88
political talk 77, 91
politics 78
public sphere attracted to 91
public used in relation to 73

Powell, Allison 7
press
algorithmic **113**, 115–116
digital press 113–115
omnibus printed press 112, **113**
printed/printing 4, 111–112, **113**
Prey, Robert 30, 34, 38
printed/printing press 4, 111–112, **113**
private, distinction between the public and
the 72, 73, 76
production and publishing technologies 170
protests 49–50
in Copenhagen 55–56
public connections 73
and lifestyles *81*
public deliberation 77
public engagement 50
public formation 5, 92, 191, 192, 194, 195
activities within citizen-led Facebook
groups 73
algorithms, information and datafication
in 53–54
counter-tactics 57–58, **59–60**, 62–65
counterpublicness 56
datafication in relation to 13–16
hybrid nature of 52–53
and hybrid quantification logics 57–67
mobilization 57, 58–62
in mundane settings 76–77
practices of 191
publicity tactics 58, **59–60**, 65–67
researching publics and 52–55
through citizen-led groups 92
public lifestyles 74, 75, 77, 79–83
Public Service Media 7
public sphere 6, 8, 32, 51, 75, 76, 78
activities in society 73–74
control of 29
definition of 11
in Denmark 83, 91
normative ideals of 196
public(s)
access to information 179–180
ad-hoc issue publics 12
affected by data and algorithmic control 16
affective publics 12
Bordieusian approach to 77–79
classical notion of 73
constructed as unknown democratic
collectives 111–112
in data 132–135
by design 130
elite/digital public 81–82, 86–87, 88
elite/traditional public 80–81
hashtag publics 12
issue publics 88
media and the 166–167
mundane/digital public 82, 87, 88
mundane/traditional public 82

networked 12
personalization logics and 121–141
public cultivation and formation 180–182
public formation and 52–55
publics-as-citizens 198
publics-as-data 198
role of large-scale providers of technological
  infrastructure in creating 17–18
and technologies, (re)imagination
  of 102–104
through emerging technologies 99–120
types of 80
use and understanding of 74–75
Putnam, Robert 50

Q

quantification logics 16, 51, 57–67, 68

R

radio transmitters 167
Radway, J.A. 43n4
reader profiles 112
recommender algorithms 170
recommender systems 124, 125, 127
  see also imaginaries
Reuters Digital News Report 2021 154
Rieke, Tom 108
RocketFuel 176
Rosovsky, Paul 110

S

Schema.org 18, 147, 148, 153, 154, 160
  and Google structured data 149–150
  NewsArticle tag 149–150
  tags 155
Schott, Anna 146
Schröder, K.C. 31
Schudson, M. 102
search engine optimization 155
search engines 43n9, 149, 159, 160
Shove, Elizabeth 168
small tech 183, 193
smartphones, communication with a web
  server 167
Snapchat 75
Snow, Robert 56–57, 123, 126
social imaginaries 102, 194
social media 1, 11–12, 58, 76, *81*, 191
  generation of news feeds by algorithms 8
  logics 56
social strata 73, 75
  public lifestyles across 79–83
sociocultural practices, gap between media
  use and 34–37
soft news 148
Sørensen, J. 174, 176
Spangher, Alexander 106
Spayd, Elisabeth 99, 100, 101
Spayd, L. 104, 106

Spotify, 'Girl's Night' playlist 146
Star, S.L. 146, 147
Starosielski, N. 184
Støjberg, Inger 82, 83
stratified public formation 72–95
Strömbäck, Jesper 7, 167
Struthers, David 68
subactivism 77
Sunstein, Cass 122
symbolic violence 91

T

tactics
  counter-tactics 57–58, **59–60**, 62–65
  publicity 58, **59–60**, 65–67
tags, generic 151
Taylor, Charles 102, 194
tech companies, and media organizations 193
tech stacks 18, 168, 180, 182, 183
  of news media 168, 169, 179
technological determinism 193
technological drama 101, 102–103
  over the personalization of the *NYT* 103,
  104–107
technological reflexivity 38
technology
  in journalism and media 189
  relationship between public
  formation and 4
  role in the formation of publics 189
Telegram 64
Think Analytics 130
third-party web services 171–179
  classification of 176, *178*
  distribution of URLs in news
  websites 174, *177*
  number of URLs and prevalence of
  third-party URLs *176*
  in users' browsers when visiting news
  websites 174, *175*
Thorson, K. 76
TikTok 146, 171, 183
Tuchman, Gaye 148, 151
Tufekci, Z. 30, 32
Turner, Fred 105
TV 2 [Danish national broadcasting]
  67, 153
Twitter 12, 52, 64, 174, **176**

U

Unesco 7
users 107–110
  agency of 28, 41
  as aggregated datapoints 130–132

V

van Dijck, José 9, 14, 171, 184
Vestager, Margrethe 5
Vincent, J. 15

W

Wahl-Jorgensen, K. 76
Warner, M. 182
Warren, Denise 99
Weapons of Math Destruction (O'Neil) 6
web metrics 170
Welbers, K. 182
Willems, Wendy 53
Willig, Ida 112
Willson, M. 30
World Wide Web 4, 147, 155

World Wide Web Consortium (W3C) 18, 147
Wright, S. 77

Y

Yandex 18
Ytre-Arne, B. 40

Z

Ziewitz, A. 4
Zuboff, Shoshana 5
Zuckerberg, Mark 133